R0061522850

02/2012

"This book is like THE ENCYCLOPEDIA FOR MEN. It covers a lot of ground and every bit of it makes perfect sense." — *David Chandler*

"A fun, entertaining and enlightening read! Wish I'd had access to this book before my last girlfriend." — *Jake Feder*

"Full of terrific data which can assist any male in becoming more successful in all aspects of his life. It covers everything from dating, clothes, table manners and roommates, to job interviews, finances, bathroom habits and marriage. And including all those lists was a genius move, especially given that so many young guys leave home without a clue about living on their own. I'm surprised no one came up with this idea sooner. In my opinion, M. Marshall deserves a standing ovation." — *Geoff Snyder*

"The majority of info dispensed here is common sense, but the way it's presented serves as a hugely entertaining reminder that all men can stand one of those friendly little whops upside the back of the head once in a while. This book should have been written decades ago." — *Michael Schoeffer*

"Very informative! I moved here from another country and it is so great having access to all of this information. It has helped me become more aware of my manners, my habits, and how I can be more accepted here. Thank you!" — *Carl Russo*

"This book should be required reading for every guy. Not only because it explains the 'what, why and how' on practically every possible guy topic, but because it gives great insight into that Black Hole that is the female mind." — *Zach Reynolds*

"I fully expected that this book would try to nag me into submission but instead I discovered that it validated many of my own thoughts and feelings, which has boosted my self confidence and reminded me that I'm actually a pretty good guy! It also helped that this author is extremely funny, in a dry, warped and twisted sort of way. She must be British." — *Robert Kerr*

"I was raised by my two older sisters, and for as long as I can remember, I have referred to them as The Manners Police. So after living for decades with the education in etiquette that my sisters bestowed on me, you can imagine my surprise as this funny little book taught me a thing or two. It is full of information that I'm fairly sure most guys don't even think about, but should. We can vastly improve our circumstances once we "get it". I've been happily married to a wonderful woman for most of my life, and even she has appreciated the new information I have received from CSFG. I am highly recommending it to every male, regardless of age, race, religion, or marital status." — *Lou Donell*

"My ex-wife sent this to me as we are still friends and she always hopes I'll get remarried. I think I stand a better chance of that now since Charm School for Guys has opened my eyes on a few different levels. It's easy and very funny, unlike most self help books I've seen." — *Brad Stonington*

"On a recent visit to the bookstore, my eleven-year-old son turned up begging me to buy this book for him. I'm sure he found the illustrations intriguing, but after flipping through the book myself, I was thrilled that it appealed to him. I see this book as a great advantage to any young man as he begins his journey outside of the nest. Reading it should be a requirement for graduating high school!" — *Jena Cook*

"Everyone could learn something from Charm School for Guys. It puts a definitive answer to the many questions that men face with regard to women, their expectations and the often confusing dynamic that naturally occurs between the two genders." — *Steve Kaminski*

From Webster's Dictionary

¹charm

a: to please, soothe or delight by compelling *attraction*
b: *a trait that facinates*, allures, or delights
c: *that which exerts an irresistable power to attract*

Charm School FOR GUYS!

Great Date Guide Included!

How to Lose the Fugly and Get Some Snugly...

The brutally blunt owner's manual and fix-it guide for every year, make and model of guy.

Written by **M. Marshall**
Illustrated by **Ryan Waterhouse**

"It is absurd to divide people into good and bad. People are either charming, or they are tedious."　　— *Oscar Wilde*

Charm School

FOR GUYS!

A Get Off The Couch Book

Written by **M. Marshall**
Illustrated by **Ryan Waterhouse**

Published by:

Get Off the Couch Books, LLC
645 G Street, Suite 100-809
Anchorage, Alaska 99501

Library of Congress Cataloging-in-Publication Data:
Control Number: 2007900778
Marshall, M.
  Charm school for guys : how to lose the fugly and get some snugly /
By M. Marshall – 1st Get Off the Couch Books ed.
p. cm.
1. Etiquette/conduct. 2. Self-improvement. 3. Health and hygiene. 4. Mens clothing.
5. Men – relationships. 6. Marriage – Psychological aspects. 7. Food habits. I. Title

ISBN: (13) 978-0-9789634-0-8
ISBN: 0-9789634-0-7

Email: info@getoffthecouchbooks.com

Book Design, Layout and Text by Krista Foley
Cover Design by Get Off the Couch Books
Author's Photo by Chris Arend

Printed in the United States of America

10 9 8 7 6 5 4 3 2

Website: www.charmschoolforguys.com

This book is dedicated to my pet project, my friend, my boss, my dentist and the absolute _bane!_ of my existence.

Also to Jon Waterhouse and Bailey, _The Mighty Fat Dog_ (who still won't get off the couch).

How this book came to be

I *love* men...

contrary to popular belief, finding something amazing and wonderful in a guy does not require an autopsy – and I can usually find a great quality in *any* man. Unfortunately, the fact that I think men are so great gives me a rash when I see how they get beat up constantly for doing or not doing the things that someone else wants for them to do or not do. We women often have absurdly high expectations of the way we think men should behave. But we don't come with instructions, and our desires are not posted on the sides of buildings or buses. So since most men are clearly not equipped with mind-reading capabilities, it is my goal to create a more level playing field with C.S.F.G.

I am a researcher, and I can tell you that all you need is a little common sense to understand why what you will read here works. If you are running low on common sense right now, you could try flagging some down on the street corner. Or you could do what I did - and tap into the common sense of your girlfriends, your guy friends, your mom, brothers and sisters, your neighbors and teachers, your dad, your sons and daughters, your bosses, co-workers, grandmas and aunts, your uncles and grandpas, your roommates, your housekeeper, your wife or significant other. They were a <u>big</u> help. (A big thanks to these people. They shared some seriously privileged information… at the expense of their loved one - YOU. Their sacrifice is duly noted and appreciated.)

They actually helped me write this. They didn't want to upset you by telling you the painful truth, so they've given me permission to do it. (I'm not worried about hurting your feelings. I know you'll get over whatever trauma I may cause.) The *simple* points that we will make in this book can easily improve your life, but only *if* you pay attention, want to learn and can tap into (or borrow) some **common sense**.

Beware that some of the items you'll find in here may be presented in a less-than-charming manner (possibly even **rude, raunchy or disgusting**). Please excuse the bad language I'll use periodically, too. But we are about to create a masterpiece (you), and when a masterpiece is created, things can sometimes get a little messy in the process. Sorry.

Read this book like we're friends...
Imagine that I'm talking to you from across the table or beside you on the couch, because that's how this book is written – like I'm talking to you. Just don't forget that *I am on your side*. I may sound like a bully, but I'm actually your new best friend.

Remember that this book was written for one reason: Your success.
You can be hugely successful in anything you try if you can be charming.

Acknowledgements

Do the people listed here really want to be thanked – or even remotely associated with this book? Probably not. But they have inspired and enabled, so they are getting thanked anyway.
Thank you to Jennifer Brubaker of Avedis for the intro to Myron Golden who opened this door. To my jagged, but motivating little reality pill, Donna Cariglio, for inspiring me then promptly leaving the state – *thanks a lot*. To the most *generous* human on Earth – **Diane Murray**, for her constant support and encouragement. Thanks to the infamous Mark Price, a.k.a.: Precious, for releasing my inner cynic. To my favorite human, Cindy Price for re-enforcing that *friends for life* concept. Thanks to Jake Price, for speaking his warped, over-developed little mind and for leading me to Jay and Sean. Thank you to Sharon Rumble, for constantly reminding me of the angels and for always sending them my way. To the fabulous Laurie Lyons for a friendship that has survived the test of time *and gravity*.

Thanks to my brilliant big brother, Jack Marshall, for seeing the value here – and for editing it. To Carol Van Deursen for the often disgusting but terribly entertaining 'mom of four boys' stories. To Bill Stringham, for the classified relationship info (and the shocking photos). To the incomparable Yomara Rivera-Sanders, enforcer of positive attitudes (through better health and avoidance of the drive-thru). To Peggy Beal for her *abundant* support! Thank you to Jim McCormick, The Kenai King. Big thanks to the very cool Kim Harmon for sharing her wisdom and great stories, and to Dr. Kat Moran (Lara Croft) for the best advice I've ever received.

Thanks to Dr. Bill Dorfman, (DDS), for leading me to the expert dream team: Gayl Murphy, Alex Carroll, Dan Poynter and Steve Harrison, who all fell out of the sky and landed on my laptop that one day when my planets lined up. Thanks to my attorney and favorite charmer, Tom Van Flein *(way to keep a low profile…)*. Thanks to Bob Shake, Jesse Jansen and David Braun at Northrim Bank. To the amazing Ryan Waterhouse, talented artist and *psychic*. To my wonderful parents, Jack and Evelyn Marshall: to Dad, for the priceless advice on guys – and to Mom, for teaching me table manners.

I'd like to acknowledge LK and PK, my original 'inspirers' and the two people who had more to do with making this book happen than they'd like to admit. As a matter of fact, they won't admit it – hence the initials. But here is my very sincere, very family-oriented 'thank you' anyway.

Thanks to Krista Foley, for sharing her vast knowledge of book building and for building *this* book! To the awesome team at Televox for their terrific web services. To Mark Grainger, Bob Nicoll, Michael Buzinski (Buzz!), and Kelly Snodgrass… my masterminds. You *rock*.

Thank you to Flora Ness, a woman of amazing grace, spirit and generosity – and the best person I know – for giving me so many opportunities and for constantly reminding me that it was *just a guy*. Big thanks to the incredibly talented Doug Ness for many great things (but mostly for marrying Flora☺).

A special thanks to my friends at Barnes & Noble for their amazing support and the many opportunities. Thank you!

Finally, thanks to GOOGLE and Wikipedia.
Therein lie the answers.
(Guys, get to know these sites and soon you may actually be
as brilliant as you want us to think you are. Peace.)

Disclaimer:
This book offers general suggestions and encouragement for any guy who wants to improve his image and become a more confident, outgoing, understanding, sexy and *appealing* individual. Reading it may not raise your IQ or make you a winner in the stock market. It will not guarantee promotions at work or that you will be the next big thing. *But it might help.*

While specific brand-name items and the names of various organizations are mentioned here, they're mention does not imply that those manufacturers or organizations endorse this book.

Web sites and contact information provided here were accurate at the time of printing.

WARNING: You may be bothered by the fact that so many of the crimes you will be convicted of here are also committed by females. But don't worry. *That* book is in progress. (And you'll be glad to know that it is *twice* as thick as this one.)

The guy asked the girl: *"Who is your ideal guy?"* She replied, *"Every guy is my ideal guy – With just a few minor changes, that is ..."*

Foreword

Greetings Gentlemen,
My name is Doug, and the guy up there facing all the complaints is me. Really. It's me. I am the guy who inspired the author, your friend and mine, to write this book. So before you begin your journey into it, please allow me to welcome you to my world – and offer you my sincere apology.

I'm guessing that "Charm School for Guys!" has landed in your hands via your wife or lover. Perhaps it was given to you by your mother or your sister. Maybe by your best friend. Possibly even by your boss. If it so happens that you have purchased it on your own… well then… let me just say that you are clearly more in tune to your potential successes — *and failures!* — than I was. But I've recently discovered that it isn't too late for either of us.

You see, this book tackles those issues with which you and I, because we're guys, are always being accused. Perceived *male clueless-ness* is a very popular, and *universal* topic. Unfortunately, it's <u>my</u> *clueless-ness* that brought you here. And no matter who signed you up, you are now in my boat. I always thought I was charming, at least in my own way. But what a guy thinks is charming and what the rest of the world thinks is charming can be so different that you could write a whole book about it. And our author did.

But I'd like to point out that even though this book is a pushy little gift, whoever presented you with it cares a lot about you and wants to help your life improve. (I'm impressed if you bought it for yourself.) And since I am the brunt of this joke, you can believe me when I tell you that reading it actually *can* make your life better – if you want it to be better.

(It may help if you remember that our author is not your mother or your wife, so she isn't nagging you because she lives with you and is constantly bugged by your irritating behaviors. She stands nothing to gain by helping you become a more appealing guy. Me? Different story... she has to be around me a lot – but YOU can take it or leave it. She is simply trying to clue us in to a few hundred tips and suggestions, which we guys can use to become more successful in every aspect of our lives.)

Personally, I'm going to recommend that you give it a shot. I challenge any of you to come back and say that you didn't learn something by reading this book. I'll also bet that the people in your life will suddenly respond to you much differently than before, if you choose to incorporate these ideas into who you are - or want to be. Just as you are asked on the back cover, what do you have to lose... other than something you shouldn't have anyway?

So read on Men. Good luck. (Oh yes, you may want to invest in a *highlighter*.)

Dr. Doug Ness

CONTENTS

Buckle Up Guys – We're Goin' In. First, there are several pages of pitches, promises and other propaganda to convince you that this book can change your life. But you've just read all that, and look! You're still here. So next, look below and see if you can't find a topic or two which you feel could *possibly* apply to you.

CHAPTER 1

Manner Up

OK guys... Here's a newsflash: No matter where you're from, or what you know or don't know, we will all believe that you are smarter, more capable, more physically fit, more emotionally stable, richer and totally better looking if you know and use good manners.

You can easily fool us all into thinking whatever you want us to think about you if you are polite and mannered-up. Guys, this is stuff that most humans learn in pre-school, so don't worry that it will be hard for you to understand. Just grab a mitt and get in the game. It's not brain surgery. Like learning your ABCs, it's very basic stuff... so elementary that it smells like *PLAY-DOH*.

First, here are a few examples of *very bad manners.*
- You spew the 'F' word or other profanities in public – or anywhere for that matter – like it's no big deal. *(Guess again, Einstein.)*
- You bump into someone but you don't say "excuse me."
- You ask someone for help but you don't say "please."
- You get something from someone but you don't say "thanks."
- You *GAK* <u>loudly</u> on your cell in public. (You think guys don't gab/yak – but when you talk loudly on a cell, you're totally *gakking*.)
- You chew with your mouth open or talk with food in your mouth.
- You cough without covering your mouth.
- You spit on a sidewalk or into an *indoor* trashcan.
  (Gee, your mother must be so proud.)
- You pick your nose in public.
- You burp in public.
- You scratch your crotch in public.

You may have had no clue that some of those things are unacceptable, but we're clear now, right?

Note: Whenever I refer to "in public" it means any place you may be that isn't inside your house – *alone.*

You can make this world a better place if you use good manners — and also to encourage others to use good manners. When you encounter some random person who is rude or clueless about their own rotten social skills and behavior, say something. Well, unless you think they might shoot, stab, strangle or otherwise stop your clock for pointing this out about them. If that's the case, then run away.

RUDENESS

Here are a few important issues with regard to charm. Maybe it's not fair to say that *all guys* like to make a production out of spitting, burping, *farting* and cussing. But it IS fair to say that the majority of people who live with those guys, are generally disgusted with the production. Doing these things around other people is <u>definitely</u> considered *bad manners,* so show some class and lose those habits.

Think about this: Don't you want to deck someone who bumps into you in a store or someplace, and then looks at you but doesn't say *jack?* (We'll talk soon about getting you over your violent urges – so chill on that for a few.) How about when someone goes through a door and then lets it go – right in your face – as you come in behind them?

Talk about irritating … did these fleas not have mommies to teach them any *manners?* Well, at the end of this chapter you (and they) will find a very long list of things you should and should not do with regard to your manners. Meanwhile, we'll hit on many topics that will involve your manners and *new-found charm.*

BASIC MANNERS

Without expending much energy or brain power, you can create a charming image by using the manners that your mom or grandma taught you. For instance, <u>always</u> say "please" and "thank you" and "excuse me." No slacking. These manners are so basic, but they are core manners that will carry a lot of invisible weight as you deal with people each day. You'll be surprised to see how everyone responds to your great manners. *After they get over their initial shock, that is.*

Here's more regarding your manners and appeal.
1. Smile. Any charming guy smiles easily and often. Try it.
2. Stand up straight.
3. Be friendly and polite.
4. Open doors for people.
5. Always look at people when you are talking with them.
6. Speak clearly.
7. Take your hat off at the dinner table (and whenever you are indoors).
8. Don't ever ask a female her age (– unless she's recently out of diapers).
9. Don't ever ask anyone how much they weigh.

10. Never ask people how much they earn, or what they paid for something.
11. Don't pick your nose, teeth or ears in public.
12. Wave to say "thanks" to people who let you into traffic.
13. Say "thanks" to strangers if they do something nice for you.
14. Help elderly ladies if they'll let you. (Be careful of the elderly men, though. They are *you* in a few dozen years – and they still think they don't need help with *anything*.)
15. If you are wearing sunglasses and someone comes up to you, remove your shades for at least a moment. It's important that people see your eyes when you are talking.
16. DO NOT spit on sidewalks – especially just as you are entering or exiting a building. If you must spit, then aim for the gutter or the street. We hate dodging your gunk.

More details about your good manners coming up later in this chapter... *I know you can't wait.*

WHAT DID YOU CALL HER?

Unless you are extremely close to a woman, do NOT ever call her "Sweetie", "Honey", "Babe", etc. If you know her name, use it. If you don't, then call her "Miss" or "Ma'am". ("Miss" if she doesn't have gray hair — *you'll score yourself some major points here* — or 'Ma'am' if she has gray hair.)

a. If You Aren't a Gentleman – You Might Be a Troglodyte.

OK, Fuzzy – Stop dragging your knuckles around. At the dinner table, you need to be clean and quiet and upright. No noise, no mess and no ripping food from the plate with your teeth.

TABLE MANNERS

These are the absolute basics of table manners, but we could all use a quick refresher, right? (As you learn, share what you learn with little kids. Maybe *their parents* will get a clue.)

Hold your silverware correctly. This is how:	*Hold your silverware correctly. This is not how:*
Right	WRONG

If your hands don't know how to hold a fork and a knife correctly, or if they and their fingernails are dirty, they'll make you look bad. So study this diagram, and be sure your hands and nails are always clearn before you're seated at a table. (Stake claim to your seat if needed by placing your napkin on your chair and go wash your hands.)

1. REMOVE your hat before you take a seat at the table - or whenever you're indoors – *no matter how your hair looks underneath it.* If you need to comb it, then excuse yourself to the restroom and 'de-hat' there.
2. Don't talk with your mouth full. If you're asked a question while eating, finish chewing before you answer. Make sure that between bites, you clear your mouth of all food debris before you speak.
3. *Always sit up straight.*
4. Keep your elbows off the table.
5. Place your napkin in your lap and leave it there until you leave the table, except when using it.
6. Wipe your mouth and hands with your napkin often.
7. When you leave the table, place your used napkin on your chair or refold it and leave it on the table.
8. **Chew with your mouth completely closed and eat quietly.**
9. When invited over for a meal in someone's home, be prepared for anything. If foods are served that you don't like or have never tried, remember that this isn't *Fear Factor*, so don't worry that any food you'd can't ID will be sauteed seagull poop. Be open-minded and polite, but be sure not to fill your plate with a food that you aren't sure about. Try it first, then if you like it, go for seconds later.
10. Never 'double dip' a chip or veggie. Break whatever you're dipping in half, then dip it. *(Learn more on this topic from Seinfeld.)*
11. Don't ask for seconds of an item until everyone has been served.
12. Don't reach across the table for anything – ask someone to pass it.
13. Don't pig out. You shouldn't feel stuffed after a meal so back off and stop eating before you're stuffed.
14. Cover your mouth if you cough or yawn (always, but especially at the table).
15. Don't pick your teeth (or anything else) while at the table.
16. Hold your knife and fork properly – keep your fork between your fingers the way you hold a pen or pencil. (Don't hold a knife or fork like you are about to stab something with it. See diagram.)
17. Don't eat with your fingers unless your host does.
18. Eat slowly.
19. Don't sit down and hunker over your food like you're worried someone is about to take it away from you. Sit up and back – lean in when you take a bite.
20. **Always offer to help clean up after a meal at someone else's home.**
21. Watch topics you bring up at the table – no gross or sad stories.
22. Save your burps and other noises for later, in the restroom, *alone.* (If a burp slips out in public, say "excuse me". Duh.)
23. Don't start eating till everyone has been served and your host starts.
24. Never take the last of a food item before asking if anyone else wants it.
25. Pull a chair out for a lady (or any female, lady or not) as you are

being seated. She may love you for it or she may slug you for it but do it anyway. Most often this very gentlemanly gesture will be appreciated.

Make sure to follow the next few guidelines in more formal dining situations, such as business lunches, meals in elegant restaurants or a formal meal in someone's home. Some of these suggestions are repeated from the previous list. **Again, your hands and nails must be clean before you sit down at any table.**

1. Place your napkin on your lap when you first sit down.
2. If you need to leave the table during your meal, leave your napkin on your chair and push the chair in a little.
3. When you've finished, keep your napkin in your lap until you leave, then *refold* it and place it on the table or leave it on the chair.
4. Cough into your napkin, but never use your napkin as a tissue for your nose or face – only your mouth and hands.
5. Place some butter on your bread plate, then butter one bite of your bread at a time.
6. Do not bite from the whole roll. Tear and butter your bread or roll, one bite at a time, instead.
7. Unless we're talking Nachos, do not take your appetizers directly from the appetizer plate. Use a clean spoon to place the appetizer on a small appetizer plate or on your bread plate.
8. Never cut your salad. Fold each bite of lettuce with your fork until it will fit into your mouth. (Yes, this will take practice.)
9. **Remember that once you have used your knife, fork or spoon, it should not be set back down onto the table. Keep it on a plate.**
10. Never order alcohol unless your host or companion does.
11. When drinking wine, hold the glass by the stem (but not with a pinky erection).
12. Cut one bite of food at a time. Steak, crabcakes, a Snickers bar, whatever. Unless you are six, you don't need to pre-cut every bite.
13. Begin cutting your meat or fish at the end – NOT in the middle.
14. Never tip your soup bowl or plate up. Don't empty it.
15. Wait till everyone else has been served before you begin eating.
16. Learn to make small talk. Take the heat off of yourself in any dining situation by asking others at the table questions about themselves. (They will probably go on for weeks… then you can coast and eat in peace.)

WINE TASTING...

If you order wine, there maybe a little ceremony involved, so here's how it should go: you order the wine. If you aren't sure of what to order with your meals, it's OK for you to ask your server for a suggestion. Reds go with beef and pastas with red sauces, whites go with chicken, fish and pastas with white sauces. Your server can help you decide. As far as your budget, simply ask him or her, "What would you recommend in the $30, $40, $50 range?" (The days of cork-sniffing are over. Set it on the table.)

Tips on your place setting: When you're in an upscale (a.k.a.: *spendy*) restaurant, and there is a confusing herd of forks, spoons, and knives in front of you, use those on the outside first, then work your way in to the center. For instance, your appetizer will typically be served first, then your salad, then your main entrée. (In ultra formal dining, the salad may be served last.) Use the fork that's farthest from your dinner plate for your appetizer and/or salad. The fork closest to your dinner plate is your dessert fork. (Unless it's large. If that's the case, then it is your main entrée fork, and your dessert fork or spoon will be above your dinner plate.) Your soup spoon is farthest from your plate on the right. Again, if there is a fork or spoon above your plate, it's for your dessert. The small plate and knife above your forks are for your bread and butter. Yeah, I know. Welcome to the Ritz.

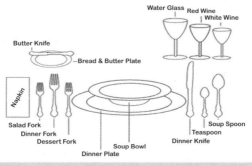

If you're totally lost in all the silverware, then you have 2 choices. Either copy what the person you are dining with does, hoping that they will know their salad fork from an F-22 Raptor, or excuse yourself from the table and find a restaurant employee. A server or hostess can tell you what is what. This happens, so they'll probably be happy to clue you in. Besides, you would rather be embarrassed by asking this restaurant person, than have to try and fake it with your date or dinner companion, right? (Remember to offer them a tip for their advice. A few bucks should do.)

SPEAKING OF TIPPING:

If you are on a date, your date will form a lasting opinion of you through the tip amount you leave a server. So when you take a date to dinner in a restaurant (or get delivery) you should always tip between 15% and 20%. *This is vitally important.* Face it – most people have worked in the food or service industry at some point in their lives – even if they only baby-sat for a short sibling when they were 12 – so chances are good that the person with you has done it, too. With this in mind, *unless the service sucked outrageously,* remember that your generosity, or lack of it, will draw some attention from your date. I can tell you that they are assessing *everything* you do (don't groan, you know you're assessing them, too.) It's discovery time - and you DO NOT want for them to *discover* that you are tight and squeaky when it comes to tipping.

Think back. Is there a great first date somewhere in your past that was going **so well** when all of a sudden, after dinner, an arctic blast swept in and turned your lips blue? Well – **now you know why.**

Sorry guys, but we all know that in any U.S. restaurant with table service, tipping is expected. And if you leave a crappy tip, then you can *expect* that your date will go home and delete you from their 'I Want This Guy' list. And why wouldn't they? If you are too cheap to leave a decent tip, that fact will tell your date that a future with you holds a whole lot of *nothing special.* No new car, no kitchen remodel, no fabulous prom dress for your daughter, no gall bladder surgery for Mom. (If you can't part with your hard earned cash and you justify your bad tipping by telling yourself that the food server gets hourly pay for what they do, then you have 3 choices. They are: 1) Never date. 2) Get good at cooking at home – *try DiJorno.* 3) Find a partner who squeaks like you.)

PAY THE BILL (When you're on a date)

OK, we got ahead of ourselves. We've already ended the dinner by leaving a good tip, so let me rewind and suggest that the first few times you date someone, *you pay.* Some guys hate this unwritten rule, feeling that it is unfair so I'm sorry to tell you that unfortunately, it's tradition. Just as it's tradition for great guys to hold doors, pick up a dropped item for someone, give up his seat on a crowded bus or subway for a female or elderly person, etc. And even though the liberal females of the world may disagree with this and want to cover their own tab (and they may not), the polite and gentlemanly thing for you to do is grab the check. (Of course everything you are reading here is 'take it or leave it' advice, so by all means... *do what you want.*)

Here is a *guarded girl secret*: When you have invited a female out to a meal with you, even if she tries to pay for her own food/drinks, if you allow it she may end up seeing you as *not so great*. Typically she wants to be polite but may expect you to say 'No way, I'm buying'. Since you have invited her out, you must come across as decisive and self-assured, so keep a smile on your face as you tell her that perhaps she can take you out sometime soon. (Plus that will mean another date.) Stand your ground. DO NOT BUCKLE! Trust me on this. We are typically attracted to people who know what they want and can get it effectively (but politely). It's all about power, Baby, and you will look like you've got it if you stand firm on this issue. Also, bad tipping and/or allowing a date to pay *OR leave the tip* are the most common reasons that second dates do not happen. (Hey - don't get mad at me over this... I'm only the messenger.) You'll find more on this *sore subject* in Chapter 12 – *The Hot Date Guide*.

Eating is frequently a social event. Food is usually involved at parties where you're meeting people and often making a first impression. That's why it's important that you know how to be clean, comfortable, polite and mannered-up at the dinner table. The proper dining process can be confusing, and even though not knowing your way around a formal table can be embarrassing, it's really easy to learn. So if you've been breaking any of the rules listed here (which many of us have), don't worry – just stop.

When you're invited to dinner in a home, take a gift for the host or hostess. A nice bottle of wine is typically a good gift, but if your hosts aren't drinkers – or you aren't sure – then non-alcoholic sparkling cider will work. To be safe, ask whether your host has a wine preference. Then take a bottle of whatever they suggest. A dessert is OK, too, as long as you clear it with the hosts first. You don't want to upstage anyone by walking in and placing your *chocolate mocha toffee truffle torte* next to the hosts' bowl of JELL-O.

What you have read here will suffice, but if you want more info on the secrets of looking great during a formal dinner (a black-tie affair) go back to the bookstore and ask for a book that addresses table manners – possibly in a book that focuses more completely on *how you can be a gentleman*. In the bookstore, find "From Clueless To Class Act: Manners For The Modern Day Man" by Jodi Smith, and "Essential Manners For Men:

What To Do, When To Do It and Why" by Peter Post. (If by chance anything you read here is contradicted by what you read there – go with Post. I'm a reformed closet cavegirl. He's like *manners and etiquette* royalty.) In the bookstore, go to the Info Desk and <u>ask for directions</u> to find those books.

b. Your Cell Phone, MP3 and Other Digital Body Parts

Calling all Cell Phone Zombies... Come back from Social Siberia. If you're around people, then give your iPod, NDS, Blackberry, whatever, a rest – and pay attention to the real world that is actually happening around you.

CELL PHONES

Cell phones seem to grow out of ears these days. And that's not a bad thing, unless they interfere with the interaction between you and the live person in front of you – even if you don't know them. When you are spending time with someone, turn your cell phone off and rely on that thing called voicemail. It actually allows you to miss a call and get it later – *wow*. Technology. Anyway, putting your cell calls ahead of the person or people you are with – is simply *bad manners*, and tells them that they aren't very important to you.

Whether your cell calls are work-related or personal, when you are with someone turn your phone off, stuff it in your pocket and focus on the live person in front of you.

If you are waiting for an important call, explain this to the person you're with and apologize for the distraction, then once you've taken that call, turn the phone off. On the other hand, when you are able to take or make a cell call, pay attention to the person on the other end. If you can't drive and talk at the same time, pull over. Don't try to read your paper or eat a cannoli and drive safely while you gab on your cell phone or text your buddy.

If you have an earpiece for hands-free talking, cool, but *make sure that if you are around anyone while on your cell phone, they can see that you are talking on your phone.* That little bug in your ear is great for all practical purposes, but it's almost invisible to anyone who may walk up and try to talk to you – or mistakenly think you are talking to them. So politely make it obvious that you are on a call by going off by yourself.

WE DON'T WANT TO LISTEN TO YOUR CELL CONVERSATIONS
Don't think that hearing you talking on your idrone or yakberry is entertaining or interesting to anyone around you. What is it with those mega-mouths who drone on and on into their cell phones, talking loudly, so that everyone around must hear what they say? They end up looking like little girls look when they get their first toy phone. *Pretending* to be a *big girl*. Listening to an idiot on a cell phone yak loudly about *himself* or his *job* or his *whatever* – simply makes him look like a loser who is under the mistaken impression that he is hugely important to anyone other than his mother.

Sorry to be in your face about this, but come on. Nobody else wants or needs to hear your phone conversations, so if you are in line in the bank, *on an airplane*, or in a crowd of people, don't blab on loudly like whatever you are saying into your phone could possibly matter to anyone who's forced to hear you. *SHUT UP!* Geez… (When you see/hear someone else doing it, try telling them to tone it DOWN.) *Always step away from other people while you're on your cell phone -- and talk quietly.*

Do NOT cough into ANY telephone – ever. This is something that clueless people do so often these days, but it hurts ears and is *really* bad manners. So before you cough, put your hand over the mouthpiece first or tip the phone away from your mouth. If someone coughs in your ear on the phone, call them on it. Say, *"OW! You just blew my eardrum!"* or you could just say, *"Ow! What the heck was* that?" Say anything to clue them in to their rudeness – so they'll stop.

> Be sure you use your keypad lock when you aren't using your cell. I get calls all the time from purses and pockets.

iPods OR MP3s
When you are listening to music, be sure that you don't lose contact with the reality outside of your play list. Not only is it rude to tune out the rest of the world (unless you are jogging or otherwise self-involved), but it can get you into serious trouble if you don't pay attention to what's happening around you. You are a prime target if you are not aware of the things going on in your zone. (I'd also like to suggest that you get your hearing checked, but that's just your mother talking.)

c. Driving: Your *Finger* is for using your *Turn Signal*.

Be nice in traffic. I know. Traffic's a pain in the butt, but getting all overheated about it does no good. Besides, you never know when you might bump bumpers or tick off a guy with an anger-management problem... and a pocket full of Glock.

When you are driving - focus on the road - not on your newspaper, not on your cell phone and not on your burrito. Your task while in your vehicle is to get from one place to another without destroying anything on your way. In order to achieve this goal, you must be completely focused on *driving*.

WHAT'S YOUR RUSH?

Do you fly by all of the slowpokes driving in front of you because they're going waaay too slow? You know, they're doing the speed limit? Then do you watch in your rearview mirror as they start showing up beside you at the next intersection? Don't you hate that? You just passed them because they were too pokey and damn if they haven't just caught up. You probably *really hate that*. Then you probably act like you're looking for something in your console or your glove box or adjusting the stereo, so that you're not forced to look over at them and get that "Hey Brainless Speed Racer Guy – *I just caught up with you*" look.

This constant occurrence just proves that unless you're doing 50 mph over the speed limit and running red lights, you aren't getting anyplace any faster than the turtles that you pass. So chill, OK?

CHANGE YOUR DRIVING MOOD

If traffic stresses you out, listen to classical or new age music, or a comic CD or cassette to diffuse you. You'll be surprised to learn that what you listen to while you're driving can totally rule your mood.

For your "I hate traffic" blues, remember that laughter triggers the release of endorphins. (Or so say Dr. Lee Berk and Dr. Stanley Tan of Loma Linda University.) Endorphins make you happy and happy is what you need to be. Even a doctor will tell you that laughter is great for your health. (And your driving record.)

So when traffic is getting on your last nerve, laughter can loosen your tight jaw and bad attitude. Go out right now and buy some comedy to keep in your glove box. Do anything that will improve your mood and make you laugh. Trust me when I tell you that this simple step can save you from exploding twice daily, around 8 and 5. If you can adjust your departure time to or from work to avoid the busy traffic times, do it. (Remember that laughter is the best medicine **FOR EVERYTHING**. Bad things don't like to be laughed at, so when you laugh at them – they lose their 'bad'.)

FYI: In or out of traffic, if you often find that you are stressed out, try changing your daily focus to finding humor. Start picking movies at the theater that are funny. Rent funny DVDs or videos, too. Funny things always will lighten your mood and can immediately switch your lousy "stuck in traffic" mood into a "Night at the Improv" mood.

Also, whenever a jerk flies by you, cuts you off, or pulls out in front of you, think of them as a speed bump. Not there to intentionally make you blow... just there.

ROAD MANNERS
Here are a few 'be a nice guy' tips to use when you're behind the wheel:
1. **Use your turn signal. It's only an inch from your finger.**
2. Be a safe driver – abide by traffic laws. Even if they're *stupid.*
3. Don't speed through parking lots. You could hit a kid.
4. Focus on your driving – not on your music, text messages or your Big Mac.
5. When you shift into reverse, back up *slowly*. You would rather bump into something while doing 5 mph than completely obliterate it (*and your vehicle*) because you floored the gas pedal while backing up.
6. Don't speed through residential neighborhoods. You may squish something with a heartbeat.
7. When someone lets you into traffic, lets you turn in front of them, allows you to do whatever you need to do, always wave to say *thanks.*
8. Be polite. Don't be a jerk by speeding up when someone is trying to merge in front of you. Geez, Dude – just let them in. Yeah, the person may be an idiot, but let 'em in anyway.
9. Unless you are PASSING – don't hog the passing lane. Slower traffic keep right. (Didn't you see that sign? Your name was on it. It said "your name here – Keep Right".)

For long commutes, learn another language. Think about the amount of time you're spending behind the wheel. Make good use of the time— learn to speak French. Or Female. Whatever.

d. Smoke. Chew. Can You Say P.U.?

Putting smoke in your lungs – who thought that was a good idea? Most people who do not smoke these days are not considered simple "non-smokers." No way. They are more like extremely militant "anti-smokers", and if you smoke, then you are an offender and they'll nail you for it.

My goal here is not to save your life – it's to see that you don't smell like an ashtray, and that your smoking habit doesn't cancel out the charm that we are bringing out in you. So if you smoke the 'occasional' pack a day, understand that it's time for you to start keeping it a secret.

If you smoke cigarettes or chew tobacco, you are probably abused on a regular basis. (And your wallet probably suffers as much as your lungs and lips.) Sorry about that. But you need to be respectful of the fact that you have a very nasty and obnoxious habit, and it will actually drive other people away (to plot your death) if you aren't a considerate smoker.

Smoking used to be accepted and encouraged. Doctors and patients even used to smoke in hospital rooms! Today, people are actually *rude* to the smoking section for many obvious reasons. Do I need to explain?

If you are single and you smoke, *beware that unless the person you are interested in smokes, too, then this aspect of your life will probably turn them way off.* So don't advertise that you smoke.

THAT SMOKE SMELL
If you've been smoking in your vehicle, have it detailed - or detail it yourself – every few months, starting now. When you smoke as you drive, keep your windows open so the smoke is sucked out and the smell doesn't permeate everything in there – especially you.

Never smoke indoors. And definitely stay out of indoor areas that are designed just for smoking – like in airports. Stink city. Just go outside to smoke (or chew some Nicorette gum). When you go outside to smoke, no matter how still the air is, the majority of the smoke will not stick to you. Better yet, go for a walk while you smoke. Three things will happen if you walk and smoke:
1. You'll smoke less because you won't want to go outside.
2. You won't smell like a smoker because the outside air won't allow the smoke to stay on your body and clothes.

3. You'll be walking, so you're getting some exercise while you're killing yourself with tar and nicotine. (Sorry. But it's true, you know.)

Unless you are a hack-your-head-off-coughing smoker, the way most people will know you smoke is by the smell on you. So again, smoke outside, pop an Altoid or brush your teeth after every smoke. Cologne and aftershaves won't cover the smell. You'll just smell like your cologne was concocted in an ashtray (and that cologne would be called "TAR" by Nicotini Stinkini?)

If you will commit to only smoking while you are outside, you know that you'll cut back and that would be a really good thing. At the very least, you'll smoke less, hence better smell, better lungs, better *sense* of taste and smell, better sound to your voice, better color to your skin and higher numbers on your gravestone. Just make a promise that if you currently smoke indoors, you will stop. The 'smoke smell' in houses, offices or any indoor area is worse than you can imagine – especially to a non-smoker. Even other smokers will admit that.

YOUR BUTTS
When you are finishing a cigarette as you enter a building, don't just flick your butt out into space as you walk inside. Find an ashtray - or drop it, step on it to put it out and then find a trash can for it. Don't litter the walkway with your butts. At the very least, kick them into a gutter. If you are driving down the road, don't throw your butts, lit or not, out of your vehicle. Littering and starting thousand acre forest fires are each a little rough on the image. Keep a trash bag in your ride for your dead butts. If you smoke a pipe or cigars, follow those same guidelines.

DO YOU CHEW TOBACCO?
With chewing tobacco, my suggestions (other than *quit*) are limited. But I'll tell you that spitting on the ground, or into a container that you carry around with you, are both nasty. And have you checked the inside of your lower lip lately? If it's all white in the spot where you hold your wad, then my friend, you are on the road to Oral Cancerville. Don't go there. It's like the end of the road for your lower lip. Do you really wanna look like a *chicken?*

IF YOU WANT TO QUIT
If you want to quit smoking tobacco, **get a patch, or get a prescription for Xyban or Chantix.** If you want off the chew, go to the grocery store's

natural food section or a natural food store and ask for a cigarette/chew substitute. They have flavored chew substitutes that will keep your mouth busy but won't gross out the rest of us, make your lip fall off – or kill *you*. These substitutes will wean you off the tobacco, and they will taste good and smell good, too. Or you can chew cinnamon toothpicks or gum. Try anything! You look better WITH your lower lip and chin than without, so don't sacrifice them to the God of *Absurd Addictions*. (If you don't WANT to quit – then you're stupid. Unfortunately there is no cure for that.)

You'll quit tobacco when you are ready – and you'll be ready someday. But until then, do whatever you must to keep that smell off your body, off your hands, and out of your mouth. Thank you, thank you, thank you.

e. The Bathroom. Wow. I Loathe What You've Done With The Place.

If your visit to the restroom only confirms that you are a messy, lazy stinker who sheds pubic hair and has bad aim, then here's a new word for you: "YuckGrossNastyDisgustingTakeHimOutBack&ShootHim."

Here it is – the bane of your existence. What? You didn't know the bathroom is the bane of your existence? Are you kidding? Lemme tell ya, if there is a guy involved, this is usually the ultimate couples' and roommates' battle zone. But here's some news for you. There's an easy way to end the turf war. You simply need to leave the bathroom like you found it – or cleaner – every time. We'll get back to this in a minute, though. First, there is a much bigger issue to clue you in on – regarding *that* room.

THE TOILET SEAT ISSUE

Forget the toilet seat – close the *LID*. Probably the biggest complaint about guys and the toilet/bathroom is about the toilet <u>seat</u>. I know. Blah, blah, blah, blah. But the *real concern* has **nothing to do with the *toilet seat*.** **It's all about the <u>*lid.*</u>** If you guys knew what happens to your bathroom every time you flush – via the airborne micro-bacteria that flushing creates – you would start locking the lid down before you hit the flusher.

Seriously. The females in your life would drop the whole toilet *seat* issue like a hot potato if they could see the results of studies done in airport bathrooms and other public facilities. These tests, performed in bathrooms in which the toilets *have no lids*, reveal that nasty, totally disgusting, squirmy, invisible things start to grow on <u>every</u> nearby surface within just a few minutes of flushing. They fly through the air and splat down on anything that's sitting still.

According to Charles Gerba, Ph.D. and Professor of Micro-biology at the University of Arizona, Tucson, whenever you flush, a fine mist is created in the air around the toilet as the water is spinning and going down (– to the sewer, I might add). Then this 'flush' mist slowly starts to settle on anything that isn't running for cover. So anything sitting on your counter gets covered with this nasty mist, too. EVERYTIME you flush with the lid open. Your towel. Your comb. **Your toothbrush.**

It's even been determined that because of this nastiness getting on your toothbrush, you will get sick more often, and you'll stay sick longer. OK, so anyway… please close the toilet lid before you flush – and leave it down whenever you are not making a deposit.

THE DRIPPY PEE THING

A guy spends a huge part of his life focused on what lives behind his zipper. But if you want the rest of us to be as impressed with it as you are, then try proving to us that it is, at least, a good aim. Pay attention when you urinate. When you begin to go, if some unseen blockage causes your stream to hit the floor, the flusher, or the picture on the wall, *then wipe it up*.

You will find that there is toilet paper in most bathrooms and you can actually wipe more than your butt with it. It works on many things, including walls, floors, baseboards and the entire toilet. If you drip on the toilet rim, wipe it up. Wherever your urine lands, if it isn't IN the toilet, *wipe it up*. Simple. Then wash your hands.

The water in toilets has nasty bacteria in it so, again, shut the lid. This will also ensure that your dog, ferret or Billy goat can't drink from it.

YOUR BATHROOM PRODUCTS

When you are getting low on any product in the bathroom or kitchen, such as shampoo or toilet paper, write it down on your grocery list or tell your butler, OK? Because getting into the shower in the a.m. to discover there's no shampoo has a way of ruining a "sky is blue, birds are singing, sun is up", kind of morning. But that's nothing compared to reaching for toilet paper to discover that there is none. This can cause a 10.0 on the Richter scale, so don't use the last of the TP without replacing it or calling the police.

CLEAN UP YOUR HAIRY MESSES

Whenever you shave, trim, pluck, or clip over the bathroom sink and counter, be sure to clean up your discarded stubs and body parts. (You wouldn't want the wrong people to get their hands on your DNA, you know.) *Keep Clorox® Wipes on the counter or under the sink in the bathroom.* When you make any mess, you can easily clean it up with these. Except on the mirror – you'll need Windex® Wipes for that, so buy those, too. (See your Grocery List, coming up.)

Rinse your soap! Don't leave your pubes or other short and curlies all over the soap when you get out of the shower. (A good reason to try Old Spice® Body Wash.) Even if you live alone, *rinse your soap bars.*

YOUR BATHROOM ODORS

When you have polluted the bathroom, spray it with an air freshener. Keep a can of Glade® on your toilet tank. If you are a guest in a home and you find it necessary to pollute *their* bathroom, there's a way you can avoid the embarrassment of walking out of the bathroom with a brown cloud. That would be to flush mid-deposit (a.k.a.: the South Park© 'courtesy flush').

If you are polluting a bathroom, and you can't light a match (really – the sulfur smell can overpower a stinky deposit), then a midway flush will get rid of the culprit before it becomes a fragrant issue. This is a good idea for two important reasons: 1. the smell thing 2. if you happen to be making noise, then the sound of the flushing toilet will cover your sounds. And you can be sure that anyone outside of the bathroom would rather hear you flushing 2 or 3 times than hear your sound effects and smell the monsters your body is capable of creating, Dr. Stinkenstein.

PUBLIC TOILETS

When you need to actually sit down on a public toilet, find a clean one. Do not sit down on a nasty john. You've probably noticed a dirty toilet with dried urine stripes going down the front from the rim to the floor, yes? Well, if you sit down on it, butt gasket or not, you'll be cleaning those stripes with the back of your pants and your wallet pocket. So just hold your urge until you can find a clean toilet… Or at least be careful not to let your clothes polish the john.

CLOSE YOUR BATHROOM DOOR

Here's one last bathroom thing. No matter how close you are to the person or people you live with, leave a few things about yourself to the imagination – even if you've been living together for 75 years. A little discretion is *still* a good thing and watching you 'take a leak', 'take a dump' or 'drop the kids at the pool' (as you often so eloquently put it) is not a charming thing, so even if you are home alone, close the door. Believe it or not, this habit can drastically improve your sex life.

Wash your hands *with soap* before you leave a bathroom. Or keep a bottle of Purell® in your pocket.

f. Hit the Road (and Travel), Jack

What does that guy on the Travel Channel say? Oh yeah, "Be a traveler, not a tourist." Good point. Do that.

Traveling can push your last button, that's for sure. It's tough to deal with the often *clueless* masses you encounter in airports and other transportation terminals, and still remain calm – much less charming. So when you are planning your travel, whether you use a travel agent or book travel yourself, try to book during slower times of day to find options that aren't full. Also allow plenty of time between stops so that you can get from gate to gate in time, without wanting to flatten anyone who gets in your way.

ON A PLANE

Since when you're on an airplane, you may end up very close to the people seated beside you for a while, be very polite. Here are a few tips:

1. While at the gate, don't get in line until your row has been called.
2. Help others with placing or retrieving their bags in the overhead bins when you can.
3. Be very careful NOT to kick the seat in front of you. Don't constantly bump that seat as you dig around in the seat pocket, either.
4. If the person seated beside you wants to talk and you don't, let them gab for a few, then lay your seat back and close your eyes. Put on your headset if you have one. If they keep talking, give short

responses without opening your eyes. They'll get it. Somewhere over Omaha.

5. Don't *fart*. That could definitely cause air rage.
6. If your connections aren't too tight, make way for the folks whose connections are tight.

BUSES, METROS or SUBWAYS
On public transit in any city, it's probably wise to be polite but keep to yourself. Don't stare at anyone. Just keep your eyes open and pay attention to everything around you. When you are using public transportation, you are temporarily hanging out with every level of 'normal' and 'not'. Probably a good idea to avoid locking eyes with anyone, because you just never know when you are looking at someone who plays with matches or runs with scissors.

HELP OTHER TRAVELERS
Once again, if you see someone who can use your help, offer to help. Especially elderly folks. However, when it comes to the little elderly couples, be careful as you offer your help to the woman. (Elderly men can be like formerly badass and territorial grizzly bears. If one of them thinks you are a threat to his little she-bear, you could get shredded.)

Mommies with small kids and babies are usually desperate for help but typically won't ask. Be charming and un-spooky to them and they may let you help with a bag. Either way, nicely offer your help and you are potentially the hero of the day (or the decade) to a little traveling family.

TRY A DIFFERENT CONTINENT
Step away from your usual destinations once in a while. Try an exotic or unusual location for your next adventure. Vegas, Maui and Daytona will still be there next year. Expand your horizon. Get a passport.

When you travel outside of the United States, be a good example of an American, OK? *While visiting other countries, be very respectful of where you are and abide by the rules, especially with regard to dress codes and taking photos. (And when you and your people are at the top of the Eiffel Tower, fight the urge to carve your initials in the paint.)*

Pay close attention to your appearance, and leave your jeans, sweats and T-shirts at home. Encourage your travel companions to do the same. In Europe, typically the only people you'll see wearing jeans or sweats are overly casual American tourists - or maybe Italians in their designer jeans. Europeans usually dress a bit nicer than we do here, and though they may sleep or clean house in sweats, they usually don't wear them to the store. So try to adjust to your surroundings. Buy some khakis or chinos and tuck in your shirts. It's painless – *I promise.*

Europeans EXPECT visitors there to be polite. So be polite! Keep a smile on your face. If you don't speak the language, take the time while planning your trip to learn to ask the locals if **they** speak English - **in their language**. Then they can see that at least you are making an effort. This will score big points for you – and the people that you interact with will probably be really nice to you. Most everyone there **does** speak some English – but if you're pushy or rude, when you ask if they do - they'll say that they **don't**.

Remember, in other countries, namely Europe, restaurants serve meals in a leisurely fashion. They want you to sit and relax and enjoy your food. Plainly put, by our American standards, *they're slow.* So don't plan on rushing through your meals. <u>Also, don't believe that if your food is not served to you in 20 minutes, it will be free.</u>

Get this. An American lady with a bus tour group in England actually told a café server in a small English village that she didn't feel she should have to pay for her food because she had to wait a whopping 20 minutes for it. He-llllo! Let's see. This staggeringly brilliant lady had just gotten off her tour bus with about 30 of her travel companions. Next, they had <u>all</u> crowded into this tiny café in this small country village, which happened to be the only one open on this particular Sunday. And since it was the only eating establishment in the village that was open, it was already full when the bus got there. And this lady expected to be in and out of there in half an hour? Hmmm… <u>Off</u> with her head.

Don't visit another country and expect the people there to cater to your American needs and customs. My aunt from Podunk, USA, took an incredible trip around the world. What a waste. She came back complaining about *everything!* The food, the hotels, the weather. Geez. Especially about the fact that nobody spoke English (yeah, right – they saw her coming and forgot every word of it.) Unbelievable. I knew we should have left her in her pen. FYI – almost everyone in the major cities around the world can speak *some* English, but you need to ask them if they do – *politely.*

(NEVER make a smart-ass or derogatory comment to a local while you are visiting another country, thinking that they won't know what you said because you assume – or they imply – that they do not understand English. They probably do, and then who knows how they might get even with you for the comment...)

STEP INTO ANOTHER CULTURE (– They Won't Eat You.)

If you are lucky enough to visit other countries, try immersing yourself in the culture there and appreciate the value of our differences. Often we Americans expect far away places to be like the US. This is very narrow-minded. You'll be amazed to discover many great things that you'll really get into, and even miss once you're back home again. So when you arrive in Athens, experience Athens without looking for McDonald's and other reminders of the U.S. Try whatever it has to offer.

You would not go to Taco Bell to get a hot dog, so don't go to Brussels to get a pizza. You might say "yuck!" and you might say "yum!" But try something new and see. **You've paid for a passport so use it. Otherwise, stick with Disneyland. The food's not bad there <u>and</u> they speak your language.**

TRAVEL RESERVATIONS

Be flexible when you travel. Roll with whatever punches your airline, hotel, or rental car agency may throw your way. Having your tight travel plans jacked around can lead to nightmares. If you are about to board an 8 hour fight to connect with a 5 hour flight that will put you in London just 3 hours before you're scheduled to watch Mick and Keith and the rest of the fabulous Strolling Bones take the stage, then you don't have much flex time do you? If one flight is delayed, well then, you are essentially screwed. And I don't see the Stones delaying their performance for you (...I mean how much time could they possibly have left?) So allow time for airline and rental car screw-ups and other mishaps when you make your travel plans.

Also, DO NOT light into a counter agent if you arrive in Las Vegas to discover that your bags stayed in Baltimore. It is not the agent's fault – and if you yell and spew and act like an ass/jerk/idiot then not only will everyone think you *are* an ass/jerk/idiot, but the Karma Bears will probably put your bags on the next plane to Nairobi. Chill, and understand that the world won't end if you have to find a Target for new socks and underwear. You can still shower. Even Motel 6 gives you soap and water and towels. So you will smell good at the casino.

If you get to the car rental counter and find that the Mustang or Magnum you reserved was rented to someone else, and you are stuck with a minivan, remain calm and ask if there are any other options. If not, be polite, tell them you'll get back to them, then check the other rental counters there. (Better yet, as soon as you get to <u>Baggage Claim,</u> call your car rental place – from that rental car phone wall - and be sure they have your car. If Avis does not have the car you reserved, tell them you'll get back to them – and then call Hertz. You can cancel your minivan and get your hot rod, Formula One racer or go-cart from someplace else.)

When you arrive at the Ritz, and are ticked to discover the room with a view you requested actually has a view of the dumpsters in the alley, don't use the toilet, don't use the sink, just use the door and go back to the front desk and politely ask for a different room. If they tell you they have no other rooms available, tell them you would like to move to a different room the next day. Then call the desk the next morning at 7am, 8am and 9am to remind them you are waiting for a new room. If you have no luck, then try it again the next morning. (The squeaky wheel gets the grease… As long as you are a nice guy about it and not an *ass,* someone will take pity on you and find you a nicer room.) Or you could just shut the curtains.

Remember that hotels and rental car agencies do not guarantee that you will get the car or the room that you request. And airlines never guarantee that your bags will go where you go. They try, but it's still a crapshoot. (To avoid lost baggage, travel with carry-on bags only. But don't be an overhead bin hog. The world hates overhead bin hogs.)

Bottom line: Remember that your attitude is what will make or break your trip. Stay positive, deal with whatever comes your way without having temper tantrums, and have a good time. Try not to embarrass the people who are with you.

g. Giving Gifts, Flowers and Birthday Cards.
Who doesn't love to get stuff? So if you are the one who's giving it, then, gee, I guess you could end up in the 'getting' line someday, too.

But that's not why you're giving. You're giving because you want to make someone's day, and make the person you're giving to – feel good.

GIFTS

Unless you are buying something for your twin, don't buy a gift for someone just because you would like it for yourself. This is a most common mistake and a regular complaint from gift recipients. Put some serious thought into the person getting this gift, and try to recall past instances or conversations that may remind you of things that person likes. Then buy a gift based on what you know about that person. You can always ask a mutual friend or someone who knows the person well for ideas or suggestions.

Here are a few thoughts on gifts:

▪ Quality chocolates (like Godiva) are usually popular, but they don't always go over well because most of us are pissed at the bathroom scales already. (And, of course, chocolate is a *really* bad idea if the person you're buying for is a diabetic or someone who has just lost 379 pounds.)

▪ You could find (or take) a photo of you and the person you're buying for, then find a nice picture frame, slip in the photo, wrap it up and give it as a gift. This is a cool gift (if they like you) and it's an obvious and constant reminder of *you*.

▪ Only buy perfumes or colognes <u>if you know for sure</u> *which ones this person likes*. Otherwise you may have totally wasted your cash.

▪ **Never buy bedroom or sex stuff for someone you aren't already sleeping with. This is beyond UN-charming.**

▪ Jewelry items can be popular, but are also very personal and can cause recipients to feel like they owe you something. (*Not* good.) Save them until the two of you are in a real relationship. Then watch out as your gift is opened. You'll probably be knocked over and get your whole face licked.

WEDDING GIFTS

Most guys hate weddings but love the idea of meeting something hot and sexy at the reception. So if this is you – the least you can do for the potential opportunity of a hot encounter with a cute bride's maid, would be to show up with a gift. The picture frame idea will work well here because there will obviously be a ton of photos taken that day and they will need frames. Buy a nice 5 x 7, 8 x 10, or 11 x 14 with matte.

BUY A GIFT YOU ALREADY *KNOW* THAT THEY WANT

A suggestion for finding the perfect gift *(huge success – guaranteed)* would be to go shopping or hang out at the mall with the person you are buying for. Make mental notes of the specific things that this person sees and obviously likes, then go back later and buy one of those items. (Or ask a salesperson to hold it for you if you can sneak this in without your person catching on. Or even buy it on the spot if you can do it without getting caught.) Slam-dunk. Not only will the recipient of your gift remember the instant you saw it together, but it will blow the person away that you actually bought it.

To give is to receive. Take my friends Chuck and Patti for example. While on vacation, they visited a gallery where they saw a painting that she totally loved. She is whimsical. He is not. He actually winced when he imagined that thing hanging in his house, but he noted the gallery name and the artist's name anyway. He then called and purchased it later by phone. When it showed up on their doorstep, Patti couldn't believe it! Now, this obnoxiously colorful painting of three little circus mice, hangs in their kitchen. Everytime Patti looks at it, she goes looking for Chuck and everytime she finds him, he's really glad he bought that goofy painting!

Be warned, however, that if you are new to this person and you discover that they are nuts over something like a Porsche Cayenne, it may not be appropriate for you to spend the big bucks to buy it for them (yet), and it may actually creep that person out.   *I know. Go figure.*

If you do not yet know someone well enough to go to the mall together, or well enough to talk about almost anything, it might be too soon to buy a gift *of any kind*. Once you know that person better, you'll know what type of gift to buy for them then anyway. Right?

SEND FLOWERS

When you have the urge to do something nice for someone special, send flowers – *to work*. Sending flowers to someone at work will get that person some special, positive attention from co-workers and anyone else that sees your flowers. This is a really good thing, because every time someone comments on the bouquet, the receiver thinks about you – in a positive way. Make sure the message you have placed on the card will make the recipient feel great. *But be sure it's OK for other people to read, too.*

There are actually two schools of thought on giving flowers to someone you have the hots for, or are involved with (cool for you if they're the same).

One thought, of course, is to have flowers delivered. This makes the giver look kind of like a big shot and makes the recipient feel kind of like a star. Delivered flowers have an air of mystery attached, too, which is good.

The other idea is that if you deliver the flowers yourself, then the co-workers and anyone else who may have heard about you can check you out and this is a big deal for the recipient. Especially if the recipient has told people about you and you sense that you are close to #1 on the recipient's popularity list.

However, if you and the recipient are new to each other, I suggest that you have the flowers delivered. You aren't sure yet that your face, walking through the door – even with flowers – will be a wonderful thing for the recipient. Besides, the delivery will pave the way for the next time flowers are in order, and then everyone will <u>definitely</u> want to get a look at the mysterious flower sender. So be on your best behavior and looking good when you make *that* delivery.

Don't ever use delivering flowers (yourself) to someone as an excuse if you have a hidden motive, like checking up on the person at work. This action is transparent and your jealousy, suspicion and sneakiness will almost always show through.

When you send flowers to someone at work, do it on a Monday. Or on their 1st day back at work after their days off, because the flowers will be there for the rest of the week for your recipient to see. If you send flowers later in the week, the recipient may accidentally forget to take them home for the weekend and find them in a sad state of affairs when they return to work the next week. Then thoughts of you will be lumped in with stinky, wilted, dead things. We can't have that, now can we?

Regardless of what you send, make it clear to the florist that you are looking for a classy arrangement that will last for <u>several</u> days. Also be clear with the florist about the mood of your relationship with the recipient. Roses are elegant, daisies are happy and cheerful, and there are loads of options in between – from sexy to comical. (Anthuriums are both.☺)

Bringing flowers when you meet someone in the park or for dinner sounds great and looks romantic in the movies, but be warned that if the recipient is very practical minded the thought could be, "Great. Now what am I supposed to do with these? I have no water. I have no vase. They'll wilt in my car. *Uhhh.* ..."

On the other hand, maybe the recipient will be so jazzed to get flowers that who cares if they wilt in the hot sun while you guys take a hike? If you are meeting someplace with plans to stop off immediately at either of your places, then definitely show up with flowers in hand.

If the recipient of your flowers has a dog or cat, ask your flower shop to include a pet treat for it. *(Make sure the pet's name is on the treat.)* Many flower shops are equipped to do this and you won't believe how many points this little thing will score for you. If your flower shop has no pet contraband, go get a box of Milk Bones, some catnip or a toy for the florist to add. Anyone who has a pet typically worships it, so for you to *care enough to send the very best* to their precious fuzz ball will immediately raise your pedigree.

Most important, hook up with reputable florists. Go and visit the floral shop that you've chosen to see the different arrangements that always will be available. Tell the person taking your order what the occasion is, too. A birthday, an apology, a "just because," or "Wow. You really *rocked* last night."

If you are close to someone who is in the hospital: Send or take this person flowers to brighten up their room. If you deliver them yourself, be sure that they are already in a vase with water. You wouldn't want to ask your sick friend to fuss around a hospital room looking for vases and dealing with a bundle of flowers while supporting a cast, a feeding tube, or an oxygen tank. Don't expect the nurses to scrounge around and find a vase for you, either. (They're busy.)

Before sending or showing up at a hospital with flowers, be sure to call ahead and ask the hospital staff *if the patient can have flowers* in their room. Often there are concerns about other patients with allergies (sneezing with stitches or staples across the abdomen ranks right up there with bamboo under the fingernails). In this case, your favorite florist probably has balloons (Mylar balloons are hypoallergenic. Latex balloons are not) so have them put together a colorful hypoallergenic balloon bouquet in place of flowers.

BIRTHDAY CARDS

Drop into a Hallmark store near you and buy a stash of funny cards for various occasions. Find the Shoebox® card section, then stand there and crack up as you pick out a few cards to keep on hand for later. Be sure to get several, so that when you hear that it's someone's birthday, you can hand them a card. Whether it's a co-worker, a neighbor or a friend, getting a birthday card will make anyone feel great, and ultimately, *THAT* is what your goal is. To make them feel great. It will make YOU feel great, too. (When you sign the card, all you need to do is write 'Happy Birthday!' or 'Have fun!', sign your first name and call it good.) **By giving birthday cards, you will be putting yourself in a league of your own. Think about it – how often do you get a birthday card from a** *guy***?**

When someone gives or sends you a card, flowers, balloons, cookies or any gift, be sure to respond with a happy "Thank you!" Even if you aren't thrilled with whatever it is, or the person who has given it to you, call – or go – and say, "This was very thoughtful. *Thank you.*"

h. Your Foul Mouth – Could Someone Please Pass the Irish Spring?

Should you clean up your language? Probably. No matter who you're hanging out with, you'll be more impressive if you lose the F-word and all of its stinky little buddies.

I got mad at my big brother when I was 6, and in my temper tantrum, I screamed a 'bad word.' My mom promptly washed my mouth out with a blue washcloth and a bar of that gold DIAL soap. I learned a valuable lesson that day. I learned that saying bad words was wrong. Especially if my mom and her bar of DIAL soap were around.

I don't expect that you will stop using bad language entirely – obviously I didn't – though that would be good. I only hope you will pay attention to who can hear you when you use it. If the people around you don't know you *extremely* well, then keep the smut talk inside your mouth.

No matter what words and phrases are acceptable in *your world*, you must consider who'll hear you when you say them outside that zone. You need to understand that bad language coming from your mouth will make many people see you as a trashy loser. No - don't say, "F- *them*". Why?

Because whoever it is that hears you may one day end up being your boss, your father/mother-in-law, or the dream person you could have married. Bottom line: your classless vocabulary could prevent an amazing person from wanting to get to know you better.

Even the little phrases like "pissed off" and "that sucks" have paved the way for "shit happens" and their big, bad counterparts. Yeah, yeah. So what? Well, here's what. None of them are charming and you know it. When you think about it, you know that cussing is scummy. Whether you're doing it to be cool around your buddies or because you've been doing it for so long now that you may as well be saying 'hello', stop it. If you want to come across as charming, appealing, classy or even slightly intelligent, don't do it. You can handle dropping the "shit," along with the "fuck" this and the "fuck" that, to develop your class and charm, OK? This is important.

WATCH YOUR MOUTH

Bad language (profanity) shouldn't be blurted out in a conversation between you and your friend, mother, boss, or anyone as you're pushing a shopping cart down a store aisle or walking across a parking lot. Show some class. Tell your friends to show some class, too. *Many people are not used to hearing skank talk or bad language, and you should respect that.* Also keep in mind that just because you hear bad words and language on TV or at the theater, doesn't mean that you should spew it, too.

Pay attention to where you are. If you are working in your garage and you drop a crankshaft on your foot, then screaming out %$@&! is understandable. If your Granny hears you, she may still slap you into next week, but at least she may understand. On the other hand, if every other word you use is 'fuck' or 'shit', then we may need to schedule your lobotomy.

Just to be sure we're clear on which words should not come out of *your* mouth, I'll share a bit of history here. Back in the 1970s, the late, great comic George Carlin told the world about the 7 words that you could not say on TV. Here's part of his quote: *"... Shit, Piss, Fuck, Cunt, Cocksucker, Motherfucker and Tits. Those are the heavy seven. Those are the ones that will infect your soul, curve your spine and keep the country from winning the war."*

OK. I would suggest that you listen to George and remove those words, as well as the following from your vocabulary: Goddamnit, bastard, asshole, dick, prick, pussy, bitch, bastard and/or any variation of any of these words.

If it's a word you wouldn't say to your granny or your best friend's mom, then don't say it at all.

Also, here is a final thought about cleaning up your mouth: *The word "shit" is not a catchall term.* If you are constantly using the word *"shit"* to describe everything, then you're dropping a rung or two on the 'class' ladder, so drop the *"shit"* instead. *"Shit"* and "stuff" are not the same.

If you are asking your buddy where he put your jacket, your pack and your book, don't say, "Hey, Man, where's my *shit*?" If you discover that someone made a sandwich and left a mess on the kitchen counter, don't say, "Hey, who left this *shit* all over the counter?"

You do not wash your hair with "shit," so if someone tells you that your hair smells good, don't say "Yeah, it's some new *shit* I got." Do not refer to the ingredients for a pineapple upside-down cake as *"shit."* And when you hear that Elvis has returned to the building, DO NOT SAY, "No *shit*?"

"Shit" is a slang word for fecal matter. Yours, your parrot's and Cleopatra's – so unless you are talking about actual feces, it is not *"shit."*

i. If You're a Boozer, You Might Be a Loser
"Alcohol, taken in sufficient quantities, may produce all of the effects of drunkenness." So said Oscar Wilde - and he would know.

Beware of this stuff. It makes you *drunk*. *Drunk* then makes you do things that you may regret later, remember? Oh, yeah. You were *drunk* so you probably don't.

One tee many martoonies will slam your image.
Call alcohol a social lubricant if you like. And we all know that too much of any lubricant typically only makes for a counter-productive mess. So maintain if you drink, because you will not impress the person you are trying to impress if you're too buzzed.

One beer, one glass of wine – no problem. That could even take the edge off if you're nervous. But stick with the light stuff. And only a little bit. Too much of any version of *booze* tends to quickly pollute the blood on its way to your brain. Polluted brains are interesting in lab tests – remember 'Abby Normal'? – but they're really bad in *'first impressions'* and *'getting to know you'* situations. Plus, when you are drunk, your Inner Idiot comes out – and we really need to keep *him* under his rock.

If you are The Party Guy. More importantly - if you AREN'T a party guy, be sure you eat something that is filling but not heavy or greasy before you go out (drinking). And make sure whatever you eat will provide a good lining for whatever booze you are about to inflict on your stomach. Also remember that certain foods will go down like velvet but may come back up with the ease of a freaked out porcupine slipping out of a silk stocking.

While we're on that subject, when it comes to drinking, if you are a light-weight or a feather-weight drinker, learn how to stop yourself before you get to the puking point. (For you proud heavyweights out there who are smirking right now, get over yourself. We've seen you hurl, too.) Once you get to that spot where a gulp is 'searched at the door', bag the drinking at that moment because your next slam will probably be 'denied entry'. That means that you're only a gulp away from getting the Wimp Award and needing new shoes. Also, if you do barf, it doesn't mean you're good for another 10 beers. Stop drinking and go home or to the Pancake Palace for an omelet.

> If your date (or friend) drinks too much, behave. Yes, even though you are in complete control of your floppy, flirty, putty-in-your hands date, fight the urge to be a scumbag. Be a hero instead. Be responsible and careful with this person. Get them home safely and be nice the next day when they are the perfect picture of the ultimate hangover. (Even though you reeeeally want to torture them with tales of the previous night and all the horrifying stories of the many things that they didn't actually do.)

If your partner complains about your drinking, *don't blow it off.* It probably means that for whatever reason, you are not a joy to behold when you drink. Think about it. If you were fun, wonderful and perfect when you drank, then your mate would probably be tapping the kegs and popping the corks for you.

So, if instead, there is worry about your drinking, maybe you should do 1 of 2 things:

1. Bag the booze and live without it   OR
2. Get a new partner who won't be bummed when you wanna party.

HINT: Pick Option #1. Because if booze is running your life – if it's included in all your time off work – a visit to AA might be in order. There are worse things to eliminate from your life than alcohol. Just don't let booze run your show, OK?

All the same can be said for drugs. No matter what drug you're doing, legal or not, YOU KNOW if it *owns you*. Whether we're talking about pot, pills or pokes with a needle, *you* are the only one who can make *you* stop. So decide that it's time for a reality check (change your reality if the only way you can handle it is *high*) and move on to other things. Try tennis. Or Paintball. Become a rodeo clown. Whatever. You'll feel better. Eventually.

> **"Drugs are just self-indulgent. Kind of like sucking your thumb."**   **-Courtney Love**

(Great point. Perhaps she learned that in rehab.)

THE LONG LIST OF DOs and DON'Ts

Did you just fall off the turnip truck? I didn't think so – I've never met anyone who did. So to put it plainly, you need to learn – and start using – good manners, to be sure you're never mistaken for a turnip.

OK, hopefully *your* mom – or nanny – taught you the basics. You know, cleaning and taking care of yourself, dealing with your clothes, house, pets, how to interact with other humans, and some basic manners ("please," "thank you," "excuse me" and so on). And if you use what you have learned to get through each day, it's really not much extra work for you, but it tells the world that you're a class act. A good guy. And you should want for the world to see you as a good guy. Not a jerk. So here are a few dozen little reminders and suggestions for you. (What? You already know all this? Of course you do. So I'll simply share it with the open-minded guys now, so that they can be charming, appealing and mannered-up like you.)

 SIDENOTE: *Charm isn't something that you can simply develop by reading this list of* Do's *and* Don'ts. *BUT, since somewhere in this book there's an explanation for you as to why it's important that you* **do** *or* **don't***, this list should – at the very least – be helpful.*

j. The Very Long List of What to Do *and Not Do* – <u>For Guys:</u>
(Yes, I know. Girls need a list, too – but that's a different book.)

1. Be polite and friendly.
2. Keep a smile on your face.
3. Make eye contact with the people you pass - and say "Hi" to everyone, including your co-workers each a.m.
4. Say "hi" to your neighbors when you see them.
5. When meeting someone new, smile and shake hands. (Unless your hand is wet – yuck.)
6. Avoid turning your back on anyone in a conversation. If you are talking to more than one person at once, step back so that no one is looking at your back if possible.
7. Pay attention to the person you are with at the moment.
8. Do not sit and text or gak on your cell unless you're alone.
9. Look at people as you speak with them.
10. Give anyone you are speaking with plenty of personal space.
11. Don't interrupt when someone else is talking. (Wait 3 seconds before you reply to any comment.)
12. Always say "please" and "thank you."
13. Always say "you're welcome" when someone thanks you.
14. If you bump someone, say "excuse me."
15. Hold doors for people as they come through or go out.
16. Don't step in front of someone, let them go first.
17. If you step between a shopper and whatever they are looking for on a shelf, say "excuse me".
18. Be sure to say 'THANKS' when anyone has done something for you – friend, neighbor, co-worker, etc. – even if you've gotta call or email to say it.
19. Be a hero every day by helping people whenever you can.
20. Offer assistance to anyone who may need your physical help.
21. Don't be known as a loud mouth – speak softly.
22. When you walk into a quiet place, be quiet.
23. Don't criticize others.
24. Don't be a constant complainer or whiner.
25. Don't be pushy or bossy.
26. Don't be overly competitive.
27. Don't be a control freak.
28. Don't judge people that you don't know.
29. Don't lie about anything – ever.
30. Don't brag about things you have – or things you've done.

31. If there's a chance that you're wrong, don't argue that you're right.
32. Don't be a know-it-all.
33. Don't debate everyone to prove that you're brilliant.
34. Bag the bad language — don't swear/cuss/use profanity.
35. Watch your grammar. "I seen it", and "where's it at?" don't work.
36. Never ask how much someone paid for something.
37. It's not OK to ask someone how much they weigh, except little kids.
38. Never ask people how much money they earn.
39. When a female is about to be seated, offer help with her chair.
40. Give up a seat to the elderly, the sick, the pregnant, or the whining.
41. Show respect to elderly (don't call them *old*) people.
42. Be kind to animals – especially if you want to impress *girls*.
43. Be nice to babies and little kids and their mommies.
44. Respect the belongings and property of others.
45. Be respectful of the beliefs of others, religious and otherwise.
46. Keep your negative thoughts to yourself.
47. Focus on the positive stuff in your life.
48. Dress well; wear clean clothes. (Unwrinkled would be good, too.)
49. If you wear baggy pants, be sure what's under them is clean.
50. Keep your butt from popping out of your pants.
51. Don't wear pants that are too tight.
    (And swim guys, avoid The Evil Speedo – no matter what.)
52. If you have a large belly, make sure your shirts totally cover it.
53. Brush your teeth in the morning and before bed – at least.
54. Shower daily, scrubbing all of your 2,000 parts.
55. Clean inside your ears with a Q-Tip after you shower.
56. Use plenty of shampoo, massage your scalp to regenerate growth.
57. Use hair conditioner if your hair is dry or stiff.
58. If you have a beard and mustache, keep them clean and trimmed.
59. Use 1 squirt (2 max) of cologne, aftershave or body spray.
60. Use lotion on your dry skin, especially face, hands and feet.
61. Keep your hands and your fingernails clean.
62. Leave the bathroom like you found it – or cleaner.
63. Rinse your shower soap. Don't leave your hairs all over it.
64. Use deodorant.
65. Be sure your fly is always closed. Check it discreetly.
66. In public, don't scratch your crotch.
67. Don't announce when you "need to take a leak." Just go do it.
68. Zip up and adjust yourself before you leave any restroom.
69. Always wash your hands with soap before leaving a restroom.

70. Don't be addicted to mirrors. (Reel in your ego.)
71. Breathe through your NOSE – not your MOUTH.
72. Check your breath before you speak up close with someone.
73. Keep mints, gum or spray in your pocket for your breath.
74. Chew your gum with your mouth closed and don't pop it.
75. Don't cough stuff up and spit it unless you spit it into a toilet.
76. If outside, spit in a gutter – not on a sidewalk or on the grass.
77. Cover your mouth when you cough, yawn or sneeze.
78. NEVER cough into a telephone.
79. Chew with your mouth closed and eat quietly – no slurping.
80. Don't pick (or floss) your teeth in public.
81. Don't pick food from your teeth with your fingers.
82. Don't burp out loud.
83. Never pick your nose in public! Keep your fingers off your face.
84. Don't clean your eye, nose, ear or teeth gunk, then stare at it.
85. Do not EVER carry a cloth hanky in your pocket. Use tissue.
86. If you wear glasses, KEEP THEM CLEAN.
87. Never wear your sunglasses INDOORS.
88. Remove your sunglasses when you first meet up with someone.
89. DON'T DRAG your feet — pick them up when you walk.
90. Stand straight and hold your head up when you walk.
91. Don't slouch or slump – sit up straight.
92. Don't litter. (Consider the health of your planet.)
93. Recycle your trash. (Consider the health of your planet.)
94. Don't stare – it's very rude.
95. Don't point at people – it's very rude.
96. Don't eat in front of someone who has no food. Share yours.
97. Be generous instead of greedy. (Be a giver – not a taker.)
98. Try to prevent people from having their feelings hurt.
99. Never try to embarrass someone.
100. Never laugh at anyone unless they want to make you laugh.
101. Be fair and remember there are at least two sides to every story.
102. When you see a chance to do a good deed, do it.
103. Always keep your temper under control - stay calm.
104. Never hit or hurt a person or an animal.
105. Never argue or fight with your mate, or anyone else, in public.
106. Don't yell or shout – even if you're mad. Stay calm.
107. Never take a HANDICAP parking spot if you aren't disabled.
108. Don't honk the horn when you pick someone up – go knock.
109. Don't yell at someone from across a parking lot. Get closer.
110. Clean up any mess you make – no matter where you are.

111. Keep your house – all of it – clean.
112. Clean up all of your spaces (desk, yard, truck, hot tub, outhouse).
113. Put things back where they belong or wherever you found them.
114. When the party's over, don't be the last one to leave.
115. Know your limit with alcohol and stay under it. Don't get drunk.
116. Never drink and drive, and never let anyone else do it, either.
117. If you drink booze everyday, there's a problem. AA can help.
118. Give compliments to people when you see they are deserved.
119. Don't give a compliment that isn't true.
120. Don't take credit for something you didn't do.
121. Listen to your critics, it will build character and improve you.
122. Drop your pride and say you're sorry when you should.
123. On a date, if you aren't having fun — act like you are anyway.
124. DO NOT talk in movie theaters or shows — be quiet and polite.
125. Never kick the seat in front of you, whether you're at a movie, on a plane or at a Josie & the Pussycats concert.
126. Tip your food servers, drivers, valets, hair stylists and other service providers (15 to 20% – unless their service sucked).
127. Watch how you behave in front of kids - be a role model.
128. Don't send emails that you don't want your mom/boss/mate to see.
129. Keep in touch with your relatives (unless they're jerks).
130. Don't avoid getting to know people because of their looks.
131. Stand up for what's right. Don't let anyone talk you out of it.
132. Don't ever make a promise you can't keep.
133. Be reliable and dependable, be on time, and *keep your promises*.
134. If you tell someone that you will call them, be sure you do it.
135. If you're ever running late, call ahead to let them know.
136. Don't have sex with her if you wouldn't want a baby with her. (Old fashioned idea? Yep. But you know that sex causes babies, right?)
137. Be a good neighbor and keep your stereo and other noise low.
138. Keep an umbrella in your car or truck.
139. On an escalator or moving sidewalk, stay to the right so people in a hurry can go around you.
140. Wipe your feet before you go into someone's home.
141. Don't put your feet on any furniture but yours.
142. Don't get a tattoo that will scare your grandkids when you're 80.
143. If you get something pierced, keep it clean and uninfected.
144. Know this: If you act jealous, you're putting yourself down.
145. Hang with people who do the right thing – not losers or posers.
146. Be a great friend to your pals.

147. Never 'come on' to someone your buddy has professed his love for or staked claim to.
148. Donate blood. Ask your friends, co-workers etc., to do it, too.
149. Learn CPR so that you can save a life.
150. Pay off your credit cards and stay debt free.

Before we move on, here are two very important manner issues which are commonly overlooked but still should be pointed out again:

• **Your hat.** You may find this hard to believe, because it's become so common, but **wearing a hat of any type** *indoors* **is actually considered very BAD MANNERS.** So if you really want to impress people, take your hat off when you go into their house. Also, take your hat off whenever you enter a restaurant, an office, a church, etc. Put it this way, Home Depot and the Sports Arena probably welcome your hat, but as far as everywhere else, take it off indoors.

• **Your sunglasses.** Your eyes are important when you are having a conversation, so if you live in your sunglasses, be sure to remove them when you meet up with someone (especially when you've run into someone you haven't seen in a while). And if looking 'cool' is your concern, get this: being charming (by lifting the shades) will get you much farther than thinking you are looking cool (by leaving them down). If it's ultra bright out, and you're worried you'll go blind, then take them off for the first few of minutes of your talk. **NEVER WEAR YOUR SUNGLASSES INDOORS.** You will look like a loser who believes you are beyond cool. To everyone else, you will simply look like a loser (who is beyond help).

Tips from Chapter 1: Your Manners

1• **Mind your manners.** Stop embarrassing your Grandma! Always say "please" and "thank you." Using good manners will impress everyone. No matter what, good manners will work in your favor.

2• **Learn now how to behave at the dinner table.** This is huge. Know how to correctly hold and use your silverware, learn which plates are used for which dishes, etc., keep your napkin on your lap and use it often (see the diagrams on pages 4 and 7). Otherwise, we'll figure you grew up under the table, in the drop zone, with the dog or the cat.

3• **Remove your hat at the dinner table.** (Yep. This means you need to have clean hair under it.) Show extra class by taking the hat off whenever you are *indoors.*

4• **In restaurants, always leave a decent tip.** If the service was average or better, do this. No excuses.

5• **Don't make a production out of talking on your cell phone.** You won't get a fan club by blabbing LOUDLY in public on your cell. Well. Unless you say, "Hello. I'm Johnny Cash". So talk quietly or go away. Also, don't put your cell calls ahead of the person with you. *Turn it off when you are in a meeting or on a date.*

6• **Unplug your ears when you are interacting with others** (and clean the gunk off of your buds once in a while...)

7• **Be mellow in traffic.** If you get explosive in heavy traffic, then avoid heavy traffic. Either leave work a little earlier or a little later. Or try listening to classical or new age music, *or a comedy CD.* Don't use your finger to flip off other drivers... Try using it to flip ON your *turn signals.*

8• **If you smoke, be discreet about it.** Cut back by only smoking outdoors. Brush your teeth often and keep Altoids or some type of breath fixer in your pocket. *Start working out.* That will aim your brain – and your lungs – in a direction where smokes are absurd.

9• **Keep the toilet lid CLOSED when you aren't using the john.** Always leave the bathroom like you found it, or <u>cleaner</u>. If you shed, drool, drip or spray, clean it up. Also replace or make note of anything that's running low – like toothpaste, shampoo and T.P.

10• **Respect the people and the places you visit, especially in other countries.** Dress nice, be polite and follow *their rules*. Leave your sweats, T-shirts and ball caps at home. Buy some *there*.

11• **When you travel, don't let problems (airline, rental car, hotel, rogue tour groups) mess with your mood.** Stay focused on having a good trip – even if you must do it from a room with a crappy view. Your great attitude will show in your photos when you get home. (Your whining and pouting will, too.)

12• **When you buy a gift for someone, try to figure out exactly what that person would want.** Not something that YOU would want. If possible, ask the friends or family of the person to give you some ideas. Wrap it up in gift paper, too – not a shopping bag. (Also, stop showing up at wedding receptions empty-handed.)

13• **When you want to score some points, send flowers to someone at work.** Flowers always attract a lot of attention, and the person receiving them will feel very special. Find a great flower shop, and charm the people who work there. That way they'll always put some extra 'awesome!' in your orders.

14• **Keep track of the birthdays of your friends, co-workers, neighbors and family.** Keep a stash of funny birthday cards for everyone, too. Giving cards is a really charming and easy thing to do — so do it.

15• **Stop using bad language.** When *"F-ing"* this and *"F-ing"* that come out of your mouth non-stop, you sound *stupid*. I don't mean that those words sound stupid, I mean that <u>you</u> sound *stupid*. As in 'room temperature IQ' stupid. Sorry.

16• **If you drink alcohol, don't get drunk.** Get a designated driver, too (but try not to hurl in their car). Always stay in control, and take care of your friends if you happen to be there when they've had too much to drink. (If you drink too often, figure out why and go to AA <u>now</u> so that you can learn how to stop.)

17• **Take your sunglasses off when you meet up with someone and start a conversation.** Get a clue, Mr. Cool. It's important that people see your eyes while you talk and removing your shades not only will show respect, but it will show that you're polite, and not a self-absorbed *poser*. (Think of yourself as a knight in shining armor. They lifted their visors.)

18• Forget everything you've learned from Larry, the Cable Guy.

CHAPTER 2

The Charm Alarm

On the Charm-Meter, would yours even register? Are your CHARM levels running dangerously low? Not to worry. We can rebuild you. We have the technology. But first, with regard to CHARM, here are a couple of things you should know about humans:

Women start out as little girls – very little girls who dream of being princesses. (Look at the most popular Halloween costumes for little girls – and the Disney movies that little girls watch **over and over**.) These very dreamy little girls have come to believe that somewhere in their future, they will meet their very own dreamy prince – and that he will be **charming**.

Men start out as little boys - little boys who do not even come close to dreaming of becoming princes. These little boys do not attend 'Little Prince School', and they could **not** care less about little princesses. Therefore, Prince Charming is not a very popular costume for boys to wear when Trick or Treating. As a matter of fact, most little boys know that on Halloween, a Prince Charming costume actually runs the risk of being beat up by a Spider-Man, Superman or Batman costume.

Little boys are sssso not into little princesses. Not for a while, anyway. But sadly, once little boys actually do begin to care about that other sex, it's too late for them to suddenly become charming. They have already become guys with bad habits and in some cases, as the little princesses compare them to 'Prince Charming', they are clearly more *'appalling'* than *'appealing'*.

But we can fix that. We can change the bad habits to good ones and soon the lovely princess who lives next door to you will start to look at you in a whole new way. And she will be looking *a lot*.

HOW OPEN-MINDED ARE YOU?

When I asked my buddy, Mark, if he would read this book, he said "Would I read a self-help book? Yeah, I'd probably pick one up… – *If it was covering my beer or remote control.*"

Gee, could an attitude like that be part of <u>your</u> problem, too? That's

OK. You're not alone. I know that you probably think you are perfectly fine, but the rest of the world may not. You are a guy, and for some reason everyone picks on you. So the goal here is to save you from that, and at the same time make your life much better – by proving that you can look great, feel great, and get great responses in any situation.

You can be someone's ideal guy. It's easier than you think to improve yourself – just ask a woman. Women are always looking for, finding and applying new ways to improve. That's good for you guys, because when you are assessing your mate or 'potential' mate, and you consider your 'Ideal Mate Check List'… bad breath, sloppy clothes, a flabby belly, and a screwed up attitude are typically not on it. But oddly, when it comes to evaluating yourself, you guys most often believe 1 of 2 things: #1 is that you can't change. #2 is that you don't need to change. Either way, (please prepare for the excruciating pain of hearing this) you're **wrong**.

So, if you agree with #1, then *hallelujah!* Your newfound success is camped outside your door. If you agree with #2 however, then what did that guy in JAWS say? Oh yes: "We're gonna need a bigger boat." No problem. Think of this book as your very own personal aircraft carrier.

a. Can you be charming?

Of course you can. You can do whatever you want. You already own the only tool required to help you develop charm. (And it's not great looks or a perfect body. It's your MIND.)

So with that, let me tell you that there are 3 things that you must know about yourself in order to successfully complete your trip to Charm City. Read them out loud:
1. *My mind* is the most powerful tool on the planet.
2. *My mind* can make me do *anything*.
3. *My mind* is the only key to my success.
That bit of information will rock your world, so please read it again.

If you don't get *that*, then try to get *this*:
Everything that man has ever done – in the history of the entire Universe –began as the idea of _one person_.

You can be the person with the big idea. Simply open your mind and remember that *you can do anything you want. Today,* you want to be charming so keep reading. Your amazing new success is waiting for you.

Speaking of ideas... check out the story of Hard Rock

To give you an example of how your success might occur or what an impulsive little idea might become, I could mention Galileo and Einstein, but instead I'll use a couple of guys who are a little closer in space and time: Isaac Tigrett and Peter Morton. These two Americans are the founders of the Hard Rock Café. They opened the original café in London back in 1971. It began as a little burger joint, where Eric Clapton happened to like to eat and hang out. One day he asked if he could hang his guitar over his favorite seat, to sort of permanently reserve his spot. Wow. Good idea. Or at least Pete Townshend of *The Who* thought so, because a week later, he sent *his* guitar to Isaac and Peter. And so up onto the wall *Pete's guitar* went. The rest is Hard Rock history.

Today, the Hard Rock Café chain has a few more guitars on the walls – and around a *gazillion* other rock and roll items which decorate their locations in every major U.S. city – and *all over the world*. So I guess we can safely say that Eric Clapton accidentally started something *huge* – with one simple idea. He probably sits wherever he wants now.

(The Seminole Nation now owns the Hard Rock franchise, but that's a different tale of success.)

The moral to this story is that the people with the big ideas are not always scientists, physicists or CEOs.

We never know when an obscure little idea might become the next big thing. So without spending years in classrooms or access to large amounts of cash, you can simply count on *your powerful mind* to let you become anything you want – and succeed.

Wally Amos, A.K.A. *Famous Amos* – Chocolate Chip Cookie King – quit high school and got his GED after joining the Air Force. Walt Disney never graduated high school either and scraped to save enough money to start his own company. He did this by eating only once a day and sleeping in a small office where he worked as an ad artist. Within a year his new company failed and Disney was broke again – but we all know that Disney didn't stay broke forever. He obviously had better luck when he started another company later. (A *mouse* gave him *that* idea.)

Bottom line: you are all you need to achieve success and you don't need a genius-level IQ or a million bucks to do it.

YOUR QUEST FOR PERFECTION

Just out of curiosity, if you are in search of the "perfect" mate, what perfection will you be bringing to the table? Most guys have a long list of requirements when it comes to what they want in a mate. And that's OK as long as these guys have as much - or more - to offer a mate in return. But here's something my guy friend said once: *"I want someone who is slim and nice-looking, makes good money – without any debt. There shouldn't be any jealousy issues, and this person must like sex and want it whenever I do. My ideal partner needs to be independent and reasonably intelligent – preferably with a degree."*

Well, that's fair enough I guess – if this list of requirements came from the mouth of a male who met all of the requirements himself – but it did not. *He* did not. Bless his pompous little heart.

So let me suggest that as you pursue a partner, and create your "Ideal Mate Check List," you make sure that you have plenty to offer in return. Because if you are a mix of Airedale, Bull Dog, Lab and Cocker Spaniel, with bad breath, a bad habit of chasing cars or digging holes – and a gas problem, you really can't expect that a national champion, a winner of the Westminster Kennel Club dog show; a beautiful, sexy, smart Golden Retriever – would pick *you* to father *her* pups.

With regard to your career and your belief that you *deserve* a high paying job, how do you think you can get it? What will make you the best candidate? I can tell you that a guy with charm can get more of what he wants than his charm-free competitor can – including the job *or the hottie* that all of the other guys are after.

Remember this: **If you are fishing for perfection, try using something that at least resembles perfection as bait...** (OR: *Don't reach for the stars, unless you've put on your deodorant first.)*

b. You Ask, "What Is Charm – and Why Should I *Care*?"
Because if you can be charming, you can have anything you want.

Here's Webster's Dictionary definition of "charm:"
[1]*charm*
a: to please, soothe or delight by compelling *attraction*
b: *a trait that fascinates*, allures, or delights
c: *that which exerts an irresistable power to attract*

OK, here's what will make a guy (you) charming:

1. Self-confidence
2. Positive attitude
3. Humor/Playfulness
4. Attentiveness
5. Politeness/Great manners
6. Respectfulness
7. Friendliness
8. Good appearance
9. Kindness
10. Intelligence

You may feel that you are missing 1 or 2 (or 10) of the qualities listed, but don't worry about it. Keep reading so that you can understand how to develop these qualities – and why you should.

Here are short descriptions of these 10 qualities, but there will be much more about each of these later.

• *Self-confidence.* **Stop sucking your thumb and quit hiding behind your mommy.** If you want success in life, the most important thing you need is the belief that *you* can get it. If you want to attract people, then live and breathe each day like you are completely OK with yourself. They will trust you if you trust yourself, and they will like you if you like yourself.

• *Positive attitude.* **Keep the negative version of you buried in your backyard.** Always display your good side. Most people are attracted to "up" not "down." You - acting like a happy guy, saying and doing nice things, will prove that you are positive and harmless (and magnetic). Angst-driven whiners are draining the planet so drop the crap – consider it *fertilizer.*

• *Humor/Playfulness.* **Put on your Scooby shorts and lighten up.** The best people are always ready to laugh. Humor makes life better and you can change into a funnier guy by focusing on the funny stuff in life. If you can laugh easily, <u>most people will love to be around you</u> – and we will all be like *Silly Putty*® in your hands.

• *Attentiveness.* **Are you listening? Did you hear me?** Pay attention and *listen closely* whenever someone is talking to you. It's painless and most people love anyone who will listen to them talk. *That would be YOU.*

• *Politeness/Great manners.* **This is a forgotten art. Being polite is HUGE, but it's easy, too.** A guy who opens doors for people, always says "please" and "thank you," and helps little old ladies (– say *"elderly,"* not *"old"* –) is a charmer for sure. **Any guy who puts some effort into knowing and using good manners these days is in the *league of extraordinary gentleman.***

• *Respectfulness.* **Treat other people like you want to be treated.** Golden – isn't it? There are many aspects of respect, but to put it simply, it means treating everyone and everything with care – like you want to be treated. Any guy who takes great care of others like he takes great care of himself is obviously trustworthy, solid and *real*.

• *Friendliness.* **"Friendly" can score points for you (and *jackass* can get your tires slashed.)** You can be a friendly guy or you can be an ass. Friendly people <u>naturally</u> attract other friendly people. When you keep a smile on your face and speak to people anytime you have the chance – even if you only smile and say, "how ya doin'?" – they'll be attracted to you.

• *Good Appearance.* **Whether you look like Orlando Bloom or an elephant seal, you need to care about your appearance.** This isn't about being a great-looking guy. It's about looking like you care about how you look, and that you look like you take care of yourself. Why? Because if you look like you care about how you look – hair, skin, teeth, clothes and all, then people will probably figure that you care about everything else in your life, too. That looks good because it may mean that if we need your help, you can take care of us, too.

• *Kindness.* **Understanding and compassionate guys are rare.** Helping someone through a problem, especially if it's something that most people won't want to help them with, makes some guys natural *pinch hitters* - and we know that they'll always step up to the plate - and hit the ball out of the park for us. Do that. We know you can.

• *Intelligence.* **Why putt through life in the *clueless* lane?** Study the world around you, check out Wikipedia where you can find the answer to everything. Learning all you can will open your mind to new ideas. An open mind is necessary if you want to succeed at *anything* - so keep learning and asking *"Why?"*

c. Rent Some CHARM

Just to give you an idea of a charming guy, I'll list a few famous ones for you to check out. Most of these guys are rent-able at Blockbuster, but I need to warn you that you may need to watch a few chick flicks to see them being charming. What? Like you're gonna find an example of 'guy charm' in the Sci-Fi or Horror section? Possibly – but it's a stretch.

(Disclaimer: Don't be judgmental about these guys. You may not be a fan, but stay focused on the message here. And keep in mind that even *Prince Charming* had a charm-free moment once in a while. So understand that the most accomplished charmer may seem a little bit 'charmless' in certain instances.)

THE CLASSIC CHARMERS
Cary Grant, Gregory Peck, Sydney Poitier, Clark Gable, Rock Hudson and Sean Connery are a few of the *true classic charmers*. I'll add **Alan Alda and Bill Cosby** because these two are not only charming, but they are also very funny – and 'funny' can be a *very attractive* quality.

All of these actors seem to possess illegal amounts of appeal – no matter what they do. They *ooze* charm – and class. So seek them out and study them (edit the 'cad' out of Alan Alda's role as *Hawkeye Pierce* in M.A.S.H. I'll explain more about the *'charming cad'* soon.) Rent "The Bishop's Wife" and watch Cary Grant as Dudley, the Angel. He was perfectly charming. Also Sidney Poitier in "To Sir With Love". Yes, these are old movies, but you can handle watching them both *from start to finish*. They have good messages...

NOW FOR THE LESS CLASSIC, BUT STILL CHARMING GUYS...
Johnny Depp (Pirates..., Benny & Joon, Chocolat, Sleepy Hollow, etc.) beyond his roles, if you've ever seen him in an interview – you'll see that he's made of one thing. *Charm*. He's polite, relaxed, curious, he's not conceited or egotistical, and he's *ready to laugh*. Copy that. (Capt. Jack Sparrow is a cad, yes, but he's one of those cads with the ability to *do the right thing*.)
Will Smith is charming in pretty much any role he plays.
Adam Sandler was not only very charming and sweet in 'The Wedding Singer', but he has created many other charming characters – and though sometimes they are rude, they also know when to behave.
Owen Wilson, John Cusack and Hugh Grant — *charming and funny*.
Jack Black (Shallow Hal, charming) typically plays guys with a notable 'smart-ass' side but, as with any charming smart-ass, he knows when to shut down his sarcasm and save the kitty that's up a tree.
Jesse L. Martin - Det. Ed Green on TV's "Law & Order"; a low-key, polite, and *classy* shot of well-dressed, GQ charm. Bad grammar and all.
Bradley Whitford and Rob Lowe in the older episodes of TV's "West Wing" are also major league charming – but often with a very cynical and sarcastic edge.

Michael Jordan and Lance Armstrong – both famous athletes who have terrific public images. They are charming and classy and they care about being decent role models for the people who look up to them. **Jeff Corwin**, the funny, charming and entertaining host of several animal/ wildlife related TV shows. His is industrial strength charm.

Keep in mind that great looks aren't required for charm. Albert Einstein had a rep of being very charming, but would you call him good-looking? Not me. Cute like a baby Rhino maybe - but you sure wouldn't find him on the Eye Candy aisle.

THE CADS.
There are many charming cads in the characters I've listed, but they also know when to get serious, be sweet and 'do the right thing'. Hawkeye in M.A.S.H. had that ability - and many of Jack Black's characters have it, too. Do not try that approach unless you can drop to your knees real quick once you discover that the cute little smart-ass side of you has hurt someone's feelings and made them cry. (You had better know how to get ultra <u>sensitive</u> and apologize at the drop of a hat – *or a tear*.)

d. Do Not Confuse "Cool" With "Charm."
You can be charming 24 hours a day and still have fun. Charm can laugh and act goofy if it wants, but cool can't. A guy can be charming all day long, but if he's trying to be cool all day long, um, borrrrrrr-ing. No fun.

The guys you just read about are charming but they may *accidentally* be cool, too. I'll explain: A guy who is trying to be <u>cool</u> cannot necessarily pull off <u>charm</u>. But if he is trying to be **charming,** he can *always* pull off a little **cool**. Example: If a guy who's always worried about looking *cool* dumps his Harley or Ducati in a busy intersection, how cool can he look as he dusts himself off, picks the bike up, climbs back on, and takes off – like nothing went wrong? Especially since he's totally embarrassed and ticked off because everyone is watching and *laughing that he dumped the bike?*

OK, now if a **charming** guy dumps his bike there, he may laugh (a little) as he panics (a little), and scrambles to pick up his bike and jump back onto it – obviously aware (and worried) that at any moment he might get smacked by a Kenworth pulling triples.

Do you see what I mean? The cool guy is so uptight and obsessed with looking cool that if he screws up and someone sees him, manic depression sets in and soon he's thinking of drinking the poison. But a charming guy realizes that he isn't perfect, he's not TRYING to be perfect, so he shrugs it off, deals with whatever he gets, and keeps on going - without wanting to jump off a building over the humiliation of it all.

(Do not try to fake charm. Reference Gilderoy Lockhart in the third Harry Potter movie. The average guy can't pull it off and he will usually end up chasing scampering customers around used car lots. If you know that guy, buy him this book.)

e. Step Out of Your *Comfort Zone*, Smile and Say, "Hi."
The guys with the true charm usually get whatever they want, and the good part is that their club is not exclusive. Everyone is welcome, and you can join just by deciding that you want to be charming. Start with saying 'hello' to us.

One afternoon my girlfriend told me this story: "I was walking down the street today and I noticed a guy coming my way on the sidewalk across the street. When we were across from each other, he looked over, gave me a friendly smile, said 'hello,' then looked back ahead and walked on. There was no flirting or weirdness, and even though he wasn't great looking, he completely charmed me by smiling, saying 'hi,' then moving on. I wanted to follow him home and have his baby!"

Wow. So can you see how incredibly easy it is for you to get people that you don't even know to feel good about you and like you? Get this: Four easy steps: (1) Look at someone. (2) Smile. (3) Say "Hi." (4) Move on. Can you do that? Sure you can. Nobody bites. Just look, smile and say "hello." It's very simple, and if you can take these 4 easy steps, then you are on your way to owning some serious charm. And ruling the world. *Or getting whatever you want.*

If someone doesn't say "Hi" back to you, who cares? Maybe they didn't hear you. Maybe they don't speak your language. Or maybe he or she is simply an idiot. Even if you say hello to an idiot and you get no response, you won't die. It's no loss to you if someone doesn't respond, because saying "Hi" didn't cost you anything and it was the right - and charming - thing to do. Keep doing it. Your charm will get you more "Hi"s than not.

If you are one of the 25% of guys whose skin crawls at the idea of speaking to strangers, get a book that focuses on your 'stage-fright'. **"Feel the Fear and Do It Anyway"** by Susan Jeffers. **Then step into the spotlight. It's OK. You may even love it in there.**

Just remember: Arrogance, conceit and huge egos aren't charming. You need to be open-minded and you should always be looking for ways to improve yourself, not trying to convince us all that you are already *great*.

If you have a buddy (like Beavis) who swears you're perfectly cool just the way you are and that no improvement is needed – *and you believe him* – you will only confirm your very own permanent seat on the Dateless or Doghouse or Dumb-ass Express. However, if you *are* fantastic just as you are, then reading this book proves that you are open-minded, too, and *that* is a *totally charming* quality.

Tips from Chapter 2: The Charm Alarm

1• **Know that you can do whatever you want.** Be open-minded and put your brain to work on being charming. You'll succeed and actually *get* whatever you want.

2• **Study the ten characteristics on page 45 to develop your charm.**

3• **Check out actors in charming roles to find your model.** No, I don't mean that you should copy every word or action of those characters but see how charm acts, then try to incorporate some of those behaviors into who you are. (Learn more about charming guys by watching *any* James Bond film.)

4• **Do not think that 'cool' is charming.** Cool can be an uptight jackass, but charm is never stuffy or conceited or egotistical. Charm is sweet and easy-going. That translates into sexy, too. *Oooh La La...*

5• **Slide out of your 'comfy' little world and try saying 'Hi' to** *everyone.* Get out there and make contact. This will only get you good stuff so don't worry about it killing you.

CHAPTER 3

Excavating Your Self-Confidence
(Get a Backhoe - Dig It Out)
Vital stuff if you want to rule the world... or get some *snugly*.

a. No Fear
Remember the dream where you showed up at school with no clothes on? I know. Cringe City. That dream simply proves that the worry of getting judged and laughed at even comes to bed and sleeps with us.

> "Most fears cannot withstand the test of careful scrutiny and analysis. When we expose our fears to the light of thoughtful examination, they usually just evaporate."
> -Jack Canfield, Co-Author of Chicken Soup for the Soul

First, understand that unless you are facing a cobra or a grizzly bear, FEAR can do nothing good for you. So how can we get you past your fears? Well. To start, let's take a look at Abraham Lincoln. Did you know he lost his bids for State House Speaker, the Legislature, the Senate, Congress, *and* the Vice-Presidency? Can you believe that? Seems like a lot of failure, doesn't it? But through all of these failures, he kept on going *(just like that battery bunny.)*

Wow. I can't believe Mr. Lincoln had the nerve to get out of bed each morning – much less run for President. But he did, because he never lost his passion, or his willingness to put himself out there. This means that either he was deluded, or he possessed great self-confidence. We can't really know which, but either way, look at all he accomplished – and now they say he even suffered from depression! Failure? I don't think so. He abolished slavery. He won the Civil War. AND his head is on *every penny*. (That's a lot of billboards.)

No matter what has happened to you up until now, as you can see from Lincoln's record – you can get beyond *your* track record, too. You need to see that you can get *anywhere* in life with self-confidence. It's the one thing that can ensure success. Do you think *anyone* who has achieved success did it *without* self-confidence? No. And if you have not seen the value of *your own* self-confidence up until this point in your life, then let me just say: **Welcome back from your coma. Hope you had a nice nap.**

> "As for VP, it would certainly be an exciting thing to consider but to me, it's so far-fetched that I don't spend any time thinking about it because we have so many things to do in Alaska." - Gov. Sarah Palin (July 11, 2008)

Whodda thunk? Look at where her self-confidence put her.

No charming guy is without SELF-CONFIDENCE – or the appearance of it. So let's begin with this bit of advice that can make a bigger difference than anything else in your life so far. The first thing you need to do in order to begin your pursuit of self-confidence is sort of deadly, but once you have accomplished this horrifying, life-threatening feat, everything else that *ever* happens to you will be easy. Without question. Easy. Honest. Everything.

Here goes:
Stand in front of your mirror (all by yourself) and laugh. Seriously. Stand in front of your mirror and laugh.

> You probably think I'm kidding – or stupid – but you know that this is true: The fear of being laughed at by others affects us throughout our lives, and it begins at an early age. So we make little decisions every day that hinge on this deep-rooted "but someone might laugh at me" fear. As I mentioned, that 'naked at school' dream proves that the fear of being laughed at even follows us to bed.

So face your fear. Look at that guy that's staring back at you from the mirror and _laugh_. Laugh at his nose. Laugh at his hair and his legs and his feet and his ears. Laugh at his belly and his eyebrows and his teeth. Laugh at his knuckles, his voice and the way he stands there, and since it seems to rule your world, then take a look inside the boxers and laugh at whatever's in there, too.

You can get over this fear by understanding that it doesn't matter if people laugh at you. You won't explode. And better yet, _if you can laugh, too,_ then you have grabbed control of the situation. Suddenly, you are not the bonehead who stumbled and fell in the Food Court, sending his tray of food flying and causing all who saw him to giggle and point. Instead, you are the guy that stumbled, sent his food flying, got up laughing and said, "TA DA!" Yeah, you're gonna get some attention, but "TA DA!" is way better than being - _and acting_ - embarrassed. What? Running away with a red face is a better idea? No. It isn't. Or you could say, "Live from New York, it's Saturday Night!" My buddy does that. (His kids don't get it.)

Big difference. Usually the people who wanted to laugh at the bozo who tripped, won't. If they laugh, don't sweat it. Laugh back at them. Direct your "TA DA" _at them._ They might even help you round up your lost fries – because you are obviously a funny and likable guy. Take a bow. Even if this gets no response, you are still looking so much better than if you were to turn red and crawl off.

ACCEPT THE WAY YOU LOOK

Then the rest of us will, too. Don't obsess over your facial features or your looks. (Look at all the beautiful women who hook up with the not so beautiful musicians – and not all of these guys are rich and famous. Most are simply confident in their own abilities, and they enjoy what they are doing. _A happy guy is usually very charming._) Remember that your success in life does not rely on any specific physical attribute or feature. Your successes are in your attitude – not in your looks. It's all about developing your self-confidence.

Now step back from the mirror and look at the whole picture. Your entire image. When you do this, you'll see what the rest of us see when we look at you. Remember, you are a package deal to us. We don't pick you apart the way you pick yourself apart, because the individual things that drive you crazy about yourself are nothing to us. We accept all of you – and you should, too. We're grown up now. Forget that you were teased in 3rd grade about your monobrow or big ears, OK?

That guy in the mirror is not such a big deal. He isn't perfect – but nobody is. It's not like the world revolves around him anyway – so why take him so seriously? Taking yourself too seriously in life just sets you up for never having any fun. Uptight sucks, so you must allow yourself some room for error – even a periodic trip and fall in the Food Court, or on the red carpet – in front of all the cameras and Jennifer Anniston.

IT'S NOT WHAT HAPPENS TO YOU — it's how you deal with it.

If you can master this terrifying 'laugh at yourself' feat, then who cares what anyone else ever does to you? You will be the best at the most difficult task *for anyone,* which is to lighten up, let go of your worries and insecurities and accept who you are. This means that when you make your next "uh oh" or "oh Geez! I can't believe I just did that ..." move, you will beat everyone else to the punch. Laughing at yourself may possibly even score you some points. Really. Think of what a great diffuser your sheepish little "Ummm, I can't believe I just did that" grin could be.

Take Hugh Grant, for instance, and all of his self-deprecation. Whether he's in a movie playing his usual, stereotypical Hugh Grant self, or he's caught on Sunset Strip with his pants down, he's a guy who seems totally OK with the fact that he's a bonehead sometimes. He's not bulletproof and doesn't try to pretend he is. (The Hollywood hooker incident didn't seem to hurt his popularity as a celebrity or his career. Probably because he shook it off and moved on, instead of setting sail for the Sea of JustShootMe.)

Still not convinced? Then go back in time to the *single most embarrassing moment in your life.* Yeah, you're probably getting all sweaty just thinking about it – but stay with me. Hold that nasty little degrading, still makes you squirm, thought. OK, now imagine how much better that moment could have been if you'd accepted your goof and laughed at it. Can you picture it? The bottom line is this: Anyone who can laugh at himself must have a heck of a lot of self-confidence, or at least he *seems* like he does. (So is it live - or *is it Memorex?* Who cares!)

Here's an example of what I mean: A guy is sitting at a table in a crowded restaurant with someone that he doesn't know well yet, and is hoping to impress. People are seated all around them, and he knocks over his full glass of water, creating lots of noise and mess. This makes everyone look at him. But instead of getting all embarrassed or mad, and worrying that he's looking like a loser, he puts a smile on his face, looks around and then says to the person he's with, "Wow. That was smooth. I wonder what else I can do to make everyone look at us."

This guy is looking much better than the guy who jumps up and shouts "Shit!" as he scrambles to avoid getting wet.

NO ONE is going to die when these things occur, so don't freak out and act like an idiot just because of a tiny screw up that got your pants wet. If your pants get soaked, don't worry. They'll dry. If you can't ignore it, then go home and change – after you've had dinner. But drop the topic and move on – *nicely*. Don't ruin anything for everyone else.

Otherwise, if you can't wait until after dinner to change your wet clothes – without ruining the meal for everyone else by complaining about it – then you are a high-maintenance guy; a.k.a.: a royal pain in the butt. *High maintenance is not charming.*

Heck, even if you spill red wine on your white pants (and unless you are in Key West, and you *are* Ernest Hemingway, do not let me catch you in white pants), it's over and done with. Having a jerk attitude about it won't undo it. Accidents happen, so deal with them with an easy-going attitude. (Back to the white pants thing, get some ivory, tan or khaki ones. Not white. As for your buddies and their pants, remember that friends don't let friends wear white pants. Unless of course, they are in Key West and they *are* Ernest Hemingway.)

If someone else spills something on you, be a class act and smile as you say, "No worries, it'll dry." Because if you act like an ass over something that is so totally, completely, and 100% non-life-threatening, you are about as appealing as a turd in a punch bowl.

Learn to *chill*. Start now. (The experts say that you can develop new habits and patterns in yourself by practicing them for just 21 days. *Twenty-one days*. Really. It may be an odd thought, but it works. *If you build it, they will come*. Sort of.) If you can start shaking off the things that would normally get to you, or if you can stop sweating the small stuff, then you are on your way to **stunningly self-confident**, and a mile above average.

Try picturing the one guy in your life that possesses more self-confidence than anyone else you know. Picture what he does and how he looks as he walks into a room full of people. What is it about him that is so different from you? Does he have a million bucks in his pocket? Does he live in the White House? Maybe. But I doubt it. Yet something gives him the gonads to step out there and grab the world by the tail.

Maybe he's simply OK with who he is. Maybe he feels that whatever is going to happen, will happen, and when it does he'll just deal with it – positively – no matter what it is. He knows he can't control it, so he accepts that the next best thing to do is to simply handle it. He's relaxed.

LEARN TO RELAX
What's it going to take to relax you? You could try *Yoga*. Really. Take a beginner class or buy a book (Barnes & Noble has Yoga flashcards) and learn it in the privacy of your own *closet*. Or try listening to new age, jazz, or classical music.

OK. Listen up. If you just rolled your eyes at the thought of you and yoga, or you - listening to any type of music that you aren't into, then you've just made it perfectly clear to yourself that you are not willing to do everything that it may take to improve. You must be open-minded here, remember? Otherwise, drop the book and step away. Let your terrific life stay just the way it is - you're perfect as you are anyway, right? (Now watch as your potential charm slowly circles the drain ... who needs it anyway...)

Be relaxed and ready for *whatever*. Because self-confidence is fair game for everyone and anyone can have it. **There are no requirements – physical or mental – for someone to possess incredible self-confidence.** Look at famous people. There are celebrities who are great looking, goofy looking, fat, skinny, short, tall and so on. They come in different shapes, colors, education levels and social standings, too. You fit in there somewhere.

If you are painfully shy, try doing something that you always avoid doing because it makes you horribly nervous or uncomfortable (right after you check out that "Fear" book I told you about before). That will help build your self-confidence. Go someplace by yourself - like a movie or a restaurant. Take this book (put it in a brown paper bag) and go eat a meal in a restaurant alone. Big step. Try saying "Hi" to people you don't know. Whatever it is that you don't like to do because you feel shy or self-conscious, DO IT. Because once you've done it, you'll see that it did not cause the Earth to open up and swallow you, and that it isn't as hard as you thought. Then make yourself do it again. And again and again. *And again.*

Order a burger with the works. Try any food you aren't certain – but think – you may not like. This is an odd suggestion, but trying a new food, or anything that you are not certain you will like, then discovering you do like, could be the stick of dynamite needed to *blow open your closed mind*. And then, pretty soon you'll want to try sky-diving and public speaking, too. This next suggestion can give you *loads* of self-confidence.

TAKE DANCE LESSONS. Yep, ballroom, swing, whatever. When a guy learns to dance, his self-confidence level shoots up. Try it. Go alone or get a friend to sign up and go with you. But don't be shy. Keep in mind that everybody else in that class wants to learn to dance, too. And dance lessons also will show you how to move smoothly – we're talkin' 007 smooth. (Rent "Dance with Me". Hey. It has Jennifer Lo-*pezzzzzz…*)

> "To be a great champion, you must believe that you are the best. If you're not, pretend that you are."
> -Muhammad Ali

You can become really good at anything – if you do it *often*. Remember the 21 day (3 weeks!) thing. Do it over and over. Soon you'll be a pro. True story. Keep doing it. Have faith, and faith will be given to you. In other words, believe in yourself and we'll believe in you, too. Also remember, if you act confident for long enough, you're actually going to become *confident*. **Fake it 'til you make it.**

Understand that there are many guys out there who are too uptight to enjoy life. These guys are *not* charming. They are addicted to their own advancement and that is their only focus. The charming guys are relaxed and happy. They're accepting of who they are *and* of who *you* are, too. They don't judge others and they don't battle with insecurities. They get over them and go with the flow. *And they'll find* **success** *because they aren't obsessed with finding* **success.**

Last, realize that you are not being judged by everyone who sees you. Because you aren't. Honest. Most of us are way too preoccupied with our own stuff, which can include our own worries and thoughts that WE are being judged, to judge you. Most of us are just a little too self-absorbed to really care.

Besides, *the people who are most judgmental are actually the biggest chickens,* and they're also pretty much charm-proof anyway. Nothing works on them, so just hold your head up and remember, that in reality, there are no <u>real</u> judges here. Nope. Nobody here but us chickens.

SORE LOSERS

Don't be one. Nobody likes a whiner, so if you lose, get over it <u>right now</u>. Because if you carry on about how "it's not fair, blah, blah, blah", you'll only make the general population hope you lose next time, too.

Take the high road and congratulate your opponent/rival/bane of your existence. Be happy for whoever won or got whatever it was that you wanted because when a guy steps up and acknowledges that someone performed better than he did – or at least convinced a 'judge' of that – that guy is looking waaay self-confident and generous and more important than if he allows a competitive situation to show his *butt* side.

SIDENOTE: If you do not have a college degree, and that fact makes you feel inadequate or insecure, please keep in mind, as you read this book, that at the time he changed your world and mine, the biggest, baddest computer geek – and one of the richest men *in the history of Earth* – didn't have a degree either. So get over that fact. Or go and get yourself a degree. Getting a degree will only take time and money. If you can read, think and pay for it (or get someone else to pay for it), then you can have a degree, too.

Tips from Chapter 3: Your Self-Confidence

1• **Face and fight your fear.** Do something that you are now afraid to do. Just do something you think of as 'out of the box' for you. Something that makes you sweat. Once you conquer your first fear, the rest will be easy. And you suddenly will find that you are oozing self-confidence! *Just do it.*

2• **Let it roll off your back.** Don't be uptight. Accept that you cannot control many things that will happen in your life. Just deal with those things with an easy-going attitude. No worries. or *self-consciousness*.

3• **Remember that you are waaaaay harder on the way you look than the rest of us are.** We don't focus on any specific part of your look. To us, you are a complete package, and the things that you obsess over probably aren't even noticed by others. It's no big deal to us. (Note that certain physical things can be fixed, like acne and crooked teeth. Start saving up for those now.)

4• **Lose the fear of being judged.** Who cares if you make a mistake or do something stupid? No one is perfect, and the guy who knows he isn't perfect will always score more points when he screws up than the guy who thinks *he is* perfect and goofs up – then tries to cover it up. (LAME, LAME, LAME.)

5• **Be the first to laugh at your screw-ups** – beat everyone else to it. This will make you more likable, too. *Remember that once you can laugh at yourself and accept your mistakes, everything in your life will be much easier. And much more fun.*

6• **Do things that you never would consider doing before.** Take dance lessons or a yoga class. Try other things that you would not normally try. I repeat: *Step out of your comfort zone.* Soon you'll be confident and great at doing the things you've been avoiding, and your fears of other unknown things will go away, too.

7• **Keep in mind that most everyone is self-conscious to some degree.** Most people are a little worried about how they look or perform to everyone else. But keep in mind also, that there are certain people who always will need to put *you* down to make themselves feel better. They'll never be impressed by you, so don't waste time worrying about these few. They'll get over themselves someday. Or not.

8• **You can develop new habits easily by practicing any new habit <u>constantly</u> for 21 days.** Remember that you learn to do things well *by doing them often.* If you never try to do something because you're worried that you'll do it badly, then you'll *never* get good at doing it *(or anything)* and you will never have true confidence in yourself.

9• **When you give credit to someone else, you are looking *amazingly* self-confident.** No matter what the situation, when you share or give someone else the spotlight, you'll gain the respect of those who see.

> "The last thing I'm worried about is looking cool. I'm such a spaz anyway, looking cool is not on my daily worries list. I'm not worried about being fooled or looking like I don't have it all together — because I admit that I don't, and I admit that I'm not cool."   -Actor Ashton Kutcher

That's pretty <u>cool</u>. And consider this: he thinks he's a spaz and he got Demi Moore. Hmmm. Wonder what *you* could get?

CHAPTER 4

Your Image (The Way We See You)

In an old TV ad for Canon cameras, Andre Agassi said that image *is everything. No, we're not talking about a camera, but your image is a big deal. When you leave a room, your image remains in the minds of everyone who saw you - and the way you* act *is as big a part of your image as the physical part is.*

You have an outer image (your appearance) and an inner image (your personality). When anyone thinks of you, your complete image is pictured in their minds. So be sure that the impression you are leaving behind is good – not obnoxious, not jerk-like, and not a toxic brown cloud.

You want for the world to see you as a great guy. This means that you should create an image of yourself that is positive and friendly, so that when you walk away from people, they are left thinking good thoughts about you.

a. The Way You Look – *It's All in Your Head*
Great looks are definitely not necessary to be charming or appealing. After all, did you ever see John Belushi in "Blues Brothers?" He was *charming. Well, some of the time.*

And he did not have the looks that Brad Pitt has, but he had a charming attitude, and that's all he needed. Of course, the way you look is important – it creates the first impression to anyone you see and meet. But you shouldn't obsess over it, because this isn't about your features or build.

Check this out: My guy recently made a trip to Sweden. (I know. Can you believe he *came back*?) He said that he was amazed that just about every woman he saw there *acted* like she was gorgeous. Granted, most of them actually *were* gorgeous, but even the women who were not physically great looking and well built – still dressed, walked and talked like they *were*. He was floored by these women. They all had self-confidence enough to know that even if they didn't look like supermodels, they could still *act and present themselves* like supermodels.

You need to see that *it's not as important for you to be tall and great looking as it is for you to be charming in your appearance and behavior – forget about your physical attributes or lack thereof.*

This simply means that you need to possess a bit of noticeably <u>positive</u> energy and confidence. The best way to project these is to SMILE. Honest. Just smile. Smiling is the ultimate charming thing to do. No matter what you look like, your smile will make you look much <u>better</u>. Mean people don't smile – so when you smile, it tells the world you're a good guy. Or that you're up to something. Either way, we are intrigued by your smile.

Smiling is THE BEST WAY for you to present a great image and make a good first impression. Again, in order for you to smile easily, you've got to be *relaxed*. It may not be easy at first, but you can evolve into it. This ability actually comes along gradually as you start making some of the positive modifications in your life that you are reading about here.

> There is one trick to presenting a natural and sincere smile. You must be reasonably happy, relaxed and comfortable in your skin. If you're not, your smile isn't real and it won't look real – it could actually look more like one of those scary psycho smiles from a horror show. Yikes. Stop that. You'll scare the kids and creep us out.

These modifications will include reminding yourself that you are going to be happy, that you will stop sweating the small stuff and that your life is good – or it will be soon. Because in America, no matter who we are or what we do, we are in the land of *opportunity*.

> Remember this: If you can be happy with yourself, and like who you are, then you can be happy forever, no matter what life happens to throw at you.

In society today, the way we look – our features – are quite varied. Generally, we are not as judgmental about the physical differences as we've been in the past. *Every generation becomes more accepting of the physical diversity that we see in the people around us.* This is a great thing!

The shape and size of your nose? Who cares? Thick lips or thin? Yawn. Do you have lots of hair, thin hair or no hair? Whatever. Do you have acne? Hey, wait a minute. Acne? Acne is easily fixable these days, so why would you have it? Hmmm. (See? This is why you're here.) We'll talk more about fixing your acne a few chapters later. But just because so much is accepted shouldn't mean that you guys put any less effort into creating a great image of yourself.

SIDENOTE: Even though there are things about you that you think we won't accept, but we probably would - like those things just listed - there are a few things that *can* create an image 'set-back'. (One is your mouth hanging open. When you are reading, driving, watching TV or performing brain surgery, close your mouth and breathe through your nose. You will look much less dunce-ish and a lot more neurosurgeon-ish. And your breath won't kill plants and small animals like it will if you always breathe through it.)

STAY POSITIVE. Up – *not down*. What's on your T-shirt?
   1) "Life's a bitch and then you die"? OR
   2) "Never knock on Death's door. Ring the bell and run away. He hates that."

You can create an image of the guy you'd like to be by talking to yourself about the way you'd like to be. *Talk to yourself*. Regularly. Say positive things, because the things that we tell ourselves, our 'self-talk,' is huge. **(Read any book by Tony Robbins.)** If you are constantly thinking that you are a loser, *then you probably are a loser*. Your mind will make you *who you think you are*, so keep thinking that you're a great guy - and you will be.

> "Whether you think you <u>can</u> or whether you think you <u>can't</u>, you are right."   -Henry Ford

Yep. You can change that "I'm a loser" idea just as easily as you read that quote. *Once you've decided to start talking positively to yourself, do it constantly. Those new beliefs about yourself will actually make you that great guy. A non-loser.* Focus on the new you and what you *want* in your life. <u>Concentrate</u>.

> **Just ask anyone who has achieved great success. Do you think Donald Trump sat around believing that he wouldn't succeed? I'm thinking not. He figured out what he wanted, and he mapped out his road to get it. He got it, all right – wouldn't you say? <u>You</u> can do that, too. (And you can do it with, uh, different hair.)**

Positive energy, Pal. That's all you need, and there's a ton of it inside you – you just don't know it yet. It may not sound easy, but you really can change your beliefs just like you change your socks. Start right away. You and your image get together at the mirror again and make some decisions and commitments to each other. *There is NO LAW that says you must stay the way you are right now.* You can change anything about your personality the minute you decide to do it. No lie.

Keep this next idea in your head AT ALL TIMES:
Whatever I focus on is what I will get or become.
Whatever I focus on is what I will get or become.
Whatever I focus on is what I will get or become.

For instance, DO NOT focus on your acne. Focus on your acne being GONE. That would be you - with a clean, clear face. Don't focus on your mountain of debt. Focus on yourself—without any debt. Think about it. A lot. Because **whatever you focus on is what you will get or become.**

When you have a positive focus on the person you are going to be, then **live it and breathe it by writing your goals down** and sticking them up everywhere you'll look. Put sticky notes on your refrigerator, bathroom mirror, the steering wheel of your car or truck, in your wallet. If your buddies see the notes and ask about them, just tell them that you are improving your image and they should try it, too. You can bet that once they notice you have changed, they will be wanting to change as well. Or they'll run away. If so, let 'em go. Use your 'One Free Upgrade' coupon now - *and get some better buddies.*

I'll remind you of this again: Your mind is the most powerful thing in the entire world. All that has happened since the beginning of time, everything done by humans, in the history of humans, simply began as the idea of one person.

Your mind is not only the control panel of your body, but it controls your future, too. It is the one thing you can always rely on to make things happen for you (– good things or bad things). *So put it to effective use and let it create the guy that you want to be.*

If you happen to have old issues from your past with your parents or from an old relationship that have been ruling you or messing with your head, then call the head doc. Do whatever it takes to clear your mind and let it be happy *NOW* so that you can really feel good, smile *and relax.*

Here's a thought. I'm sure you've heard someone say, "Smile, you'll feel better." It sounds stupid, doesn't it? Hmmm. Try it. Check this out: My guy and I were in a very *heated* discussion one day, when amid the temper tantrums and the flying vases, the doorbell rang. At the door was our favorite of all doorbell ringers, our paperboy (remember them?). This kid was like a puppy – there was just no being pissy while he was around. So anyway, through our anger, we had to smile and be polite for the minute or so that the puppyboy was collecting his money and telling us all about his great new stepbrother. (See what I mean?)

He finally left and we could resume our battle. Well, what do you think? We closed the door and looked at each other and busted up. Our moods had completely changed in the few minutes that we had to smile and be nice. Man… a perfectly good rage was gone. Smiling and being nice for those few moments completely zapped our 'ticked.' Geez. So there a lesson was learned. Smile, and (as crappy as it may be) you will just be forced to feel better.

In brief, the way you look comes from inside your head, so think positively and be happy in there. That way you will look happy, and the rest of us will be chanting "Red Rover, Red Rover, send *(your name here)* over". Plus, if you can keep your focus on being a positive thinker – keeping a smile in your mind and on your face – you will automatically look *fantastic.*

b. Are Your Brain and Your Mouth *Connected?*
If you think a "thesaurus" is a dinosaur, then, Dude, we reeeeeally need to talk.

FYI – to the guys who do not know what a thesaurus is, no worries. It's a book that lists alternatives to words. If you look up the word "car" in a thesaurus, it may list: vehicle, automobile, auto, ride, rig, sedan, coupe, van or wagon. Very helpful if you like to write. *Or talk.*

I understand how intimidating grammar issues can be – especially for many guys. But we are not talking about getting an "A" in college. Our goal is simply to help you speak like you could. And it's <u>way</u> easy.

A dictionary, a thesaurus and a book on grammar will help you improve your vocabulary and improve the way you sound when you speak. Use them – they'll make you a much smarter guy. Visit Barnes & Noble or amazon.com and order the **Webster's New World Pocket Desk Set**. It's a one-stop shop with a dictionary, a thesaurus and a section on improving your grammar. So get it. It's important that you know the right thing to say. Picking the right way to say it is important, too.

> **The best-dressed and most visually appealing guy on Earth can walk into a room and grab everyone's attention in a very charming way, but if he opens his mouth and "I'm a dumb-ass" falls out, then we'd better fade to black fast.**

You can impress us with an amazing vocabulary, but you need to be sure that you *have* one. Don't use words and phrases you think you know the meanings of, but aren't sure. Get sure. *It's easy.* (With a dictionary, a thesaurus, and a book on grammar.)

Many years ago, I had a neighbor with a chronic vocabulary problem. He would use phrases such as, "When will the *'Statue' of Limitations* run out?" and "That kid seems to have an *inferiority 'complexion'*." He was a little mixed up — and although he was really good at many things, when he opened his mouth and spoke, it seemed pretty clear that somewhere, a village was missing it's idiot. (FYI: **'Statute** of Limitations' and 'inferiority **complex'** were the points that he was trying to make.) And hey! Hammer Girl on TV! The phrase is not "...opening Pandora's *BREAD* box". (But that could be a great name for a bakery.) "Nip it in the butt"? No. The saying is "nip it in the bud", Bud.

Another way to expand your vocabulary would be to start doing crossword puzzles. Don't groan... it's true. Crosswords are the perfect, healthy brain candy. Pick up a crossword dictionary, too. (It'll increase your odds of puzzle success.)

Remember this: Sometimes we're better off just keeping our mouths shut. My point? *If you're going to try to present yourself as someone that you're not, but want to be, do the homework first so that you can succeed.*

> "It's better to keep your mouth closed and be thought a fool than to open your mouth and confirm it."
> —Mark Twain

Watch your grammar.

You would not want to let one wrong word lower your perceived IQ by 50 points would you? If you are resisting my suggestion to get the Webster's 3-volume set, then you can get a basic clue about proper grammar by paying close attention while you are reading the newspaper or watching the news. There are always exceptions, but most journalists use correct grammar. *You really should consider getting that Webster set...*

Here are two *common* **examples of bad grammar:** "I *seen* it" and "Where is my coat *at*?" These mistakes are heard all the time, but they still are wrong. Instead say: "I've seen it" or "I saw it." And drop the "at" from the end of any sentence. Just leave it off. Instead, ask, "Where is my coat?" Do not ask "Where are you AT?" Just say "Where are you?" No *at* on the end, please. (If you feel clueless about grammar – what's right, what's wrong, then I repeat, read more newspapers and magazines, call on 'Mr. Webster', or check out www.dictionary.com.)

When you answer the phone...

Whenever you answer a call, and the person calling asks for *you* (*Mike*), don't say: "This is HIM", and don't say: "This is ME." Say: "This is MIKE." or "This is HE." (Or you can just sound stupid.)

Important! Learn to pronounce words correctly. Here are a few words that are commonly pronounced *incorrectly:*
• "Escape" is pronounced 'S-cape' – **Not 'X-cape.'**
• "Especially" is pronounced 'S-pecially' – **Not 'X-pecially.'**
• "Espresso" is pronounced 'S-presso' – **Not 'X- presso.'**
You'll notice that there's no 'X' anywhere around these words, or even down the street from them. Following are more examples of common words being pronounced *wrongly:*
• "Naked" – if you have no clothes on, you are **nay-ked**, not **neck-it**.
• "Nuclear" is pronounced 'noo-*KLEE*-er', **not** 'noo-*KEW*-ler' (or noo-*Q*-ler'.) No matter how many politicians you hear mispronounce it in their speeches on TV, *it's still wrong.* " Nuculer" ISN'T a word.

• "Realtor" is pronounced 'reel-tore' not 'reel-a-ter'.
The word has only two sylables – not three.

   Also, you really need to be certain your sentences aren't loaded with
"like"s, "uh"s, "um"s, and "ya know"s.

Like, uh, ya, um, know, what I'm uh, sayin', ...right?

Start paying close attention to what you say, and edit those out. Dude.

   Whatever you say, be sure that you speak clearly. Hold your head up
and look at your target audience or person. Don't mumble.

DON'T INTERRUPT

   When someone else is talking, let him or her finish before you speak. You
would rather miss the opportunity to say something than interrupt
someone or cut them off. To ensure you've let this person complete his
or her thought, use this handy tool for good communicating: Wait for
3 seconds after someone has spoken before you talk. Simply count to 3
– silently, of course. This will work, so try it.

   Some people think nothing of interrupting you or talking while you
are still talking. Over-talking is a *really unappealing* habit. If you are close
to someone who does this, point it out and tell this person to stop. Help
rid the world of this irritating noise pollution.

> **Are you the expert on Lamborghini vs. Ferrari or Budweiser
> vs. Miller? How about mayonnaise vs. Miracle Whip? It's
> important for you to be tolerant and fair, letting others voice
> their opinions, even if you're in a casual debate about your
> favorite subject – one in which you believe that you are the
> World's Resident Expert. Respect another person's point of
> view, and let them speak their mind - even if you completely
> disagree (and you know that they are <u>clueless</u>).**

THINK BEFORE YOU SPEAK.
   Be patient in your conversations and think about what you want to
say before you speak. *Practice some communication skills on your family or
close friends.* We are typically most comfortable with them, and so we are
usually not on our best behavior. Try the 3-second-wait thing on them.
They don't need to know what's up, but they are a good place to start
practicing. They're also likely to push your buttons, so you can practice
restraint with them, too.

If you have trouble talking to people because of nervousness, contact **Toastmasters®**. This organization can help anyone become more comfortable when it comes to speaking with – or to – other people. It's also *affordable for everyone*. If you have something to sell, then you need to go hang out with the *Toastmasters®* for a while.

> **Anybody who wants to develop better speaking skills is welcome at Toastmasters®.** Members include everyone from coin collectors to garbage collectors, and they can help you, too, so call. Or visit www.toastmasters.com and enter your city or zip code for a list of the locations and meeting times near you.

For comfortable subjects to talk about, try FOOD topics. Talking about food and restaurants almost always makes for easy conversation. We all eat, right? So we can all relate to food talk. Speaking of food, learn to cook and get good at it. Having someone over for a <u>great</u> meal that *you* prepared will impress anyone. (As long as it consists of more than brownies and ramen.)

HaHaHa...

If you are a couch potato and you like to sit and stare at the TV (I don't encourage that...), I'm going to offer a suggestion: Watch funny stuff – sitcoms and comedy shows. Check out the Comedy Channel (Jon Stewart lives there and if he can't make you laugh then just wait. Stephen Colbert is on next – he's the guy with the floppy ear – and if you can survive him without laughing, then you may need to see a doctor). If you want to get a laugh AND a clue about females, watch Sex And The City. (There's your chance to snag some insider information about women.)

If you're into old stuff, then TV Land and Nick at Night networks have old sitcoms. Also check out BBC. Listen to comedy CDs. The benefits of funny stuff are numerous. For one thing, they'll change your outlook on life and put funny thoughts in your head. Then whenever someone makes a comment to you, you're more likely to have a witty comeback ready – and that's a good thing.

> **Laughter makes us feel good, so try to surround yourself with it, watch comedy. Our goal here, after all, is to make you feel good, because you can't be charming if you don't.**

c. Keep Lying and You'll Go Blind

Don't lie. You'll get caught, and getting caught in a lie will make you look like a total <u>loser</u>. So tell the truth. It's OK. I promise your penis won't fall off.

Exaggerating your abilities, jobs, accomplishments, education or experiences is not charming or appealing. It's pathological. Accept yourself for who you are and we will accept you for who you are, too.

What do you have to lie about anyway? Then stop doing stuff that you have to hide. Life is so much easier when you are only dealing with the facts – and those are hard enough to remember. Why would you want to complicate your life by having to remember the many ridiculous stories that – for whatever absurd reason – you choose to tell?

If you are the tall-tale teller, then your friends probably think of you like they think about a third-grader. Don't make up big stories that you think will make you seem like the big man on campus. Just live with your real image, no matter how much bigger you wish it was, because once people know you are a constant fibber, yours will suddenly only be about two inches – your image, I mean.

Once you are caught in a lie, no matter how small or unimportant that lie may seem to you, the cockroaches have just made off with your credibility. So now you may be thought of as a LIAR — forever.

Not good. Totally not good. Plus, the lies that people tell are usually so pointless. Are you the guy at the party who tells one person in the living room that you were born in New York City, and then an hour later you tell someone in the kitchen that you were born in New Orleans? What's up with that? Don't you know that people might compare notes? If you lie, and people discover it, then you lose any hope of gaining their respect or being considered credible to the people who hear you. You'll probably be leaving the party alone, too. <u>Do not</u> lie.

Trust is vital for any good relationship – whether it's with your dad, your lover, your best friend or your boss. So never get caught in a lie. Just tell the truth. Even if it feels like a paper cut for a second.

d. Uh Oh. What Did You *Do?*

Don't wait until someone comes crashing into your face asking, "DID YOU DO THIS?!" If you've done something wrong - either by mistake or by bad judgment - cop to it now. Just fess up <u>immediately</u>.

It's time to face the music, Beethoven. And follow your confession with an immediate and SINCERE apology. Do not hide under your desk or your bed if you've screwed up. Just go to the person you have screwed up on and say, "Hey, I made a big mistake. Here's what happened: ____. I'm sorry." Because believe me when I tell you that if you try to hide your screw up and that person spends lots of time and energy trying to find out who did it, and fix it, it's gonna be waaaaay worse for you when they discover it was you. And chances are *really good* that they're going to find out it was you.

But here's a fact: People are usually pretty impressed when you admit you've made a mistake. Think about it. Most of the time you hear **"I didn't do it"** or **"It wasn't me"** or **"It's not my fault."** So for you to admit that you screwed up is not only going to show that you are a standup guy, but also that you aren't afraid to take whatever punishment is deemed appropriate for any damage your screw-up may have caused.

> When you fess up, the person you made the mistake on - and all the witnesses - will appreciate your honesty. Plus, you probably won't be punished because you did the right thing by confessing. Besides, your accuser or victim will probably be too shocked by your confession to pound you.

MASTER THE APOLOGY.

Everybody makes mistakes. Most mistakes are forgivable, so when you fess up and admit that you've made one, you are proving that you are a responsible *and confident* type of guy. A sincere apology can be very charming and shows a certain amount of vulnerability. This is good for the rest of us to see in you, because a little vulnerability in any guy is actually very appealing.

BUT! If you happen to make a really big mistake, like you've somehow caused a sun-size asteroid to head straight for the Earth, forgive us for not forgiving you. Some mistakes are impossible for people to easily let you slide. In this case, simply offer your deepest and most heart-felt apology, but don't expect forgiveness. You may get it, eventually, but prepare to wait a century or two.

In the case that you don't understand why someone you have ticked off is so upset – because you don't believe whatever you did was *that* bad – just accept that <u>to this person</u> - *it **was** **THAT** **bad***. So apologize, then give them directions to the rock you'll be waiting under, if and when they ever decide to get over it and speak to you again.

But remember that sometimes they might not get over it – ever.

Accept that – because for some people, some things are simply unforgivable. We all nurse our wounds differently. Try to make your case and cross your fingers, but <u>never</u> attack someone for not forgiving you. Just try to carefully and *apologetically* negotiate your way back into their no-longer-pissed-at-you zone.

e. Feed Your Gray Matter – Or It Will Turn to Mush
"Life is tough, but it's tougher when you're stupid." John Wayne said that. Giddy-up.

If you want to create a smarter image of yourself, you need to feed your brain more than *candy*. For instance, you could try paying closer attention to Washington, D.C. and your state senators than to Hollywood and the pro ballplayers. (Even celebs will tell you that.)

> "Why do people know more about actors than they know about the guys who are spending their tax dollars?"
> -Bruce Willis

Does it really matter that a famous rocker is being sued by a famous supermodel for fathering her famous baby behind her famous lesbian lover's actor husband's back? **PUH-leeeeze!**

We're using our *I.T.* to 'Google' bimbos and boneheads. Wow. *How brilliant is that?* Entertainment is the fun filler stuff we should use periodically to help us unwind after pushing our brains on the things that really matter. You know, those things we do to make ourselves happier and more successful. Better in bed. (Good. You're *listening*.)

Keeping up on Jackass's latest antics or on 'celebrity' blogs will not do anything to get you to a higher spot in the food chain - or on the ladder of success. You are wasting RAM on that stuff, so turn on the Discovery

Channel instead. Your brain requires exercise and attention to maintain it and keep it healthy. Just like your car and everything else in your life that's worth *diddly-squat.*

To grow your brain, check out these free web site encyclopedias; www.wikipedia.com, www.about.com, www.answers.com,. These sites are all 'ANSWER' sites. Enter any topic that interests you and you'll have a wealth of info at your fingertips. Learn the history of any company, product, country, War, dinosaur, any person - alive or dead. If it exists, or ever did, you can probably learn more about it on any of these sites.

Read everything. Newspapers, magazines, & books – anything that will hold still for you and improve your vocabulary while it teaches you about the things that matter. (Not the latest news on Paris and her current purse pooch, please.) If you are a fast reader, then read a book a week. If you are a slow reader, find a book that will grab your attention and *try* to finish it in a week. OK, take two weeks. You can do it. Make this your goal, and soon you'll become a fast reader. Reading about a variety of topics will open your mind and make you much better at making conversation.

We know that you can <u>learn</u> because we see that you can walk and talk. You learned to do those things because you wanted access to stuff. But remember that now that you are all grown up – nothing has changed with regard to learning. You want something? Then LEARN what it will take to get it.

(My own example: I wanted to help guys get more of whatever they want, and be picked on less by women, so I wrote this book. When a publisher read my manuscript, he wanted to publish it for me. But I decided to do it myself. Easy task? No. But I wanted to do it so I learned how. You can go to UCLA or NYU, or you can learn on your own like I did, in my living room on my computer.)

If you are uncomfortable around some people because you feel that they are smarter than you, then start researching and learning. And remember that we all put our pants on the same way. You can be a smarter guy by simply deciding to open your mind and start learning. On the other hand, if you are able to broaden someone else's horizon with *your* knowledge, then kindly share it – without coming across as a know-it-all.

Whenever you have the opportunity to learn from someone who's been around a different block than you, open your head up and catch whatever is tossed your way. Ask questions. You will learn, and the person who is sharing an experience will get center stage for a while. Cool for that person. He or she will think <u>you are great</u> for asking about his or her experiences, too. People love to hear themselves talk, so let them talk to you – and *you* will become very popular. *You will also learn something.*

> **"A wise man doesn't need advice. A fool won't take it."**
> **-Benjamin Franklin**

> **"A 'word to the wise' isn't necessary. It's the stupid ones who need the advice." -Bill Cosby**

Knowledge is power, but be aware that your ego can build a wall around your brain. This is usually due to the fact that you don't want to admit you don't already know everything. This can cause you to miss out on some great stuff. I have buddies who are the mighty, self-proclaimed computer geeks. They are notoriously guilty of this. Yes, *you are.*

GET SOME CULTURE

Visit museums, aquariums, planetariums, and art galleries. Force yourself. The experience is good for you. If you happen to live in or near a city with these places, *lucky you.* You have the world at your feet. Make a point of checking out one each month. Make a day or night of it. Combine it with lunch or dinner and make it happen. Drag a friend along. Mind your manners, and experience something out of the ordinary for you.

Visit a library. Go to a college campus and check out the theatre there. See what might be playing along the lines of plays or performances put on by the students. (They are typically good, cheap entertainment.) Check out unique buildings and different architectural styles, too.

With regard to what you watch on TV between your comedy shows, try the History Channel, the Discovery Channel, TLC and the National Geographic Channel. Laughter is important, but learning is also.

You are going to come across as a much more intelligent guy if you can balance a wide range of topics. Again, start reading about different subjects. This is important. You may have a Ph.D. or you may be a high school dropout **(get your GED)**, but whether your preferences in magazines are *Rolling Stone, Scientific American, S.I., G.Q., Gourmet* or *Hot Rod*, be sure you keep a balance. Read the news every day, or watch your favorite news channel, because having a clue about what's happening around the entire globe is very important when it comes to having a reasonably intelligent conversation.

EXPLORE YOUR WORLD. (Don't be boring. Get your passport and use it.)
Speaking of the globe, do you want to be a worldly kind of guy? OK. **Buy a globe**, a National Geographic or a good travel magazine, then go to the post office and get your passport application. (Yes. You are going to get your passport.) Start studying the world through your new globe, magazine and the Internet. Find the spots that interest you, and Google them. Then watch your globetrotting future unfold. Do your research on the faraway place of your choice and make your dream plans to go.

> **When you pick up your passport application at a U.S. Post Office, ask if they take passport photos there. If not, then JC Penney's or Sears, Kit's Camera, Costco and Wal-Mart do. You can also check the Yellow Pages under "Photographers" and find one who takes PASSPORT PHOTOS. One will cost you around 10 bucks. Complete the passport application, include the photo and a check or money order for $90 (save up) and mail it. Your passport will arrive in 6 - 8 weeks. THAT'S it!**

When you have a clear idea of where you want to go, head over to your favorite bookstore. (Don't buy a <u>used</u> travel book because it may not know that a hotel or inn has recently become additional parking for a nearby soccer stadium – or stables for the Lipizzaner Stallions.) Look for a "Lonely Planet" or a "Frommer's Pocket Travel Guide" on the place you've chosen. It will provide all the detailed travel information about where to stay, climate and things to see and do once you get there. (For honest, blunt and informative reviews of hotels, etc., go to www. tripadvisor.com. *Get the truth – then go.* They'll give you the real lowdown on any overnight accommodations - so you'll know what to expect when you open your guestroom door.

How can you afford to go? It's easier than you think. While you are waiting for your passport, start feeding your travel fund. Here's how:

You probably spend about $5 a day on coffee or lattes, sodas, Sweet Tarts or something that you can live without, right? So start living without it. If you put $5 each day in a box or jar on your dresser, along with change you dump from your pockets every night, you will end up with at least $1,825 in just 12 months! That's almost 2 grand...(if it takes longer — so what?)

To be safe, take this saved cash to your bank or credit union a few times each month and stuff it into a new savings account – not to be touched until you are headed for the airport. Oh. When you pick up the cash at the bank, exchange most of it for traveler's checks. And take a VISA credit card. Although there are many places that don't accept credit cards at all, VISA seems to be the card most accepted around the world. *Yep. Just like their ads are always telling us.*

I would say that not only will the one year (for planning the trip and saving money) fly by, but it's about the perfect amount of time to plan the first phase of your exploration of the rest of the world. Before you know it, you are standing on C Concourse, at Gate C-3, with your travel guide in one hand and your ticket to Bali or Prague in the other. And all it's costing you is a little caffeine and/or sugar. Woo hoo! Later Dude! Namaste! (Look it up.)

"As you walk around, assess where you are, reflect on where you have been, and dream of where you are going. Every moment of the present contains the seeds of opportunity for change. Your life is an adventure. Live it fully."

-John Francis, the Planetwalker

f. Earth to Badass Wannabe...

Important note: The coolest people are the ones who aren't trying to be cool. You know, like your new neighbor – the Buddhist biker.

Many guys are convinced that if they act tough, detached and cocky, then they'll get whatever want. Hmmm. There's no argument that there are people out there who, for whatever reason, like the "bad boys" who will treat them badly. This is a mystery to me. (Kind of like the popularity of bleu cheese.)

> **Some people will even admit that they are attracted to "bad boys." What's up with that? And do you really want a relationship with someone who wants you to treat them like crap? OK, everybody. The couch is open. Therapy's on me.**

The people who want bad boys have issues, so get a real relationship with a *mentally stable* person. Lose your bad-boy approach and keep looking for a person with a healthy brain, because the type of person who likes 'bad boys', ie: abuse and/or neglect, can bring lots of baggage and very scary things with them to a relationship.

If you insist on relationships with the type that wants a bad boy, then you better put away everything with sharp edges and see that your First Aid Kit is handy and well stocked. And be sure your <u>WILL</u> is in order, too.

Remember the "no judges here, just us chickens" statement in Chapter 3? Well, there's a catch. If you are trying to out do everyone else in a bad-boy manner, which could actually be considered obnoxious, then you are pushing your luck with that guideline. Some of those chickens will turn into vultures who will want to see you fall so they can devour you. When you tumble, they'll cheer. So you may want to keep your 'bad' in check, Hot Shot, just to avoid being challenged – *and to keep the bad Karma away.* Be a nice guy instead. And keep in mind that nice guys <u>don't</u> finish last, but *boring* guys do.

g. Ha! You Make Me *Laugh*

If more people were laughing, the Grumpasaurus would be extinct, because laughing makes people feel good. Riker's, Joliet, Alcatraz and Sing-Sing. Imagine if these places only piped in food, water and <u>cartoons</u>.

Surround yourself with comedy. As suggested in "Are Your Brain and Your Mouth Connected?" earlier, watch funny stuff on TV, listen to comedy CDs, go to the theater and see funny films. Doing this will change the way you see the world around you, and it can also change the way the world sees you. It can change your personality in a very positive way, too.

When you start paying attention to funny things, you're likely to start thinking funny thoughts. Then you'll start doing and saying funnier things – which will make you more charming. Just start hanging out with the funny stuff and you'll see. Think back to elementary school or junior high. The way you got the attention of your dream hottie was by teasing them. Well, teasing grew up and became flirting. (More on flirting in the next chapter.) Teasing your target was a sure way to get their attention, as long as it's done in a fun and good natured way. Just keep in mind that your ability to get your target to laugh will increase your ability to get them to do other things, too.

Granted, you won't suddenly become Chris Rock, Jim Carey or Carlos Mencia, but comedy will make you laugh more. Laughing makes you relax, and that will make the people around you relax, too. Eventually you'll be a more light-hearted, funny guy, and you'll smile more. Laughing and smiling are two great things, so incorporate them into who you are *ASAP*.

SIDENOTE: If you are stuck on the movies, books and TV shows that are serious, dark, depressing and/or crime-related, it's OK. I'm addicted to Law & Order so I understand. It's an epidemic. But pry yourself away and take a leap into the comedy zone for a change. *Give it just ONE MONTH* and see how different you'll feel.

Tips from Chapter 4: Your Image

1• **Care about what other people think of you.** You want to be sure that when people think about you while you aren't around, they have a good picture of you in their minds. Also, you want for the people who see you, but don't know you, to think that you look like a *nice* guy.

2• **Smile, think positive, and you'll always look *better*.** Your looks are defined by your actions – and by what your brain is doing.

3• **Focus on the good things and the things that you want.** Not on what you don't like or want. Concentrate on becoming the guy you want to be. Talk *very* positively to yourself and put up sticky notes to remind you of how you want to be. Remember this: *Whatever you focus on is what you will get or become.* If there are issues from your past that are causing you to feel bad, get help. Call a counselor or a doctor. Especially if the issue involves your parent(s) or an old relationship. You can get over these things more quickly and completely with the help of a trained professional. You know, a *ghost-buster.*

4• **Be sure you know the meaning of the words and phrases you use.** Improve the way you talk and the words you use by getting a book on grammar. Try Webster's New World Pocket Desk Set. Speak clearly. You also can ask your close friends, family and co-workers to monitor what comes out of your mouth. *Important note: Becoming relaxed enough to ask these people for their help is key to your success. It's all part of making you OK with who you are and admitting to the world that you aren't perfect and that you aren't trying to be perfect. Just a good guy.* **(Start doing crossword puzzles. *Don't groan.*)**

5• **Communicate well.** Don't interrupt or argue with people. Let them speak their minds and complete their thoughts before you speak by counting to 3 after they finish a sentence. Respect the opinions of others by being more open-minded to their thoughts or ideas. Look into Toastmasters® if you want to be an impressive speaker or communicator.

6• **Stop lying.** Your lies change… the truth does NOT. Never lie about *anything.* You won't always remember what you have lied about, but the people you have lied to probably will. They may not act like they know you have lied to them, but they will not trust or believe you, even if they pretend that they do. You will simply be one of those guys who is full of <u>crap</u> and everyone will know it.

7 • **Fess up if you screw up.** (Begin your admission with, "I've screwed up royally and now we're all gonna die." Next to THAT – anything you *really* did will have an easy fix.) Show you have the testicles to take responsibility for your actions, and you will earn respect. Mostly because the world is full of guys who would rather lie and wet their pants than tell their daddies that they were kicked off the ball team or wrecked the car, or tell their wives that they broke a dish or lost a job, or tell their bosses that they lost an account or missed a deadline. Good people will forgive you and/or help you work it out, so don't be afraid. Be brave instead. *Just apologize.*

8 • **Get good at saying "I'm sorry" and you'll get more of the things you want.** Also, let people forgive you when *they* are ready to forgive. Don't push this. You can NEVER demand to be forgiven. Don't forget, if you are the one who is waiting to be forgiven – then *you* obviously created the problem … so chill.

9 • **Be a good teacher by sharing what you know, but be a better student by learning what you don't.** Become a more confident and *interesting* guy by reading and learning all you can. Let others share what they know with you. Keep up on current world events so that you can talk about many topics – and prove that you really know what you're talking about.

10 • **If you've dreamed about far away places – then go.** Buy a globe, get a passport, save your money, plan your trip and *go*! It's actually waaay easy.

11 • **"Bad Boy" simply translates to "Butt for Brains."** So get over your idea that being a bad boy will get you any place that you would actually want to be. Worry more about being charming and positive than being tough or cool. A true tough guy doesn't *try* to *act* tough. A true cool guy doesn't *try* to *act* cool. So get over your badass wannabe self, bitch!

12 • **Work on the funny side of your personality by surrounding yourself with comedy** – TV shows, CDs, movies.

CHAPTER 5

<u>Your Personality</u> (Impress Us with It)
You can be funny, creative and generally brilliant, too, but NICE is the easy one, and it requires no additional training. Plus, the best way for you to show a great personality is simply by being a really nice guy. (No matter what your buddies may say, nice guys *do not* finish last. Forever we have been confusing two words: "Nice" and "Boring". There's a big difference!)

The way you treat people tells the world who you are, so don't be a snob or scumbag. Be a friendly guy to everyone you meet, including the person who delivers the pizza and the people who empty the trash.

a. Who Died and Left *You* in Charge?
Do you judge people before you know them? You do <u>know</u> that there are fake Rolex watches out there. You also know that millionaires have died after living their lives as bums. Keep these things in mind the next time you get the urge to judge someone by guessing about their power – or their lack of it, OK?

It seems that most of us subconsciously divide the people in the world around us into two categories. First, there are the people that we are not intimidated by, but actually feel *superior* to – like maybe the kid who delivers the paper and the "will work for food" sign person on the corner. Second, there are the people that have our complete attention – people who we may feel *inferior* to – like perhaps the CEO or owner of the company where we work. This is not a good thing, but it seems to be fact.

Are you intimidated by the gods and goddesses of the world? You know, the well-dressed, successful-looking "beautiful people" that you cross paths with from time to time? For instance, could you hold your own if Madonna – and her entourage of personal assistants, bodyguards, and PR people – suddenly walked into your workplace and began talking to you? Sure, she's just a person – but she probably has a *very big presence*.

On the other hand, how about the little elderly lady with the cat who lives next door to you? How do you feel about talking to her? Hmmm. Not so intimidating is she? Can you see what I mean about the differences we see in everyone around us?

We are all just <u>people</u>.

Think of this: Did the kids at her elementary school call her *Catherine Zeta-Jones*? I'm thinking that Cathy Jones sounds a wee bit more *elementary* – also a little more average. And I could be wrong on this one, too, but I'd venture a guess that someone out there may call Harrison Ford, um… *Harry?*

The line that divides these two imaginary groups could be based on many factors such as age, income level, physical build, religion, education, social status, clothes, marital status, skin color, lifestyle or name. But whatever the reason, our assessment of others – right or wrong – usually takes place pretty soon after our initial contact.

If you judge people this way, like most of us do, then you need to recognize that this habit can prevent your success. But if you can learn to treat people equally, no matter what your initial impression of them, then you will develop a lot more than charm. For one thing, you will learn to respect anyone you meet instead of judging them, and *this will create a powerful respect for yourself.* This is what will ultimately give you major doses of self-confidence – and it's automatic in any charming guy.

Don't judge others. You don't know what the person you are judging has achieved in his or her life so far. Admitting that you have no clue about them – and accepting the fact that you really don't know who is living inside of this person's appearance – is where you start.

Also, remember that even if you are faced with people like Madonna or the owner or CEO of the company where you work, and you treat them just as you would treat *anyone* else, then you are likely to gain their respect. (Why would the powerful types respect you if you pee on the floor when you see them? Think about it.) Simply be respectful and helpful to everyone – including the person you pay when you buy your gas and the Santa guy who rings The Salvation Army bell at Christmastime.

With regard to judging others, I know a man who treats homeless folks like they are royalty. Do you know why? Because he's sure that one day Jesus Christ will show up as one of them. OK. In this guy's defense, maybe he's right. I mean, I <u>can't</u> imagine that if JC ever does show up, **HE** will appear as a television evangelist with sprayed hair, a cheap suit and a 4a.m. spot on cable TV.

Give everyone your respect. Don't be star-struck over anyone that you believe to be a big shot. And don't act like you are better than anyone that you see as "a nobody."

b. Charm, Meet My Friend, Guy

To be charming, it's necessary for you to be <u>liked</u>. *'Like' is huge. Like is the most important thing. Like is halfway to checkers, dentures, rocking chairs and Metamucil martinis. Sex, <u>love</u>, and rock and roll will all happen on the way to your senior citizen discount.*

Like must happen before love or anything else. (The **major** problem with many relationships these days is that couples stop *liking* each other. BIG problem. Don't *ever* let the *LIKE* go away.) LIKE IS HUGE! If you are having trouble here, then you need to repeat: "I want to be liked" 483 times. (Hey – you could do this in the mirror right after you laugh at yourself.) Just remember that you need to <u>like yourself</u>, before you can get anyone else to like you.

Here's a tip about a charming guy: He's a hero any time he gets a chance to be a hero. This doesn't mean that he would rush into a burning building to save an old cat. Though he would probably do that. It means that if he sees someone drop something, he'll always reach down to pick it up for them. If he sees an elderly lady trying to walk on an icy sidewalk, he'll give her a smile and then ask if he can help as he offers his arm for support and assists her to her destination. He doesn't see doing this as an inconvenience or a pain in the butt. He actually wants to help her.

A charming guy is considerate and respectful of everyone and everything around him. If you want to see an example of what charm looks like, refer back to the list of "Charming Guys" on page 47, then go to Blockbuster and rent one of them.

> **We all act. The only real difference between the professional actors and the rest of us is that the pros are paid to convince us that they are someone they're not. We amateur actors do not get paid to act, but that's not to say there isn't a payoff for us if we act convincingly. And NICE. So ACT nice...**
> **(When necessary, that is. You do not need to be phony or deceitful. But you should see how charm looks, study it and then try it.)**

BE ATTENTIVE

All charming guys are. THIS means he pays close attention to anyone he's with at the time. Ask him what Sarah's favorite subject is and he'll tell you, *it's Sarah*. Ask him what Mark's favorite subject is and he'll tell you, *it's Mark*. Most people – whether they'll admit it or not – want to be the center of *someone's* attention. So a charming guy caters to that desire and always gives the person he is with his full attention.

A charming guy also treats anyone that he speaks with very well. For instance, if he's with someone in a restaurant, of course his main focus is on that person. But that doesn't mean he isn't equally polite and attentive to the server. He just keeps his main focus on the person he's with at dinner.

Since we're on this subject, <u>please</u> <u>hear</u> <u>this</u>. Don't be checking out other packages when you're out on any kind of date. This is slime in its most disgusting form. It's true. Can you not see the stinky green cloud surrounding a guy who does this? Very classless. Geez. Where's a good alien abduction when you need one?

If you happen to have an addiction to checking out others, then you could learn how to get a good look without turning your head. "Women have mastered this peripheral vision thing. Without taking her eyes off of you, she can see another guy enter her space up to 100 yards away - check him out - examine his ring finger - find his faults - run a credit check and get his rating - mentally weigh the pros and cons of leaving you at that moment for him - rehearse what she's going to tell her mother (- who happens to love *you* -) and make her decision. All in 3 seconds flat." *That from my charming buddy, Tom.* No comment.

Remember: Charm can get you voted into office *and* charm can get you out of sticky situations. Ya want an example? Bill Clinton. *Very* charming. Evidently.

c. Learn to Listen Like a Shrink

Listen up. *If you can become a good listener, then you can become Master of the Universe. (If you want people to listen to you, then the very simple trick to get their attention is to start by saying something good about them.)*

Being a good listener is a charming quality and if you are one, that can make you *everybody's favorite*. People will *really* like you. That's because most people like to talk for days about themselves – even you, probably, but fight that urge. If you can be the guy who actually enjoys listening to them – and encourages them to keep talking – then you are the man.

When you are listening to, and talking with someone, always look at the face – the eyes – of that person. A charming guy shows true interest in whatever people have to say. Looking at them as they speak is the best way to show interest. Most people love the spotlight, and if you can do this, people will likely love being around you.

(If your date gets home and still feels a little clueless about you, this is good. It means that you listened more than you talked, and *that* means you will probably be very popular with this person – who will no doubt be clamoring to see you again.)

Also, by giving up the spotlight, and not talking about yourself, you will not only be seen as a great listener, but you'll be considered a bit of a mystery. Hmmm. This is very good. Again, it's funny how often people will say *"he's so interesting"* or *"he is so nice"* when talking about charming guys – a.k.a.: great listeners. Actually, a more accurate statement would be: *"He let me talk and talk and talk - about* myself!"

"Knowledge speaks, but wisdom listens." -Jimi Hendrix

(And you thought he was just a doped up rocker.)

A charming guy smiles and listens. Again, *he really focuses completely on the person he's with*, even if they're in a crowded room. Without flirting – or drooling – he looks at the person he's with as he listens closely to whatever that person is saying. *He thinks about what he's hearing and responds to it.* He is focused on their conversation - not on the current price of tea in China.

Yep. Listening well is the most impressive and appreciated part of charm, and I know that even you can do it. Remember that 3-second idea? Here it is again: When you are in a deep, one-on-one conversation with your target audience – you know, the boss you want to impress, or that hottie of your dreams – always allow 3 seconds to pass, before you respond to what has just been said to you. Silently count to 3 in your head. Keep in mind that it's more important to miss a chance to say something than it is to interrupt or miss part of what someone else is saying to you.

When you are talking with someone, and you wait for those 3 seconds to process what you heard, you can avoid blurting out some funky or whacked response that might not be appropriate or sound so good. *Get into the habit of asking questions about what you have just been told.* That's responsive, and it makes the person talking feel like you are really interested in what they are saying.

If you suddenly come back to Earth and realize that while someone has been talking to you, you've actually been thinking about the due date on that bill you forgot to pay, then snap out of it and say, "I'm sorry! What did you just say?" Don't try to pretend you <u>were</u> listening if you <u>weren't</u>.

Do you know someone who is always hogging the microphone? You know, you can't get a word in edgewise? This type of person usually makes you feel like everything you say – when you finally get an *opening* to say something – is ignored. Like only what *they* have to say is important. Often this person is only waiting for you to stop talking so that it will be their turn to talk again. And instead of replying to what you said, this person starts off on some subject that may not be even remotely close to what you said. This is the worst kind of communicator. So if you do this, stop it and start *listening* instead.

> **Check this one out:** There was a very charming guy who worked in a hardware store. He was hearing impaired - or deaf. Of course he could use sign language, but since most people who came into the store couldn't, he read their lips. He would watch the lips of the people who spoke to him, never taking his eyes off their faces. Even when he responded to them, he kept his eyes on their eyes to be sure that they got what he was telling them – and to see the responses. Looks-wise, he was just about average, and he wasn't a flirt by any means. But to the women who went into that store, this guy was just plain <u>sexy</u>.

That's because there simply was something unintentionally sensuous about this guy intently watching the mouth and looking into the eyes of the person he was assisting, even if the person was actually only asking him about – whatever – lawnmowers. Understand that he was not meaning to be sexy or seductive. He was just communicating in the only way that he could. The expression on his face was one of real interest – clearly he didn't want to miss anything said. For this reason, he totally charmed most everyone - by accident.

Here is the point: this is how we all should communicate. *We should always watch the face of the person we are talking with.* We don't. We often look around at everything else there is to see, letting our eyes dart here and there while we listen and while we speak to another person. This is just *rude*. Mr. Read-My-Lips had it down – a highly functioning communicator, he was. (The next time *you* find yourself communicating with someone who hears you by reading your lips, you'll understand. Learn from these folks, because, as you'll see, <u>they are the best listeners</u>.)

d. Your Attitude Will Make or -----*Brake* You

(Meaning that the negative vapor oozing from your pores will bring your charm – hence success – to a screeching halt.) When you are in a great mood, people will crowd around you. When you aren't, you may as well be wearing a dirty diaper.

I know I've already talked about your attitude. But it's a huge issue so get used to hearing about it. It's huge. *HUGE.* So you can be sure I'll talk to you about it again… it's huge. Bear with me.

Nobody wants to hang out with a grump. Of course, not everyone wants to hang with a hyperactive cheerleader either, but a happy person is much easier to be around than a chronic, angry complainer or whiner. And a happy person typically won't pull an *Uzi* on you if you tell them and their happy butt to go away.

> Keep in mind that **your attitude rules you**, meaning that it is typically responsible for your successes AND your failures.

Positive thinkers always know that their glass is half full – not half empty. How do you see your glass – half full, right? Good. Because if you feel you are not relatively well adjusted and content with your world, then you can't really smile. This means that you can't be charming. So make the needed changes - even if it means making an extreme change – so you'll be happy.

If you don't like the view from your living room, then *move*. I'm serious. Pack up your stuff or call Mayflower – and *move*. If you hate your job, get a different one. You spend too much of your life at work to be miserable at it each day. If you feel like you never have enough money, and that's getting you down, then find a _free_ credit counselor in the Yellow Pages, they're _free_ – and find out where your money is going each month. That will make your life *better*.

Make whatever changes needed to give yourself a life that makes you happy. (But remember that you can be happy without being rich. A Rolls Royce is not a requirement for happiness so be happy with who you are, with or without the Rolls…)

This next point that I am about to hammer in is vital for your success, so please focus on what it means to you. And *get it.*

You are in charge of your attitude.
You are in charge of your attitude.
You are in charge of your attitude.

You get the credit for feeling good and you get the blame for feeling bad. THE BIG FAT TRUTH: No one can make you feel something that you don't agree to feel. Don't believe that anyone else has any power over your feelings. You get the credit for feeling good. You get the blame for feeling bad.

When you hear someone say that somebody has ruined his or her day, or someone has *made* him or her "feel bad," *it's a lie.* This person simply *let* someone ruin his or her day. For instance, you don't need to dive into depression if you are rear-ended in traffic on the way to work. Drop the "Why me?" and the *drama queen act.* Deal with your insurance company, the auto body shop and whatever else you must, then shrug it off and move on. Be thankful that it wasn't worse. (Keep in mind that even if it WAS worse, your constant whining "Why me?" is NOT going to suddenly cause a booming voice from the heavens to say to you, "Oh my gosh! You're right! There's been a mistake! This shouldn't be happening to you! It should be happening to *David!* Sorry!"…)

Even if someone says to you: "You are a stupid, ugly, stinking, loser," remember it's coming from a person who is clearly miserable and hates the world. Good people don't spew off at the mouth with that. Idiots do. So never let an idiot ruin your day. Don't give them the power to screw with your mood – or your self-confidence.

And if the case really is worse, like a *really bad* accident, or worse yet, what if it's something like - you - with cancer… OK. That would be a biggie. But still, ***you will have a greater chance of surviving everything in your life with greater success if you maintain a positive attitude*** – including beating that one. Your doctor will confirm this if you don't believe me.

Nothing will *ever* be gained by your bad attitude – so make up your mind to lose it now and never let it be part of you again.

You aren't paranoid. Everyone really IS out to get you - if you're an ass. Let me add this in simple but very blunt terms: Being an ass will only make everyone want to stay away from you or make your life suck. So if you are one, then nobody will be cheering for you. They'll want to see you fail because you're a dark, depressing, mean, irritating waste of good air. So lighten up, cub. Be nice and let everyone be <u>with</u> <u>you</u> instead of <u>against</u> <u>you</u>. Then your life won't suck anymore.

DEALING WITH JERKS

How does a person with a bad attitude affect you? Let's see. Perhaps you refuse to deal with a certain business because somewhere in your past, you had a bad experience with someone there. OK, so you've decided never to go back into that pit, but your boycott may be keeping you from something you want.

For instance, perhaps Sparky's Market is the only place in town that sells your favorite food item, Cindy Loo Hoobeedoo's Red Hot Chile Peppers, but Luther, the Assistant Manager blew you off, or pissed you off one day. So you have let that fact keep you from going back to Sparky's. But Luther doesn't care if you come back or not, so why let him keep you from your peppers? Instead, to avoid issues like this, be nice even when you are faced with a Luther-like ass. Simply stay in your 'nice guy mode' …and *get what you want*. Here's how:

When someone acts like an ass to you, you can call them on it – in a friendly and *disarming* way. The person is obviously having a bad day so be a nice guy and say, "Wow. You must be having a rotten day". Cut 'em some slack. That will usually catch the person off guard, and ultimately, bring them back to normal. Or close. They will probably apologize. (But if he or she gets worse and actually tells you to F- off, well then… at least with that you can probably get 'em fired. So see? There is a bright side.)

Anyway, there's a lot to be said for being 'a man of principal', but don't forget that there are probably many 'men of principal' out there who are doing without their peppers. So take your pick. Be a man of principal and live without your peppers, or be a man of *flexibility* – and *get what you want*.

"The strongest tree is the most easily cracked, while the willow and bamboo survive by bending with the wind..."
-Bruce Lee

AVOID GRUMPS

Listen to this: One of my neighbors is like the troll who lives under the bridge. She makes Ebenezer Scrooge look like Barney or Sponge Bob. Anyway, all my other neighbors know what an acidic little grump she is, so unfortunately, many try to avoid her. But since we live in condos, there are times when we run into her – like when we check our mail.

One day, as I checked my mail, I saw her outside of our main entry door, struggling to find her keys in her bag. So I walked over to the door, opened it for her and said, "Hi there." But she looked at me, and in a nasty tone, said, "I have my own keys to get in."

Shazam! She wouldn't come in! So without replying, I closed the door and checked my mail. Meanwhile, "Wonder Woman" out there continued to search for her keys so that she could get into the building. Why would she refuse my help? What was she trying to prove anyway? That she could open the door by herself? Geez – she's 50-some flippin' years old! It's not like I doubted she could do it!

That incident really bugged me, and I was feeling pretty wigged out about it as I got into the elevator afterward. But then I caught myself. Why was I was getting tense? Here's why – because that woman had just been a jerk, and I was letting her get to me. I had done nothing wrong. So what if I'd just been nice to a total ass? She didn't hurt me, but I almost let her ruin my day. That would have been a total waste of time – and it would have been *my fault.* Not hers.

> **The point: If you have the misfortune of running into a seriously toxic personality, <u>do not let them get any on you</u>. Be nice and helpful from a safe distance. If you can make them smile, awesome you. If you can't, then keep your smile, take nothing bad with you, complete your transaction and step back. (Then hightail it for the Straits of Gibraltar. And stay inside your psychological condom till you get there.)**

BUT! If you are ever the one with the toxic attitude, stop it. Figure out why you hate the world, and then solve your problem. Let the doctors help you if that's what it takes. You can get over your 'ticked off at the world' approach to life, because there are many people out there who will help you change – if you want to change.

I say this: *If you hate the world, no matter what torturous treatment you try to inflict on the folks around you, it's nothing compared to what you are doing to yourself – and that will* screw you up *– big time.*

"Holding on to anger is like grasping a hot coal with the intent of throwing it at someone else. You are the one who gets burned."   -Buddha said that.

If you have your own version of that grumped up little neighbor of mine, then the next time you bump into it, put on a big, fat, happy smile and say, "Hey neighbor! How's it goin' today?" It will make you feel great — and it will drive them nuts — until they finally decide to let their guard down and start enjoying life, that is.

CHOOSE HOW YOU FEEL

Many things may happen to you, but no matter how much the rest of us try to dump on you, or influence the way you feel, only you are in charge of your feelings. And if you suddenly find a big, black cloud has been placed over your head, keep smiling anyway. It won't be there forever. We all deal with garbage once in a while, but those crappy times are usually temporary. It's important for you to remember that.

If your mother-in-law moves in with you, and for that reason you have decided that your world sucks and you are getting the fuzzy side of the lollipop, then remember that several things could happen. Here are four:
1. She may soon decide to forgive your father-in-law and go back to him.
2. She may meet a man and move with him to Nova Scotia.
3. She may decide she likes you better than her daughter and make her Cinnamon Sugar Apple Dumpling Pie for YOU.
4. She'll die. (Then you're a turd for being a jerk to her.)
So be an easy-going guy. Fight the urge to show your butt.

You get this, right? Good, because you'll probably live longer if you do, no matter what battles you face. Lighten up and make the best of any sucky situation. You *can* do it you know, it's all in your attitude. Remember that in the big picture, everything is temporary. If you won't get that, then you need to go. Here's your passport to *Pluto.*

MANY FOLKS HAVE IT WORSE THAN YOU DO.
Do you want an example? Oh look. Here's one now: In San Francisco in the 1970s there was a 20-something guy who had a job as a cable car operator. Riding to work one morning on his motorcycle, he was hit by a laundry truck that had run a stop sign. The 'splat' was enough to break his pelvis and one arm, but then two or so gallons of gas leaked out, and you can guess what happened next. Yeah. He ignited.

His unconscious body burned for several minutes before an onlooker jumped in and extinguished the flames that had engulfed him. When this guy woke up in the hospital much later, not only did he have the broken arm and broken pelvis, but his fingers and most of his face were *gone.* Burned off. Sixty-five percent of his body was severely burned.

After his long hospital stay, he had to learn to live and function in this new, very limiting, very painful and very trying condition, which he did. But it was extremely rough for him to go from a normal young guy to someone who not only struggled to do the simplest things – try to do *anything* without your fingers – but who also was stared at and avoided by anyone who saw him because of the way his face looked. (Imagine going through your life with a face that's been broiled. *And I'll bet you complain about a pimple.*)

Anyway, you would think that this was bad enough, but stay seated. This guy's story actually gets much worse. Four years later, he was in a small plane that had just taken off when wing ice caused the plane to slam back down onto the runway. Well, the other three people in the plane hopped out without a scratch, but not this guy. Though he felt OK and looked fine, he couldn't get out. He thought that somehow his legs were pinned, keeping him in his seat. But he soon discovered that he couldn't feel his legs at all.

You guessed it. The impact of slamming back down onto the runway had broken his back. Now, not only would he have to live with the already unimaginable nightmare of his burn injuries, but now, paralyzed from the waist down, he would have to live that nightmare of a life from the seat of a wheelchair. Forever.

Now please stop and think about the ridiculous things that you – and the rest of us – find to complain about each day. Can we not get over the little bits of crap that enter our lives from time to time? Faced with tragedy on the level of this man from San Francisco, how would you do? Yeah, I know. So keep your own familiar little bits of crap, and hope that if you ever discover yourself in a real cesspool, you'll have the attitude and willpower to pull through it like the cable car guy.

"It's Not What Happens to You, It's What You Do About It." That is the name of a book written by a motivational speaker, and it teaches people how to focus on the good stuff instead of the bad. The author of the book is W. Mitchell. He was a pilot, a city mayor and a cable car operator in the 1970s. Yep, our accident victim has blasted past us all – scars, wheelchair and everything else that goes with them. Here's a quote from his book: *"When you are feeling cursed, try counting your blessings."* (You know, the little things – like your fingers and your face, for starters.)

With that, remember that your life is what you make it. So don't wait to *have* a nice day. *Make it a nice day.* You are in control. **This is America – the land of opportunity. Don't forget that all that holds you back here -** *is you.*

e. Oh, My God! You Have a HUGE ... *ego*
Do you suffer from a severe inflammation of the ego, or abnormally high levels of self-esteem? Then please allow me to recommend a visit to reality *for a wee bit of "Get Over Yourself" therapy.*

Arrogance is not the same thing as self-confidence. There are many guys in this world who really believe that they are better than everyone else. Are you one of them? OK. So maybe you are better at chipping out of a sand trap than others. Maybe you are better at mixing margaritas than others. You may even be better at fly-fishing for great whites, but there is no reason to think that you are more important than anyone else.

Perhaps your parents created this egomaniac called YOU, or maybe you have just rocketed into our atmosphere from the planet, 'MyPoopDoesn'tStinkAndYoursDoes'. But no matter what created you and caused you to believe that you are so much better than anyone else, you aren't. On this planet—your poop stinks — just like everyone else's.

Don't sweat it, you have simply been misinformed. Even if you do have the credentials to be full of yourself – don't be. (Wow, you can speak 5 languages? Wow, you can bench press 500 pounds? Wow, can you pin the tail on the donkey, too? *Wow.*)

To act arrogant or conceited is completely lame, and if you are a *walking ego*, then beware that while you are thinking you have dazzled the people you just walked away from, they actually may be laughing at you and rolling their eyes behind your back as they watch you go. No matter what makes you so great in *your* mind, remember that the people who deal with you may not be quite as impressed with you - as you are.

Often, the only people to witness your unbelievable love for yourself are the people who live with you. You know, the ones who have to fight you for *mirror time.* And they could decide to spill the beans about you to the tabloids one day. Eventually your love affair with yourself will become evident to the rest of us, and then you may start to lose your credibility. Only because you may not actually be able to *prove to us* that you are as great as you want us to believe you are. ...*or as great as you think you are. (Sir? Would you like a nice pair of concrete booties to go with your conceit and arrogance today?)*

To avoid being challenged on your greatness, change a few of your habits. Here are some suggestions:
• Don't brag about yourself.
• Don't brag about what you've done.
• Don't brag about what you can do.
• Don't brag about what you have.
• Don't brag about *anything* to do with *you.*
• Spend less time admiring the mirror.

You can undo your prior bad acts by doing these things:
• Compliment *others* on the good things *they do.*
• Do nice things for people, without expecting anything in return.
• Stop yourself when you have an urge to tell the world how great you are.
• Do a good deed, but remain anonymous. Don't tell anyone.

This'll be hard. You will need to bite your tongue a lot. For some people, it is completely natural to blow their own horns, but it is a very bad thing and it is almost the opposite of *charming*. Even if you have just invented the amazing, new, improved wheel, computer or Fig Newton, you must step back and keep your mouth shut. Be humble about it. Give the credit to your incredible team of amazing new, improved wheel, computer or Fig Newton designers. Let the people who discover how great your ability is, do your bragging for you. Better yet, get used to not *taking – or getting* – credit for *anything big* that happens on your shift.

I understand that if you are King of Your World, complete with kingdom, castle, peasants to bow at your feet and rolling heads whenever you say "cut!", it may be difficult to come down off your throne, but you really need to force yourself. Because there is NO WAY that you can make us decide that you are great just by telling us that you are great, or by trying to force it on us.

IF YOU WANT TO CONVINCE US THAT YOU ARE AMAZING,
THEN YOU NEED TO PROVE IT WITH YOUR ACTIONS.

No matter how much you have, what you've done, or who your daddy is, we will not believe you are incredible unless you NEVER tell us that you are incredible. So you won at Le Mans? So you dated Jessica Alba or Julia Roberts? So you made a zillion bucks in the stock market last year? Well. Guess what. If you have to tell us that you did them, then the fact that you did them won't get you the credit you think it will. Just let us discover the great and amazing stuff about you on our own. (And don't leave all the newspaper articles about how YOU have recently solved the RIDDLE OF PERPETUAL MOTION, on the table for us to 'accidentally' see. We will smell a rat. A really smart rat, yes, but still – a rat.)

OK, so if you are interviewed by Katie Couric, and she asks about your grand accomplishments, do not respond with, "Yeah, I did this" and "Yeah, I did that", and "Yeah, I am the greatest one of all" and "I know you wish you were me". You should say, "You know, I've been lucky. I've been able to follow my dreams and experience many good things so far, and I'm really grateful for the things that have happened in my life." Give credit to God or Santa Claus or the folks who invented the bike you rode when you were a kid. But don't ever agree, when someone tells you how great you are. And when someone gives you a compliment, simply say "thank you". Not — "I know".

If you suspect that I may be talking about you, then you probably have an ego problem. Perhaps you have a friend or relative with an out-of-control ego. Well, whether the ego issue is yours or your buddy's, get a book by Jim Stovall called, "The Ultimate Gift". If there is the tiniest glimmer of hope for you, then that book will open your eyes... *and make you a better person* — by putting your ego on a diet.

Last, think of the mirror as the sun – staring at it is dangerous. Also remember that you are <u>not</u> the center of the universe, except maybe to your mother.

f. Do the Right Thing and Get an Upgrade to *First Class*

To get there, you need to be a gentleman and <u>show</u> <u>some</u> <u>class</u>. All the time. This means, for one thing, that you cannot spit on the sidewalk (or pick your nose in public. <u>Ever</u>. Have I already mentioned this? Sorry. But get used to it because I'll mention it again.) You'll also need to start giving up your seat to women, kids and elderly folks.

Being a classy guy does not require a million bucks or a degree. Any guy can be 'classier' if he'll just think before he speaks and before he makes a move. Think about James Bond. He is a classy guy. Would he yell across a parking lot at his buddy? *Nope.* Would he gab loudly on his cell phone while in line at the bank? *Nope.* Would he treat anyone in his world like he didn't care about them (other than his evil enemy - that is)? *Nope.* So you shouldn't either. (In the back of this book are the names of other books which might help you morph into a *real gentleman* — like BOND, which will help.)

If you want to see what real *class* looks like, go back to Blockbuster.
Rent "To Kill A Mockingbird" and watch 'Atticus Finch' played by Gregory Peck. This is class on steroids. Great movie, too. As a matter of fact, pay close attention to the whole story, if you've never seen it, just to help our efforts here. You'll have to deal with the fact that it's in black and white. There's no color remake with Matt Damon yet, but watch it anyway, because it's a *great* film.

STEP UP

Please tell me that chivalry is not dead. *You can be a hero everyday just by being a nice guy.* Offer to help people who are physically struggling with grocery bags or other stuff. If someone gets on the elevator and their hands are full, ask which floor they need and push their button for them.

> **Don't be afraid to speak to and help strangers if you see that they could use your help.** Just ask: "Could you use some help?" But be sure you ask first, instead of just rushing to the rescue. (Especially to elderly people. Otherwise, you might scare them, and then I hope you know CPR). What are they going to say? "Screw you?" If they do, it's no big deal, and you did the right thing by asking. So what if you were nice to a jerk? I was, and it didn't kill me. Chances are good that most people will be grateful for your help and <u>this</u> <u>will</u> <u>make</u> <u>you</u> <u>feel</u> <u>great</u>.

Just because you can, doesn't mean you should. Remember, if you choose to do lame things in order to try and look cool or to move *yourself* ahead, it won't get you anywhere. But any good thing that you do to help people, or just because you know it's the right thing to do, will be remembered and rewarded by the Karma Bears.

Here's a quote from the cable car guy – keep reading it until you get it, OK? *"You can have anything you want in life – if you'll just help others get what they want first."*

To live a great life, you do it minute-by-minute, day-by-day and year-by-year. The time all counts, and it adds up to the person that you are. Think about who you'll be when you're 80, and what people – and the trail you leave behind you – will say about *you* when you're gone.

IF YOU WITNESS VIOLENCE

Anytime you see someone acting violently toward another adult, a kid or an animal, do something. *If you see someone being physically threatened or hurt, here's how to stop it*: <u>Call</u> <u>911</u>.

> **If you know or suspect that someone is abusing an animal – or a child – you can now call the American Humane Society at (303) 792-9900 or fax (303) 792-5333. (Yep, they help kids. It's been determined that animal abusers will eventually take aim at kids. And women... etc.)**

Be nice to elderly people, animals and little kids, and hang out with other people who are nice to elderly people, animals and little kids.

DEFEND YOUR *NICE GUY* ACTIONS

Don't let the fact that your buddies are constantly rippin' on ya for being polite to everyone and using good manners stop you from doing it. Just tell them that you are moving out of your 'thug' mode, and *they should, too.*

> "Try not to become a man of success, but rather to become a man of value."   -Albert Einstein

Maybe you've been associating with people who drag your class down. Think about this. If you're hanging with friends who don't focus on doing the right thing, you should seriously consider exchanging these pals – guys *or* girls – for new ones. If this step is too drastic, then just make it clear to them that you're raising your standards and changing your ways and that *they should, too.*

LAME JOKES

Be selective about which jokes you laugh at and which ones you tell. When you're with your buddies or co-workers, and the talk or activity takes a nosedive, split. You know what's right – so do it. If they ask where you're going, tell them that you aren't into what they're up to, or just say you gotta go. Rise above it – even if it means you've got to leave and possibly miss something interesting. Think beyond the moment and think of who you want to be – a good guy who is known to everyone as a good guy, or a basic waste of oxygen who likes to put others down.

> Don't be a racist or a sexist. This means that you should not believe that you are better than someone else because of your skin color or because you managed to sprout a penis.

As far as human beings, we are all your equals, no matter what you learned from Archie Bunker or Eric Cartmen. Don't worry. I'm not dissing 'your people' any more harshly than I diss my own. I'm embarrassed to say that I share blood with a few racists and sexists, so I can tell you from personal experience that **nothing drops a person's IQ down to 12, faster than when he or she blurts out a racist or sexist remark.**

> **"Racism isn't born, folks...I have a two-year-old son. You know what he hates? Naps! End of list."** -Denis Leary

Maybe it's natural to be a little distrustful of people different from you. I don't know. But whatever creates the issue, we can all get past it if we use our brains. You do not need to share skin color or reproductive organs with a person in order to share the same views or class status. Let your brain and your heart help you see others for who they actually are inside – not outside.

Make friends or get to know 1 person out of this group or race in which you are so prejudiced. Once you have allowed 1 little alien from Mars into your world, and you start to learn about that little alien — you'll start to see their whole planet in a much better way, and you'll discover that you are not so different after all...

> **"The less secure a man is, the more likely he is to have extreme prejudice."** -Clint Eastwood

If you suffer from low levels of self-confidence and self-esteem, understand that putting other people down to make yourself look bigger, badder and more important doesn't work. *It's not working.* When a guy must put someone else down, he is only making himself look like a loser who will do or say anything about someone else to try and draw attention away from the fact that *he* couldn't get it all together if his pathetic little life depended on it. (And people may wonder if his penis is ultra teensy weensy.)

So grow up instead. The fairer you are to everyone around you, no matter what their sex or skin color, IQ or job status, the more together you are gonna look to the rest of us. Be fair, Dude. Your brain and your heart automatically want you that way because they automatically know that we are really all equal. *You are fighting two of your own vital organs to act like a racist or sexist.*

g. Now, Now. Temper, Temper
Some guys <u>brag</u> about having a bad temper, so please allow me to tell you that doing that is about as screwed up as a football bat. This is so lame. They may as well just say, "When I get mad, I act exactly like a spoiled rotten 14-year-old <u>girl</u>. (And I'm afraid of clowns, too.)"

News flash: **You do not <u>ever</u> want for anyone to be afraid of you or 'your temper'. You want to be one of the guys that people run to if they're afraid of someone else – <u>or someone else's temper.</u>**

We've all lost it before. Sometimes things just push us over the edge. But you must figure out a way to release your steam slowly and steadily so that you don't explode, embarrassing yourself and poisoning the environment around you. Please keep your temper in check – always. Because the truth is, bad tempers and the tantrums that go with them are reserved for the frustrated little kids who haven't yet learned how to manipulate their grown-ups.

BAD TEMPER = GIANT TURN-OFF
Besides all of the obvious turn-offs that your out-of-control temper will bring on, it will also make people wonder, 'what else can't he control? I mean, *does he wet the bed*, too?'

Think about the things that seem to set you off. If you are more stressed and easier to snap at certain times of the day, then start taking a break during that time. Try to find the common factors that piss you off or push your buttons. Investigate the cause of your anger and try to remove yourself from the causes. Also talk to yourself. Tell yourself to chill. Use logic. It will make your anger seem absurd – even to you. Imagine yourself explaining to the judge that you ran that bus off the road and killed 34 people because it pulled out in front of you. Good grief, Chuck.

ENVISION SOMETHING TO RELAX YOU BEFORE THE 'BOIL' BEGINS.
Like *you,* on a nice, white-sand beach with a cold drink on a hot day. Whatever. Just calm yourself and end the anger thing before it begins. You can do it. It's called mind control and you can do it if you choose to. *It is YOUR mind after all.* When you can feel your anger rising because of something that has just happened, or is starting to happen—catch yourself. Tell yourself, "Nope. I'm not gonna let anger beat me on this one. I am in charge of my response." If the drive home from work raises your blood pressure, listen to classical music, new age, Tony Bennett or a comedy CD. Or wait for traffic to thin out by staying at work a little later. (Now *that* would piss me off.)

HAS YOUR TEMPER SCREWED WITH YOUR RELATIONSHIPS?
If you know that there have been too many times that you've lost your temper, and your anger has gotten you into trouble, get help. If your relationships and your job situations have suffered because of your bad

temper, you really need to fix your anger problem. Just like any other psychological or medical problem, you need to admit that you have a problem, and then do whatever it takes to get rid of it. It's ALL *fixable*.

> Of course you realize that violent felons are usually diagnosed with serious anger issues. Duh, like I needed to explain that. But my point is that having an explosive temper will only get you into trouble – and into places with lots of other "pissed off and waaay bigger and waaay badder than you" guys.

So C.Y.A. Look under "Physicians" in the Yellow Pages for Anger Management, Psychiatry or Psychology. *DO IT*. Remember that I'm on your side. **(There's a book called ":60 Second Anger Management: Quick Tips to Handle Explosive Feelings" by Michael Hershorn.)** You will like your life much better if you're not in a rage or on the verge of a rage all the time. Plus, do you really want to be Spike's butt boy of the week? I don't think so. (Then we'll get to see what you look like when you're really pissed - but you won't be able to do *JACK* about it.)

Also remember that *always* and *never* are two words that often come into play when we are ticked off about something. Those words are usually used in an impractical way when we're mad. We all know that it doesn't ALWAYS rain right after you wash your car or truck. Or that people aren't ALWAYS pulling out in front of you in traffic. We know that saying you NEVER get a good deal on - *whatever* - isn't true either. Push these two words aside, and you will start to think a little differently – more logically – when you end up in a ticked-off situation.

NO PUBLIC DISPLAYS OF AGRESSION

In public, or in private, count to 10 before you blow. Stop and think about what you'll let out before you allow your mouth to spew **anger**. You should be embarrassed if you lose it and have an outburst or tantrum in public, too. I would rather see you eat boogers than blow a gasket in front of anyone. OK, that was a complete and total lie, but you need to understand that your outbursts are gonna make you look like a full blown loser. And you should care about how you'll look to anyone who sees how much like a 4-year-old you act when you don't get your way and have your temper tantrum.

So your girlfriend, buddy or little brother hit the wrong selection when getting a drink from the soda machine for you. So what? Get over it. Drink it or don't but figure out that in an hour or a week it won't matter anyway. Peace out, man.

Tips from Chapter 5: Your Personality

1• **Instead of judging people, try treating** *everyone* **well and with respect** – whether the person is clearly rich and powerful or clearly poor and powerless. *Don't kiss up to some people and look down on others.* Give all a chance, and everyone will know you are a fair, friendly and naturally cool guy.

2• **It's important that people like you.** So really focus on the people that you're with, and care about how they feel about you. Even if it's someone you only have a quick interaction with, like a teller at the bank. Be nice.

3• **To be charming, you must be** *likeable and liked.* There are lots of guys out there who *think* they are charming, but we know they aren't. Don't go there. **Never try to fake** *charm.*

4• **Become a great listener.** When you are speaking with someone, let that person have your complete attention. Watch that person's face as you listen and speak. Let anyone you speak with know that you are interested in what he or she is talking about by asking questions regarding what you are hearing.

5• **Remember that we like to talk about ourselves.** Lisa's favorite subject is *Lisa,* so if you want to impress her, try catering to that. Encourage her to keep talking by saying things like, "really?" "tell me more" and "wow, that's interesting." Don't worry. You'll get your chance to talk once she decides that you are amazing (*and she will* – because you let her talk non-stop about herself).

6• **Always be positive** – even if you must make major changes in your life to accomplish this goal. You need to be happy, so if it means changing jobs or moving to a new place, start making plans to do it. (You've got to stay within legal and moral bounds, though, so you can't kill and destroy. Use your common sense, OK?)

7• **Remember that** <u>you</u> **are in charge of your attitude, so** <u>you</u> **get the credit for feeling good and** <u>you</u> **get the blame for feeling bad.** Don't let anyone else control how you feel. Even when someone steps on your toes, you can choose how you handle it, so chill and be nice and calm about *whatever* happens to you.

8• **Put on some *Jerk Repellant*.** Never let anyone bring you down or kill your good mood. Rise above ALL outside influences.

9• **If you hate the world, then figure out why and work it out, because if you are an *ass*, you aren't hurting anyone but YOU.** Your negativity will not only make people avoid you, but it will *really screw you up*. It'll mess more with you than them, so wassup? You're expecting others to die when you drink the poison? Uh... they won't.

10• **Know that there are *continents* of people with bigger problems than yours.** Keep things in perspective and jump over your hurdles or problems instead of being dramatic about them. Practice this. (If you are just plain miserable and you don't know why, call 1-800-273-TALK).

11• **If you are a legend in your own mind, it's time to for you to reel in your ego.** It's much easier to convince yourself that you are fantastic than it is to convince the rest of us. So start being a great guy to everyone, and then learn to let them do your bragging for you. Just remember that they won't brag for you unless *you show them* that you really are *that great*.

12• **DO THE RIGHT THING.** Wrap your brain around this: You can be a hero everyday by being a friendly, nice, **real** guy – and by helping people whenever you see their need. If you are a charter member of the Psycho Friends Network, then join a different club.

13• **Get over your *superficial* racism.** Yes, it's superficial. If you are in a serious car crash and the only way for you to survive is by receiving a donated organ from someone of another race, are you saying you'd rather die? Get over yourself.

14• **Keep your anger under control.** And don't explode in public. Never lose your cool - especially if anyone can see you. Buy a book on how to understand and control your anger. See the list in the back of this book. When you feel the start of an eruption, close your eyes and count to 10 because public *spewage* and outbursts are totally unacceptable. You want to be a charming guy – right? **So, leave the tantrums for the little kids and the creative people.**

CHAPTER 6

What Are You Wearing? (How To Look Sharp)

Even though you learned at age 4 to kick and scream about wearing a suit or getting dressed up, remember what ZZ Top told you back in the 80s: "Every girl's crazy 'bout a sharp-dressed man."

That's a fact, Jack. *(So take a walk on the* styled *side.)* Your clothes play a huge part in your image. Not only does what you wear affect how people think about you, but also how you feel about yourself.

a. How to <u>Shop</u> Without Dying

Let's be blunt here. Many guys feel that shopping for clothes is right up there with circumcision on their list of fun things to do. If that is your opinion, too, then relax, this is easy, and you'll lose NO skin *over it.*

When was the last time you bought new clothes? *If you can't remember that last time, then you could probably use a little help in the closet, so go get it.* Take a very simple step and ask a friend, co-worker, third cousin twice removed or *anyone you know* to come and help you. Who do you know that always looks great? There you go. Ask that person to help you pick out some new clothes. (Most of us think we're the experts at everything, so you think someone's going to turn down a chance to provide you with their 'expert' advice on picking out some new clothes? Get real, silly boy.)

You could start at Barnes & Noble, Borders or any big bookstore and check out the men's magazines. I mean men's *fashion* magazines. 'GQ' comes to mind, but if that's too (designer) extreme for you, there are many other magazines to check out for different looks in clothing. (Check out a Spiegel catalog — they're in bookstores too.) All you need is an idea of what you like — whether the looks are in style or not. You can figure out which look you like just by flipping through a magazine and looking at pictures and ads. Is that easy or what? (Buy the magazine.)

If asking someone you know for help to shop for clothes feels too needy for you, no problem. Just grab the phone book and call any of the larger department stores. The employees at many of the top department stores are extremely knowledgeable and helpful when it comes to putting great looks together and still staying within your budget.

SALESPEOPLE (...are your friends)

There are thousands of guys who never pick out new clothes. These guys are either too busy or just not into it, so they have someone else pick out new clothes for them. Then they go try them on and buy whatever they like. The salesperson in any good men's department can set you up with this type of 'shopping assistance.'

Call and ask the men's department at *Nordstrom, Dillard's, Macy's, Sears, JC Penney's* — or any of the larger stores — if they have someone who can help you pick some new clothes when you come in to shop. They may suggest that you make an appointment. If so, tell the salesperson your sizes and whether you are looking for jeans, casual slacks and stuff, a suit or more formal things. Then set the limit on how much you want to spend. *(Note: Even the high-end stores can fit a wide range of budgets – though most people don't know that.)*

Again, the salespeople who work in stores like Nordstrom are absolute professionals when it comes to choosing clothes for fit and style – even if we're only talking jeans and T-shirts. You can trust them to make you look good. This means that they will look good, so you can rest assured that they'll take great care of you.

Why do guys freak when they are approached by a salesperson? It seems that whether you are looking at sharkskin cowboy boots or a Winnebago, if a salesperson gets near you, you break out in a rash and run away. Wassup with that? They are only trying to, uh, help. And believe it or not, they actually can. So unless you are a fabulous dresser, and you always get exactly what you are looking for when you shop, then perhaps you should just face the scary salesperson and let them assist. Be direct and tell them what you need – even if it is simply to be left alone while you look. Otherwise, when they sneak up and ask, "May I help you?" you can always reply, "I'm beyond help. But thanks for asking."

Stores like Burlington and TJ Maxx have great prices and selection, but may not have the sales force to focus on you specifically and hook you up. In otherwords, they have great stuff, but you're on your own.

Once you're thinking of buying something, check the tag or ask about the laundry or care instructions. Unless you are used to clothes that are "Dry-Clean Only," and the money it takes to maintain them, avoid those – other than suits, of course. If you can't resist something and find that it's dry clean only, then buy a DRYEL home dry cleaning kit. It's easy. I'll add it to your Grocery List.

Look for washable, wrinkle-resistant items such as clothes made of fabrics like cotton blends. (Washing shirts and pants that are made of more uncommon fabrics can be a hassle. And they sometimes come out of the washing machine looking like eels or walking sticks.) Just tell your salesperson that you are only interested in the easy-care, low-maintenance stuff. You're a guy. They'll understand.

Getting new clothes will be completely painless and can improve the way you feel about yourself – as well as change opinions of the people who know you – or only see you.

Don't jump too far out of your fashion comfort zone. Be <u>totally clear</u> on what you <u>won't</u> wear to anyone who helps you – friend or stranger. If the salesperson assisting you suggests you take something that you just aren't into, and **you know it will make you uncomfortable to wear**, don't buy it. Don't be talked into something you don't feel OK about, because it will only waste your money and die of neglect in your closet.

On the other hand, be open-minded to styles that you may never have considered before. Don't be afraid to try new looks. Put it this way, unless you are a perfect dresser, and you get compliments all the time, try something different and see what the responses may be. It's not likely you'll end up in a green leather suit, and you may actually be transformed from a dud to a stud.

YOUR SHOPPING BUDGET

If money is a major concern for you, but you DO need some new things - no worries. Get onto the computer and go to EBAY or any auction site. Then enter whatever you're looking for. Let's say a brown leather jacket, size 44. On the EBAY homepage, enter "brown leather jacket size 44, then select "Clothing, Shoes and Accessories", and hit search. That's it. Your jacket choices (new and used) will pop right up. (I just found one for $19.00. See, I would never recommend something to you that I had not sampled on myself - or on some guy I know.) You'll find a great selection of shoes and boots on EBAY, too.

FYI: People sell all kinds of stuff on EBAY and a leather jacket for 19 bucks does not mean it's junk. Oddly, you may discover the original price tag is still on your purchase when you get it, indicating that the original price was $300 more than you just paid for it. *Go figure...*

If you aren't into computer shopping then visit your local Salvation Army. Don't roll your eyes... you can get great stuff there, or in thrift stores or consignment shops. If the idea of wearing something that is used creeps you out because you have no clue about where it's been, just take it straight to the Dry Cleaner and have it fumigated before you wear it. Odds of your getting cooties or the Black Plague from used clothes are fairly slim. Look for these used clothing stores in the Yellow Pages. They usually have good stuff. You don't think that Gov. Arnold's suits go into the trash do you?

b. Get Yourself a Kick-Ass Closet
If someone asks you out to grab a burger, you are probably ready to go. But what if you are invited to dinner at the boss's house – or at their *boss's house? If you are scratching your chin on that one then let's go get prepared, Boy Scout.*

Not every situation calls for the same type of clothing and you need to be ready for anything. Whether your stock uniform consists of Cashmere or Carhart, flexibility is the key.

We all have our comfy stuff. Shirts, pants, jackets and shoes that we've had longer than our license to drive, and I'd never suggest you get rid of these things. Only that you save them for special occasions. Don't miss my message here. I'm all for the old, comfy stuff. Heck, I had my red swoosh Nikes way before Forest Gump got his, and I still am very close to them. But we need to keep in mind that beat-up, gnarly, old shoes bring to mind images of beat-up, gnarly, old feet. That's bad. Put it this way, save these guys for outings with only your closest friends – people who already know your feet aren't gnarly. (If your feet *are* gnarly, keep reading. We'll fix them soon.)

Try the one-year rule. If you haven't worn something in a year, get rid of it. When you actually decide that you can part with any of your old clothes, don't toss them in the trash – take them to The Salvation Army or a local shelter. You can drop them in a box there (plus anything you donate can be used as a write-off when you prepare your tax return). Don't forget: "one man's trash is another man's treasure." *And somebody out there can use your old stuff.*

(You should have a wide variety of clothing styles. Remember to let the sales people help you put your look together. *Trust them. They're pros.*)

DRESS SHIRTS NEED UNDERSHIRTS
Always wear a clean undershirt underneath your dress shirts. **Always!** (When you shop for your undershirts, try a sleek, stretchy fit. They're shorter, too, so they won't bunch up in the waistband of your pants.) An undershirt serves several purposes. It absorbs sweat. It prevents your dress shirt from having a "see-through" look, which makes it look cheap, and the undershirt also will hide your nipples and man boobs – moobs – if you have them.

When you buy a dress shirt, be sure to buy the correct sleeve length and neck size. The salesperson can easily and quickly measure you if you don't know your size. They do it all the time.

Be sure your dress pants are the correct length, too. They should not quite touch the floor. When buying pants, the salespeople can usually have them custom fitted, often at no charge to you. Pay attention to this. (If your pants won't stay up without a belt, then they're too big.)

Here are the 5 clothing categories.

These items will give you a great — and complete — closet (but you don't need to go out and purchase all of these things at once. Start a collection):

Dress and Semi-formal:
Weddings, funerals, job interviews, dinners in upscale restaurants and anything in a church.
1. A dark, medium-weight suit. Dark-gray, navy or black.
2. A dress shirt, typically lighter in color than the suit, but similar to the suit's color is OK.
3. Silk necktie, dark color (or a mix of the colors in the suit and shirt).
4. Dress shoes. Black will match everything, but burgundy can work.
5. Dress socks, either the color of your suit or the color of your shoes.
6. A black dress belt. Shiny gold or silver buckle. The buckle should match your watch or any other visible jewelry.
7. A nice watch.

Dress Casual/Business Casual:
• **First option:**
Weddings, funerals, job interviews, dinners in casual, popular restaurants, and anything in a church.
1. Medium-weight or tweed blazer (jacket), navy or gray.
2. Pleated slacks. Gray with navy jacket, black with gray jacket.

3. Button-down shirt, lighter color than blazer and pants.
4. Silk necktie. Solid color (or mix of jacket, shirt, and/or pants colors.) And a tie tack if you're into them.
5. Black or burgundy leather loafers or lace-up shoes.
6. Dress socks to match pants or shoes.
7. Smooth, black leather belt to match shoes. Shiny buckle to match your watch, etc.

Dress Casual:
• **Second option:**
Dinners in casual, popular restaurants, movies, ballgames, barbecues.
1. Khaki pants, pleated, with or without cuffs. (Try Dockers. They're very low maintenance.)
2. Denim shirt, long sleeves, button-down collar. (Polo shirts are OK, but the collars can become wavy after a few runs through the washing machine. Also knit fabrics used for Polo and T shirts show every bump and bulge, ie: bellies and moobs - so unless you are tight all over, wear those at your own risk. If your bi's and tri's aren't buff, then be sure your short sleeves aren't too short.)
3. Casual shoes. Loafers or lace-up shoes in brown or rust color work well. (Boots are OK as long as the leg of your pants doesn't hike up when you sit down, and stay stuck there on the top of the boot when you stand up.
4. Socks to match your pants or shoes.
5. A casual, leather belt to match your shoe color. Dull or brushed metal instead of a shiny buckle.

Totally Casual:
Movies, ballgames, picnics and barbecues, and anything that doesn't require that you completely behave yourself.
1. Jeans, Dockers, any style and color.
2. a. Bowling style short sleeved shirts, plaid, striped, etc. — you could wear it open, with a T under it.
    b. Polo or T-shirt.
3. Tennis shoes or sneakers.
4. White or light-gray athletic socks. (White with white sneakers or tennis shoes.)
5. Casual belt. Leather or nylon. Any color. No shiny buckle.
6. Baseball cap if you want (without a bonehead message).

I REPEAT: Re-think a tight T or Polo shirt unless you have rock hard abs, pecs and all the other rock hards to go with them. Droopy pecs-turned-moobs and other rolls aren't good visuals. My girlfriend saw a guy from her work one weekend wearing a T-shirt and jeans. It freaked her out to see a roll around his waist, and slanted, droopy moobs – along with some other flabby defects. For almost a year, she had worked with him, and he looked great in his work shirts and pants, but via the T-shirt, she discovered that instead of being a hard body, he was a soft and squishy body. If you are **that**, then **start working out** and/or try some loose shirts.

Formal (black tie):

Galas, the opera and theater, balls, certain fund-raisers, formal restaurants and private clubs, or dinner at Buckingham Palace, the White House, Bruce Wayne's mansion or the home of any other world leader or Super Hero.

1. A tuxedo. (Buy or rent one with the needed accessories, including **patent-leather shoes (these are a must – no plain leather allowed)**, bowtie, cumberbund, formal dress shirt, and studs or cuff links. The salesperson, whether you buy or rent, will set you up with all of these extras – and probably a few more.)

    …And remember this as you dread putting on that penguin suit: In the *sexy* minds of many, a tuxedo on a guy is as good an aphrodisiac as any.

Keep in mind that it is ALWAYS better to be overdressed than underdressed. So if you aren't sure, wear more formal than less formal because you'd rather be seen as "that sharp-looking guy," than "that slob in the T-shirt." Besides, being well-dressed will build your confidence, so never fear being better dressed than the next guy.

What's on your T shirt? Be careful about the T-shirts you buy with regard to the pictures and big, bold statements printed on them. Never wear a shirt with a message on it that you wouldn't show to everyone you know – including the 2nd grader next door. (Skip "I'm With Stupid", too.)

Here are a few more tips:

1. **Snag the Armor All Leather Wipes out of your car or truck to use on your leather shoes and boots.** Wipe down every visible part of the shoe, even the rubber sides of the soles. This will make them look brand new (or close), so use them whenever your shoes start to look dull, dirty or old.

2. Use a shoehorn when you're putting your shoes on instead of shoving your foot in with force, and they'll look good and last longer.
3. Buy a pair of cedar shoe trees for your dress shoes to help keep their shape, and to keep them odor-free.
4. Pick your feet up when you walk. This will save your shoes, reduce static, and help you look less *lazy*.
5. Again, all guys will generally look better in shirts with collars than in collarless shirts. The shirts with button-down collars are great because the buttons help the collars maintain their shape.
6. Tuck in your shirt and wear a belt when you need to look nice.
7. Be sure your pants are long enough, because pants that aren't long enough tend to make a guy look clueless. The backs of your pant legs shouldn't be more than one inch from the floor. This is *very important*.
8. Check your fly *to be sure it's closed* once in a while.

TIP: Regarding your clothing style, it's your call. You can be trendy and fashionable or you can be classic and low-key. Your choice. My only concern for you is that your clothes are in good shape and clean. If you want to impress the fashionistas and supermodels, then read men's magazines and always enlist the salespeople to dress you. They will keep you in the 'cuff or no cuff', 'pleats or no pleats', 'wide tie or skinny tie' loop.

c. <u>This</u> is Your *Washer*, <u>This</u> is Your *Dryer*

Clean-looking, unwrinkled clothes are an absolute necessity, unless you are washing your ride or cleaning a trout.

Guys — your clothes must be clean. If they aren't, then we'll think you are a pig. So when you spill or otherwise create a 'mark' or 'stain' on your shirt or pants, *get it off*. And do not wear that shirt or those pants again until you *get it off*.

Clean and unwrinkled clothes are nice to see, touch and smell. Cheer has a really great, long-lasting scent and Bounce fabric softener/anti-cling sheets will help your clothes smell great, plus they'll keep socks from sticking to your back.

DOING YOUR LAUNDRY

Read the tags in your clothes before you throw them in the washer. If a tag reads 'dry clean only", it means that item can't swim. You'll kill it if you put it in the water, so take it to the dry cleaners or buy a Dryel kit.

To avoid white clumps of powdered detergent speckling your stuff, start your washer so that it's filling with water, then add the detergent and let it dissolve before adding your clothes. Or use liquid laundry soap. Either way, mixing the soap and water before adding your clothes cleans everything evenly.

Make sure the washer settings for your load size and temperature are correct, and be sure to separate your dirty clothes before washing them. Wash darks with darks, lights with lights and reds alone – unless you like pink. Pay attention to the settings on your washer. A cold or warm temperature is safe for just about everything. Use plenty of detergent – at least use whatever the container recommends. Again, check your settings. Stuffing the washer full, without changing the load size indicator from 'small' to 'large' will only get you muddy clothes. Also, load it loosely because if it's overstuffed, nothing will get clean.

No Sock Balls!

A chief complaint from moms, wives, significant others and really nice roommates who will actually wash the dirty clothes of their often piggy co-habitants is *balled up socks in the laundry.* So unroll them before you hand them over to your laundress or learn to remove them without balling them up. Do I really need to tell you how? Just stick a finger in the top of your sock in the back, and push it down the back of your calf with your finger past your heel. Wow. No ball and its right side out, too. Again, no rocket science is required - but this simple effort on your part will no doubt please your servants.

If you wear sweaters, turn them inside out and wash them on the gentle cycle. Never wash them in the same load with zippers or anything that can snag them. Also, don't dry your sweaters – lay them out flat so they won't shrink (or I hope you have a *mini-you* person in your life).

IRON YOUR CLOTHES IF THEY ARE WRINKLED

Oh, don't say that your shirt isn't wrinkled if it is. You know you can tell the difference between wrinkled and not. You can reduce or prevent wrinkles by taking your things out of the dryer immediately after it stops drying. Immediately. Then fold, hang up or lay your things out flat. NOW. Remember to buy wrinkle-resistant pants and shirts. Here's a tip: If your laundry gets trapped in the dryer for hours after the cycle ends, unable to get out and fold itself and is totally wrinkled, then put a *damp* – not dripping - towel back into the dryer with it and turn it on again for about 20 minutes. This will help de-wrinkle your neglected stuff.

BUY MORE CLOTHES OR FIND A **LAUNDRY SERVICE**

If you hate to do laundry, or if you are too busy to put any great effort into it, then go shopping and buy more clothes. Call your neighborhood laundromat and ask if it offers a service to wash, dry and fold your clothes, towels, sheets and stuff. This way, you'll never have to do laundry and you will always have clean, unwrinkled, fresh-smelling stuff. Take your Cheer and Bounce, bag up your dirty stuff and head for the laundry service once a week. *Easy.*

> If you wear your pants all week without a wash – I am sssso not encouraging that – at least hang them up or lay them out flat – even if on the floor – when you take them off at night. This way they will get to air out a little. (You could also spray them with Febreze.) Just don't make them sleep in a heap on the floor. They'll tell everyone the next day.

Most of the larger department stores carry 'wrinkle-free' or 'wrinkle resistant' pants and shirts. Look for khaki pants and the button down collared shirts that are wrinkle resistant or 'iron-free'. Ask the sales people. Tell them you could not iron your clothes if your life depended on it, and they'll hook you up.

CHANGING YOUR SOCKS AND UNDERWEAR

I don't mean to insult anyone's intelligence with a reminder to always wear clean socks and underwear. Of course, this is an absurd reminder. You're not a little kid anymore. (Of course YOU wouldn't wear them two days in a row - or turn them inside out to get a little extra mileage out of them, would you?) Ha! Even though this rule of fresh socks and underwear was probably pounded in for most guys in 2nd (and 10th) grade, I know for a fact that when some of you moved out and had to start doing your own laundry, you had a bright idea, didn't you? (You know who you are.) That's OK, you can change. Everyday. Your socks and underwear. Just buy more. And please do not let your shorts wear out before chucking them. Once they are see-through and fringed, it's time for new Hanes, Jockey or Fruit of the Loom.

When you take off your dirty clothes, be sure you always place them in a private spot that you specifically designate for your dirty clothes. Go to Target or Pier One and buy a clothes hamper. Don't risk mixing clean clothes with dirty ones – big, smelly mistake *that* would be – and definitely don't leave dirty clothes (– especially your underwear –) scattered around the house for your visitors to discover.

Buy more socks and underwear if that's what it takes to guarantee clean everything — every day.

Tips from Chapter 6: What Are You Wearing?

1• **If you aren't into shopping for clothes, find photos in magazines of the clothes that you like.** Then ask a friend who dresses well to go shopping with you and help you find those looks.

2• **You can find off-the-charts great deals for clothes and shoes on EBAY, or in thrift stores.** Brand new or used.

3• **Let the sales people in the department stores help you put shirts, pants, belts, socks and shoes together.** Before you buy, check the laundry instructions to be sure they are easy-care items and not "dry clean only." If you can't budget dry cleaning, but you still want a DCO item or two, then buy a Dryel home dry-cleaning kit. That works.

4• **Be open minded to different styles.** Try a few new looks, but don't buy anything that you know you absolutely will not wear.

5• **Go through your clothes and donate anything you haven't worn in a year to a local shelter or the Salvation Army.** Don't try to determine what's junk or isn't. Wash it all, then drop it off. They will find use for all of it.

6• **Be sure your pants are long enough.** No more than one inch from the floor in the back. **Be sure your pants aren't too long.** If your pants drag the ground when you walk, then you're lookin' like you belong in the Work Release Program.

7• **Have clothes for every occasion.** Create a complete closet, so you have the right clothes for whatever may come up – weddings, nice dinners out, gatherings with friends, or lunch at the Ritz with Oprah.

8• **Don't forget the rule for looking good in a Polo or T-shirt: Hard body… very good. Flabby body… – *not so much.***

9• **If you aren't sure about what to wear, dress more formal than more casual.** It's *always* better to be overdressed than underdressed. Guys who make a habit of dressing well get lots of positive attention.

10• Use Armor All Leather Wipes to clean your shoes and boots.

11• **Your laundry – do it right.** Separate lights from darks, and take your stuff out of the dryer immediately and fold it or hang it up so it doesn't get wrinkled, or learn to IRON.

12• Take your stuff to a laundry service if it's the only way to guarantee that everything will look and smell *good.*

13• Change your socks and underwear every day.

14• After you take off your dirty clothes, *put them in a clothes hamper till you wash them.*

CHAPTER 7

Your Personal Hygiene And Body Maintenance

If you don't shower every day, then you get to smell like a wet dog blanket and the rest of us get to experience something hugely unpleasant whenever you walk by.

There are two things that must happen every day. Your body gets a shower (with suds and bubbles) at least once, and your teeth get brushed at least twice. There are many other things that should happen each day, but these are the biggies.

a. The Power of a Shower – *Every day*.

If you don't shower everyday, then please ask yourself "what is preventing me from showering everyday?" Hmmm, could it be that you keep your baby alligator or goldfish in the tub? Or could it be that you concoct your home brew in there? Maybe the creek is too cold this time of year?

Whatever your excuse may be, it won't fly. You can't convince me that you're good to go - without a wet and soapy scrub once a day.

Showering every day is important for two reasons. First, it gets you clean. Second, it makes you feel good. You know, clear-headed. You can shower in the morning or you can do it before bed. I don't care. A shower can adjust to your needs. Before work, it wakes you up and clears your head. Before bed, it relaxes you and clears your head. Before bed is good if you have trouble sleeping, since you don't need to rush through a shower at bedtime. This means that you can just stand in the shower, eyes closed, letting the hot water pour over you, unplugging you and setting you up for a great night's sleep. Try it.

Pick up some body wash today. Old Spice High Endurance Body Wash has a great scent. (And with body washes, there's no dropping the hairy soap.) You're going to love this stuff, especially if you don't like using cologne or aftershave. It's very fragrant while you use it in the shower – and your bathroom will smell fantastic. But after you've dried off and are dressed, the scent will be very subtle on your skin. *Yum.*

Remember that fragrances work. People typically love to smell good things. (This is why the perfume industry makes billions each year.) But if you are stuck on bar soap, then visit the men's cologne counter in any large department store. Usually the popular after-shaves and colognes have bar soap in that scent, too. Otherwise, for grocery store bar soap, Irish Spring and Lever 2000 have a good, clean, long-lasting scent.

Good smells are appreciated by most people, but bad smells are a turnoff to everyone. (Except dogs. They love stinky stuff and they roll in it, and they want you to roll in it, too.) Don't make the mistake of thinking that you can hold yourself a safe distance from clean people and keep them from noticing your "I didn't shower today" smell. It won't happen. Some people can smell the mustard you spilled on your shirt at lunch today from three buildings away.

When you shower:

1. Make sure to scrub ALL of your 2,000 parts – every guy nook and every guy cranny.
2. Keep a small scrubbing brush in the shower for your fingernails/ toenails.
3. If you have dry skin, there are shower lotions to use just before you rinse off and hop out of the shower. Like *Olay Moisturinse In Shower Lotion*. Baby oil works before you dry off, too, but it will make your towel slightly oily. Or you can use regular lotion after you've dried off (though many guys believe that this will kill them).
4. Use plenty of shampoo on your head. Even if you don't have a lot of hair, you still need to make sure your scalp is really clean because it will have a distinct, greasy-scalp smell if you don't. **Massaging your scalp for at least two minutes when you wash it can help regenerate growth. I think this only works on scalps for hair regrowth...**
5. Use conditioner on your hair if its texture is stiff or dry. (Or if you rip half of it out as you try to comb through it after your shower.)
6. If you have a beard or mustache, be sure you scrub it with soap or shampoo, too. No stinky fuzzy faces allowed (and facial hair will stink if you only get it wet and don't use soap).
7. At the end of your morning shower, run cooler water over your body to *really* wake you up and close your pores. (Then run very cold water over your feet before you step out. Why? To help improve your circulation. Thomas Jefferson soaked his feet in icy water every morning. Check out where he landed.)
8. Always use deodorant or antiperspirant.

Pretty obvious points, right? Well, not really. Some guys get into the shower and 'rinse off' without using soap or shampoo. But, without soap, why even bother? When dogs get wet in the rain or in the creek, they typically don't use soap either and they end up smelling like - wet dogs. You can, too, if you don't use soap.

Repeat: Rinse your soap... Don't leave your pubes or other short and curlies all over the soap when you get out of the shower. (Another reason to use body wash.) Even if you live alone, *rinse your bar soap.*

COLOGNE OR AFTERSHAVE

One squirt. That's it. One squirt. Whatever you use, buy it in spray form, and then only use one squirt! OK, if you're used to 36 squirts, then you can use two squirts, but only if you do it like this: Spray the cologne (two squirts) over your head, and then let it fall over you. Let the mist land on your hair, face and shoulders. This will give you a perfect, great-smelling *aura*. And it's your *aura* that should smell good. Really. There's no need to saturate all of your clothes and every inch of your skin.

Many guys are clueless about how much cologne they need to use. Maybe their nostrils aren't working. You know those guys – they smell like they have a Glade Plug-In in every pocket. And their scent enters a room before they do. This is not a good thing, so please stick with just 1 or 2 squirts. Save the industrial-strength scents for your bathroom. (Also, some people have allergies to fragrances, so for **their** sake, lighten up.) We don't need to smell you 2 hours before you arrive – or 2 hours after you're gone.

If you are on a tight budget and can't afford colognes, then try some TAG or AXE body spray and see how it smells on you. (You'll spend less than 5 bucks for either of these.) Apply only two squirts (above your head) – after your shower, before you get dressed. Again, be sure you shower each day. *Nothing* will cover up your "I didn't shower today" smell.

SHAVE EVERY DAY
Most multi-blade razors have pivoting heads and strips of aloe or lotion. Use them! The cleaner and smoother your face is, the more likely you are to get stroked. (And we all know that guys *live* to get stroked.)

In the store, with shaving supplies, be sure to grab some moisturizer to use after you shave. Many guys have razor burn after shaving – or really dry skin. Soften it up with any of the **skin care products for men**. Try L'Oreal, Neutrogena or Nivea. Many department stores have Clarins and other high end brands for guys, too.

And if you have a beard or mustache, trim around them so that your face will look clean. Lose the scruffy stuff on your cheeks and neck that wants to be part of your beard but can't get with the group – unless you prefer the granola look. If so, that's cool, too. *Just keep everything clean, because if your face smells like last night's pizza, then Houston, we have another problem.*

Some guys prefer to shave in the shower. If you do this, be sure to check your entire face after you're back at the mirror – to be certain you didn't miss anything. Unless you are going for the two-day beard look

(...like George Michael, Don Johnson - - - - _1980s_). TIP: If you keep your disposable razor in the shower – place it away from the water. Believe it or not, those blades will last for a year if they aren't constantly wet.

(If you have a hairy back – try getting it waxed. Not the front though, that would hurt. Ask Steve Carell.)

b. Hair – It's Always Leaving

Whatever you have, accept it and be happy. Or get a hair transplant. But remember this: Many guys intentionally shave the hair from their heads these days. So does a guy do that because he's totally self-confident or because he'll be bald soon anyway? _Who cares._

If you are experiencing a hair shortage, welcome to the club. Every day, every hour, every _minute_ we see guys with receding hairlines, thinning hair and bald spots. So if you are dealing with one of those issues, God bless you for still getting out of bed each day. **Come on! It's only hair. Or not. It just clogs the drain anyway.**

> If a bottle of DRAINO is getting more action with your hair than your comb is, don't sweat it. You're not alone. Studies world wide are concluding that human hair actually prefers drain pipes over scalps. So what can you do to help stop this pandemic? You could try surgery. You could join the Hair Club for Men. Or you could try a few simpler and cheaper suggestions, like Rogaine foam (reportedly reduced loss **and** promoted re-growth in about 85% of the guys who tried it), zinc, vitamins E and B-5, B-6, and B-12 **or -- an electric shaver**. Any of these could change your fate.

Vitamins, minerals, eating healthy foods – such as whole grain cereals – on a daily basis can help, too. Nothing will work big miracles overnight, but you may see a difference before your next birthday. These are long-term remedies and typically they could take 12 to 24 months to show clear results, but look at it this way, they _will_ show results more often than not. And wouldn't you rather start trying these solutions NOW and possibly start to resemble your graduation photo again, than sit by and watch as you start to look more and more like Dr. Evil or Mr. Magoo?

Keeping your scalp clean will promote hair growth. Many guys who are losing their hair have been thinking that washing it every day could actually be causing hair loss, but the opposite is true. Shampooing (and MASSAGING) your scalp each day will promote better circulation, which can cause you to sprout more hair. Oil and build up on your scalp blocks your pores/follicles. We can't have that. And as I repeat about 92 times through out this book, you need to keep every inch of your body clean and that is especially true when it comes to your scalp. Massaging your scalp (for two minutes each day) to improve blood flow is easiest when it has shampoo all over it. Regular exercise will also help with circulation. Google 'hair loss remedies for men' to learn more.

Whatever you decide with regard to your head, as I've mentioned before, your attitude is what will make or break you, not your hair – or lack of it. So don't hide it. Accept what you have or don't have. (If you can't accept your hair loss without getting depressed or hiding under your bed, then you need to start saving up for a hair transplant. The only requirement for this is money, so anyone with cash or a credit card can soon be looking like Cousin IT or Don King.)

DON'T HIDE YOUR HEAD

The self-confidence you show the world by *not* trying to hide your hair loss will more than make up for the fact that you don't have as much hair as you wish you did.

My girlfriend met a guy who was very nice, cute, in good shape and fun. She was out with him on a 3rd lunch date – every time he had been under a ball cap – when he repositioned his hat and she saw that most of his hair was MIA. But the problem wasn't his missing hair. It was the fact that he was missing the self-confidence he needed to not be ashamed of his missing hair. You cannot keep your head a secret, and waiting until later to reveal the truth could end up leaving you high and dry.

Once your terrific personality wins someone over, (yes, you are getting a terrific personality – keep reading) your hair loss becomes nothing more than a tiny little blip on the screen. It's a waaaay bigger deal to you than it is to the rest of us. You cannot spend your life worrying about what we will think of your head. WE DON'T CARE. Your head without hair looks fine to us, *so lose the ball cap* and hold your head high. Go get a tattoo on it. Or don't. (I saw a guy in an airport with a full-size tattoo of his own face on the back of his head. Bizarre. But hey – it was a great use of the space.)

SIDENOTE: Do not wait until bedtime before revealing your head without a hat. It is very important for you to get to know someone before you go there. If you like someone, and you think you might want something more than a quick roll in the hay, then you must give that person time to get to know you. All of you - including your lost hair and that tattoo on your chest that says, "Mother".

Just do whatever it takes to drop the stigma that our goofy society has attached to your hair, and be OK with the way you look - no matter what - because to us, *you* are fine. Besides, if some judgmental person is so shallow that they will not find you appealing because of *your scalp*, politely drop this person off at the nearest campus of Dipstick U.

YOUR HAIR *STYLE*

If you need to find a new hair stylist, then ask the people you know with great hair for the name of their's and make an appointment. Or get into the Yellow Pages, find a salon then call and make an appointment. Otherwise, ask whoever has been cutting your hair if you might need to try a different cut. Step out of the box. (*Remember that your bi-level haircut only tells us that you may have been really cool in the 80s.*) It's not like you can't change it back in 3 weeks anyway. Unless you've got dreds. Big decision, then. But they'll grow back, too, *eventually.*

If your hair is thinning, then VERY short is VERY good. No comb-overs. Don't try to stretch your little army of 8 strands of hair to cover 5 football fields of head. Just face your fears and cut or shave it. We will all still like you, and you will look much better, classier, smarter, richer and cleaner. This will make you look younger, too.

SHAMPOOS AND CONDITIONERS

If you have plenty of hair, lucky you. Make sure you keep it looking good. If it's dry looking, or it doesn't feel soft, then be sure to use conditioner after you wash it. Shampoos and conditioners are not all the same, and some conditioners do not leave your hair as healthy looking and as soft as it should feel. So consider spending the extra bucks for salon stuff every once in a while.

You still can use what you use now, just keep a couple of different brands in your shower and alternate between them every few days. Many salons offer 2-packs of liter-size shampoo and conditioner for $25 or so. (Do not balk at the idea of spending big bucks on your head. You can look like Dr. McDreamy or you can look like a Geico caveman, but putting some effort into your appearance – and smell – will get you more of whatever it is you want. For some reason, 'sex' keeps coming to mind...)

Infusium 23 and Suave have great salon formula hair care products, and you can buy them for just a few dollars at many drug stores. Also, several shampoo manufacturers now offer shampoos and conditioners specifically for guys, including formulas that can make your hair look thicker. So look around at the different options the next time you shop for hair products at the salon or at the grocery store.

If you have dandruff, try Head & Shoulders. Use it in your beard, too, if you're flaky there. No big deal – it's usually just dry skin. Easy fix. Because there is NO excuse for oily hair and a flaky scalp - at least not as long as there is soap and water on the planet. If your dandruff kicks butt even on the industrial strength dandruff shampoos, then try this 3 day routine:

Day 1: use Nizoral brand dandruff shampoo (from a salon).
Day 2: use Head & Shoulders shampoo.
Day 3: use any mild, everyday shampoo (try Infusium 23).
EVERYDAY: use hair conditioner but rotate brands.
Repeat this week after week, and you'll see waaay fewer flakes.

c. The Weight of the World is on Your Shoulders
– It's Your Head
OK, beyond your hair, let's discuss the other occupants of your head. Your eyes, ears, nose, mouth – and the ABSOLUTE rule when it comes to any of them. DO NOT PUT YOUR FINGERS inside any of these places and then stare at, play with or smell whatever you get out.

• **Your face.** You know, if you're like most guys, you don't think much about the skin on your face, but there's a good chance that the person you may be talking to or touching – or hope to be talking to or touching – will be thinking about the skin on your face. So here are some suggestions to help ensure that you have good skin to look at and to touch.

As with hair products, manufacturers of cosmetics for women are now making items for men to use on their faces. Again, L'Oreal, Nivea and Neutrogena each have a great line of men's skincare products, usually found with men's shaving supplies. (Ask the pharmacist if you can't locate them in the store. They aren't cheap, but if you have skin issues, a solution is worth the cost.) Go to Walgreen's or Eckerd's.

If you have acne (or constant breakouts), here's a thought. *GET IT FIXED*. Because there is no such thing as a sexy red, puffy, pus-filled zit, and don't think that a zit on your face is not going to be noticeable. *Please!* A woodpecker glued to your forehead would be less noticeable.

We can fast-forward to the dermatologist if you want, but there may be an easier fix on the way there. First, as with everything else in your world, keep your face really clean. Keep your hands off of it. Dirt or bacteria is often the culprit behind skin problems, so shield your face from unnecessary contact with *anything* – even things that look clean. Especially your hands and telephones, because those two things can cause major breakouts in the spots they touch.

(Many celebrities who have had acne swear by Proactiv, so visit www.proactiv.com and do your research.)

Sometimes problems with the skin on your face, which is almost always some form of acne, is diet-related. Greasy foods can cause many skin problems. Caffeine, too. I know. Bummer. But either way, here's great news: *There are prescription medications in pill form available now that can zap zits and acne-type skin issues quickly* – like in a matter of days. There is no reason for you <u>not</u> to try this stuff, unless you're pregnant (and if that's the case, then acne is the least of your concerns). Get a prescription from a dermatologist. You can afford it <u>if you want</u> it.

1. Keep your skin clean. Wash your face in the a.m. and before bed.
2. If you only get zits once in a while, ask the pharmacist for a good ointment or other over-the-counter products that work well on acne.
3. Use lotion/moisturizer on your face if your skin is dry after you shave.
4. If your skin is oily, keep tissue in your pocket to use periodically during the day. Oily skin is not only *gross*, but it can also contribute to bigger skin problems. The good news is that it's fixable! (Again, check into Proactiv.)

• **Deal with dry lips.** I can't think of anyone who sits across the table from dry, split or cracked lips and fantasizes about kissing them. Lips must be *soft*. Yours included. So use Chapstick, Carmex, or Blistix. You don't need a purse for this. It will fit in your pocket. Also, if you're prone to having saliva stick in the corners of your mouth, wipe it off *often*.

I'll repeat this while we are still on the subject of the gross gunk that your body produces. Please stop picking or wiping stuff from your eyes, nose, ears and mouth – <u>and then staring at or examining it</u>. What are you looking for? The meaning of life? A Smurf? Pamela Anderson's phone number? Don't sniff it, or roll it around in your fingers and play with it either.

• **Nose.** Don't pick it. If there are things flapping around in there, get a tissue and blow it out – don't shove your finger in to get it. (What would you do with it then anyway – wipe it on a wall?) Look, I know that the physicist in you has already discovered that the tip of your index finger and the opening to each of your nostrils are exact in diameter. *Eureka...* A perfect fit. But you need to do everything humanly possible to prevent these two from coming together. *Keep your finger out of your nostrils.* Simply make periodic trips to the men's room and keep tissue in your pocket for nose emergencies. If your response to *that* is the cloth hanky you carry in your pocket, then...

DON'T KEEP A CLOTH HANKY IN YOUR POCKET. If this has been a habit of yours, then you need to ask your therapist for some high octane, anti-hanky medication. That is about the nastiest habit ever developed by man. (You may as well be recycling your toilet paper and keeping <u>that</u> in your pocket.)

Warning – brutally blunt, disgusting point... coming right up. I realize that what I'm about to say is even more disgusting than what I just said, but there are some guys out there who need to hear it anyway (you'll know who you are): I'm not sure if it is a split personality issue, some other form of mental illness, or simply a very horrifyingly bad habit you've brought with you from 1st grade, but if you happen to move one of your fingers directly from your nostril to your mouth, then you have three choices. 1) you could swear to us both, you and me, that you will break this habit NOW, 2) you could have your nose or your guilty finger(s) surgically removed 3) you can go to the backyard and dig a hole for someone about your size, get in it and <u>stay</u> - until the cows come home and the pigs fly - and they all team up to pull you out. (We see you do this, you know, and when we do, we suddenly start to believe that you have landed here by mistake and cannot get back to your disgusting home planet.)

One way to avoid dry nostrils, which is typically the cause of your finger's need to mess around inside your nose anyway, could be as simple as keeping them moist inside. Though Vaseline, Neosporin or any of the petroleum based products may not be the long-term answer for this issue, they could be a temporary solution to help you train your fingers to stay out of your nose. Use a Q-Tip to lightly line your nostril.

• **Ears.** Since you just met Q-Tips, then try one to clean and dry your ears after your shower. Clean every nook and cranny – after every shower (but be careful not to push it in too far). If you like the thought of someone whispering or breathing in your ear, it's more likely to happen if your ear is free of funky, flaky debris and stinky earwax.

• **Trim your eye-brows, your nose hair and your ear hair.** If you don't, then gross things take up residence there and they'll slink out and wiggle at people when you're not looking. This is important, because these things can make the rest of us run screaming from the room. Invest in a real hair trimmer. Ask the pharmacist where to find one in the store, or call the 800 number you'll find on the infomercial at 3 a.m. READ the instructions. If you have bushy brows, nostrils or ears, you'll need this handy tool forever anyway. As we get older, some of our body hair gets wild and crazy. Noses, ears, eyebrows and any of your hairy warts, with their increase in psycho whiskers, demand a little of your attention. *Or they will get a lot of it from everyone else.*

• **Watch your tan.** If you're looking like saddle leather or beef jerky, you need to step into the shade. Find a happy medium. Too tan and you'll look like George Hamilton. Too pale and you'll look like Marie-Antoinette. Reduce your bake time – or try some of the self-tanning creams/sprays to replace your time under the sun or the bulbs entirely. Skin cancer isn't pleasant, and looking 60 when you're 32 isn't either. Understand that I think we all look healthier with a little color in our cheeks. You just don't need to lube up and broil to achieve a *slight* tan. L'Oreal makes a self-tanning lotion called Sublime Glow and there are actually two benefits to this stuff. It moisturizes, and it enhances your skin tone. (Self-tanning lotions can also improve acne break outs.) But be sure to wash it off your hands because for some reason, your palms will turn orange.

You'll want to heed the advice on the issues you've just read about, because it could mean the difference between breakfast for two and life sucks – for 1.

d. Eyes, Glasses, Contacts
If you wore glasses in the 60s or 70s, you were probably called "four-

eyes." If you wear glasses now, there is a T-shirt worn by teenage girls that says: "I Like Skinny Guys With Glasses." Wow. Lucky you. (You're skinny, right?)

Yes, this book is about developing charm. So why would I talk to you about taking care of your eyes? Because if you want to be charming, it will help if you are healthy from head to toe. And since the goal here is to help you get what you want, we'll also focus on helping you <u>see</u> it.

Take care of your eyes. See an eye doctor every year. Eye exams aren't too expensive, and if you have health insurance, the exams are probably covered. (But as with any health issue – do not let your insurance dictate what you do for yourself.) You may take your ability to see for granted, but I'm sure that any man who has lost his sight would happily kick your butt for not taking care of your vision. Most people will agree that pitch black is good for one thing. That would be *sleeping.*

Here are a few simple things that you should do for your eyes:
1. Make certain that when you read, you have plenty of light.
2. Limit the hours you spend at a computer monitor if you can feel the strain on your eyes.
3. If you have a job or hobby that puts your eyes at risk of injury, always wear your safety goggles. This is a no-brainer, right? (Kind of like when you get into a vehicle you wear your seatbelt.) Goggles are *cheap* and you can buy them at K-Mart, Wal-Mart, Target, Fred Meyer, True Value, Lowe's, Ace, Home Depot or just about any other all-purpose store. And did I mention that they're *cheap*?
   (Especially compared to the cost of:
       Your Emergency Room visit
       Your twenty-two eye surgeries and follow-up appointments
       Your white cane with red tip
       Your Braille training
       Food for your new, 85 lb. Seeing Eye Dog
   And the numerous other costly components of your new life in complete and total darkness.)

IF YOU WEAR GLASSES
Be sure to keep them clean. Dirty eyeglasses are gross and will make people think that that you are a slob. Also, make sure your glasses frames are not left over from 1972. Get a classic frame style. If you can afford to buy new frames as the styles change, and you like being trendy, go for

it. Glasses can be as much of a fashion statement as a necktie or jacket. Reference: Elton John.

If you hate wearing glasses, get contacts. Single-use, extended-wear, etc. There are colors and funky designs, too. For easy and inexpensive vision options, look for a *Lens-Crafters* in your local mall.

> **If you want to end the issues involving your 'less than 20/20' vision, ie; glasses, contacts, walking into walls, mistaking your hemorrhoid cream for your toothpaste, etc., then GOOGLE "Lasik surgery". Lasik facilities can often be found in shopping centers, so you can buy a CD, eat a slice of pizza and have eye surgery- all in a trip to the mall.**

e. Your Smile: A Dealmaker or Deal-*breaker*?

An awesome smile is a killer asset when it comes to charm. But we are not all blessed with dimples and perfect teeth, and THAT *is why God made dentists.* They are equalizers.

Why will we spend the next several pages discussing your mouth? Because it's the one part of your body that jumps out at us when we see you. Unlike your eyes, your mouth has many components to make it appealing (or appalling). And although your eyes may be an outstanding feature, we don't typically stare at and assess your eyes like we do your mouth. Also, eyes are rarely ugly or full of issues. But mouths? *Issues.*

Please get this: a disgusting mouth is not likely to help you get dates. Or friends. Or jobs. (Or sex.) And though it's true that your dog typically loves anything that smells like a dog butt, most humans do not. So start using the money you now waste on silly things like food – I'm joking – to start your dental care fund. Then get ready for better job opportunities, better relationships, better seats at restaurants (and more sex).

Question: Does your mouth look, feel, taste and smell great? If NO is the answer to any part of that question, then your mouth is probably not healthy – or very inviting.

You would not believe how often the following things are said about guys after a first date or first meeting:
"He is totally hot, but I can't stop staring at that one tooth."
"God! He's gorgeous! But he *really* needs to get his teeth fixed."

"He's really nice, but his breath is sssso disgusting."
"I won't be seeing him again because his mouth is a total train-wreck!"

Hmmm. Could any of these things be said about your mouth? Well, here's some happy news: These days, anything that's wrong in your mouth can be fixed quickly. All it will cost you is *MONEY*. (You know that you can afford the things *that you want to afford*. So prioritize.) No flesh, no sweat, no years off of your life, no selling your soul to the devil. But what you can get back – once you have invested in your healthy, great-looking smile – is limitless. More on the cost soon.

Dealing with gnarly looking teeth and nasty breath is cruel and unusual punishment, whether you're the person presenting this grossness or you're the person looking at it and smelling it. So you should simply do whatever it takes to get your mouth healthy and clean, and then keep it that way. A healthy mouth consists of two things ('fuzzy teeth' isn't one of them): healthy gums and healthy teeth. That's it. If you can brush after every meal, perfect! (Tip: This is a great diet aid, too.) Otherwise, brush in the morning and *before bed*, floss once a day and go to the dentist regularly. (After your initial overhaul, that is.)

I'll tell you that if you have **dental insurance**, that's great, but DO NOT let it dictate the amount of dentistry you will accept. Most insurance plans will cover a certain amount of care each year (usually around $1500), but if you need dental care, it may exceed that amount in a heartbeat. So prepare to find financing and/or raid your savings.

FIND A GREAT DENTIST. If you don't have a dentist, ask a friend, co-worker or the people next door for the name of theirs and get a complete check up. (Or visit the web site of any school or institute such as LVI – the Las Vegas Institute for Advanced Dental Studies.) If you need to use the Yellow Pages to find a dentist, do it. Call around and make an appointment. Once you go, the dentist will check you out and then make his or her recommendations. Then you follow them. Bada bing, bada boom.

If the dentist finds that your mouth needs an overhaul, get it. **Invest the millions it may cost and do it**. Get a loan. Really. You can find a way to afford it. Dental offices are like car dealerships now. They can offer 532 different financing plans with easy, nothing-down, interest-free options, spreading low monthly payments over a period of 241 years.

OK, slight exaggeration there, but beyond the age of 12, it's not likely that cash will appear under your pillow when you lose a tooth. As a matter of fact, if you lose a tooth at your age, it's BIG bucks to replace it. And yes, you need to replace it, Jethro, because once one is lost, the rest just seem to follow... *like lemmings off a cliff.* (Well, that 'suicidal lemmings' thing was just a fabricated *staged* occurrence in an old documentary, but the domino-effect-like loss of your teeth is not.)

Bottom line: You can't be charming without teeth. Well, I guess you can – *until you open your mouth to speak, smile or eat.* But, the tooth fairy would much rather help you get financing to *fix your teeth* than leave mythical lemming poop under your pillow for the ones you've lost.

(Tell your new dentist that you don't want to treat one tooth at a time, but that you want your mouth totally healthy and looking good NOW - regardless of your insurance coverage, your own work schedule or the temperature outside. Seriously. Just get a loan and *gitter dun!*)

FYI, there is nothing remotely sexy or charming about a guy with a floppy denture, so if you happen to have 1 or 2 of those, then ask your new dentist about **dental implants** to anchor your teeth.

ARE YOU A 'DENTAL CHICKEN'?
Yeah, you and everyone else. Practically anyone over the age of 25 has had an uncomfortable (or nightmare) visit to the dentist, but times have *changed.* These days, the dentist can get your gums numb with gel before poking you with that skinny little needle that *you think* is ssssso big. Also quiet lasers can be used in place of noisy drills. These two facts alone have just convinced you to make a dental appointment, yes? Be honest when you call and tell them that you are a dental chicken – if you are.

If you can't bring yourself to open wide without being a little, let's say, incoherent, I'm sure the people in your new dental office will provide nitrous oxide (laughing gas) or a pre-treatment pill to relax you for your dentistry. Don't be embarrassed, you aren't alone in your worries about dental work and the dental crew will understand. But think of your final result. That would be you, finally, with a mouth that looks and feels great. How would that be for you? You can sit down snarling like Freddy Kruger and stand up smiling like Freddie Prinz. Yeah, Baby!

MOUTH BREATHING

Do you breathe mostly through your mouth instead of your nose? Why? Figure that out, because breathing through your mouth will pretty much guarantee that you always have bad breath. Also, you probably look like your only word is 'duuuuuuuuh'. So close your mouth. Breathe through your nose. Practice. Place a strip of Scotch (or duct) tape from the tip of your nose to under your chin to train you to stay closed. (Do this with the curtains closed.) If you can't breathe through your nose only, then go to a doctor and find out why.

BRACES

If your teeth are crooked, get them straightened. *There are many alternatives to the old-fashioned metal mouth.* Check them out, because if your teeth are crooked, braces definitely won't make them look any worse than they do now – metal or not – and people who notice will know that you are improving yourself. Eventually you'll have a great, straight smile. This means you'll feel better about yourself, too. Ask any adult guy who's had braces to fix his crooked teeth. He'll tell you it was a *brilliant* move.

DO YOUR GUMS BLEED?

Bleeding gums, typically caused by gum disease, ARE NOT HEALTHY and will cause really bad breath. Is a bleeding hand OK? No. A bleeding ear? Of course not. Bleeding gums are not OK, either – no matter what your 93-year-old dentist or hygienist may tell you. And remember this: Statistics prove that your teeth will not fall out because of tooth decay. They'll fall out because of gum disease. And if your gums bleed, you probably have it (but it's controllable...) Check out the OxyFresh™ products I'll mention soon.

Be sure you *always* use a SOFT toothbrush. A soft brush is best for your gums – and your teeth couldn't care less. They don't need scrubbing. (A *washcloth* can clean your teeth but the edges of your gums need the massaging of a soft brush.) Remember this: you only need to brush the teeth you want to keep.

After you have invested the necessary big bucks to make your smile charming, and you are back in great dental shape, I suggest you have your teeth cleaned 3 or 4 times per year. **THREE OR FOUR TIMES PER YEAR.** Not once or twice. Pre-schedule your cleaning appointments and never miss, because this will keep your mouth looking, smelling, feeling, and performing at its best. And it will almost guarantee that you will keep your own teeth forever – even if you live to be 200.

BAD BREATH

First, let me tell you that whenever someone offers you a breath mint or gum, take it. It may be a hint. Bad breath is one of the biggest turn-offs and common complaints about guys. (Yeah, yeah, girls get it, too. *Different book.*)

Here is a simple way to eliminate your bad breath… *forever.*
Get your hands on some **Oxyfresh™ products.** You can't buy them in stores but you can go to www.oxyfresh.com, and under 'Oral Care Products' order the 'Patented Zinc Kit' and the "OxyCare™ 3000'. That's an oral irrigator… like a water-pik on steroids. It will remove the crud from below your gum line – the gunk which causes your bad breath. You could practically wash your car with this thing. (Picture a sand blaster here, but it uses water and it's actually great for your teeth and gums.) You'll need to sign up when you place your order, but if you want to avoid the newsletters and product emails, then when asked how you heard about the products, under the 'drop down', select Media Resources, then select **Charm School for Guys.** *I'll protect you.* Many dental offices sell Oxyfresh, too.

You will be amazed to discover that *once a hygienist has gotten your gums healthy*, with daily use of the OxyFresh™ stuff, you will never have bad breath again. *Not even in the morning.* You probably can't even imagine what it would be like for you to wake up and roll over to say "Good Morning" each day without *morning breath*, huh? Yeah, neither can your partner. The words "it's time to get up" could take on a new meaning in *your* bed. Wow.

Keep in mind that bad breath can also come from stomach issues, so after you've tried the Oxyfresh™, if you still have bad breath, there could be a deeper issue. (Go get checked.)

TOOTHACHES

When you get a toothache, you need to see a dentist. And as I mentioned before — avoid 'one tooth at a time' dentistry. Keep whatever bugs are in one corner of your mouth from migrating to the other three corners (or into the mouth of the person that you like to kiss.) Also — **don't ever apply an aspirin to a toothache.** It can make matters <u>much</u>

worse. Bite the bullet, find the money and get your mouth healthy to avoid future toothaches.

BRIGHTEN YOUR SMILE

If your mouth is healthy and you've just had your teeth cleaned, then get BriteSmile™ or ZOOM™. Many dental offices offer them, and there are also whitening centers in many malls (just like Lasik for your eyes). Go to www.britesmile.com to find a location near you. For a cheaper, easy way to whiten your teeth, try *Crest White Strips*. They work. But you'll need to divorce the coffee. Go to Kroger and buy some EuroMints. They have caffeine. (Stop smoking, too.)

> **Teeth, unlike bumblebees and little sisters, will go away if you ignore them. So get your mouth completely healthy, and keep it healthy. You maintain your car or truck, right? You change the oil, right? OK then, there you go. Take care of your mouth, too. Geez. It's part of your body. You can't just park it and take the bus.**

You get the message. Dentistry has come a long way, Baby - so go out and get yourself some.

f. Your Body *Armor*

ROUGH skin is a turn off. *I can almost guarantee that your scaly, dry skin is not helping you get some snugly. So put some effort into getting it soft, smooth and snug-able.*

There is this great product called *lotion,* and contrary to popular guy belief, it will not cause you any pain at all. There are hundreds of brands, and they all make great promises, so try a few for yourself and see which you can tolerate.

You might start with **Aveeno**. (No, they are not paying me.) It takes a longer-lasting approach to softening skin, and from the feedback I've received, it works. Also, it doesn't leave your hands or skin feeling greasy. This is good, right? We all know you hate that greasy feel. Try the lightly scented formula. Cover yourself with it after your shower.

Itchy skin. Try Gold Bond Medicated Lotion if your dry itchy skin is driving you crazy. If you cannot handle the thought of using lotion, then try these options for men: Old Spice Body Wash, Gillette Hydrator Body Wash or Nivea Men's Body Wash. They moisturize and smell great, too.

GET A MASSAGE

A great way to figure out the skin on your body is by getting a full body massage. Really. Pro massage therapists know skin. If you've never had a massage, you are in for a treat. Don't worry. They cover you with really big, thick, <u>heavy</u> towels so you'll have no reason to be self-conscious – no matter what ideas may pop into your head (think about a carburetor). A massage therapist has probably seen it all, anyway.

Fees for massages will vary depending on where you are. A massage at Cindy's in Arma will cost less than one at Donna's in Boston or LeeAnn's in Anchorage. You can usually choose from a 1/2-hour, to a 1-1/2-hour session. Call around to health clubs, hair salons/day spas, and physical therapy offices to get rates and make an appointment. After you're finished with your session, ask the massage person for suggestions to improve or maintain your skin. Professionals can see areas of *you* that *you* can't see - like your back, so if there are any funky spots, they'll make suggestions for fixing them. Or they can rush you to the hospital.

ASK THE PHARMACIST

If you think you have skin issues, but you can't bring yourself to get the massage *or* see a dermatologist, then you have one last resort. That would be your friendly neighborhood pharmacist. A pharmacist is like the all-powerful medicine man (or woman). *Pharmacists aren't doctors (usually), but often they will listen to your problem and recommend non-prescription medications that might help you.* (And check this out, Zorro... they can do this by phone so your identity will never be revealed.) Also, they don't have a box full of *one latex glove.*

> Whether your skin is too dry, too oily, itchy, bumpy, red or blotchy, whatever, the pharmacist can often help. There are enough over-the-counter remedies available these days that just about everything from noisy neighbors to a problem with your tax return can be dealt with by using one of them. Anyway, if you're too far gone for the pharmacist to help, I'm sure he or she would be happy to call an ambulance for you.

g. Hands, Fingers, Feet, Toes

Your rough hands are no good for anything to do with another human, but they might work well for brushing your dog or your cat. And your rough feet could actually cause bodily injury to the unsuspecting person who shares your bed.

YOUR HANDS

First, keep them clean. (Keep a small bottle of **germ-X** *or* **Purell** *hand sanitizer* nearby to use periodically throughout the day.) Next, take a good look at your hands. It is common for guys who live and work in cold climates, or who have never heard of that thing called *lotion*, to have dry hands. **But dry hands are definitely avoidable, and I highly recommend that you definitely avoid them.** Test your hands on your own face. If they feel scratchy and rough and look dry and cracked, you really need to lose the tutu and get acquainted with hand cream or lotion. Because your rough hands are sure to scare away the soft things that you may wish you could be touching with them...

Lose your lotion phobia. Rough hands are a turn off and very bad for your sex life. Try Cornhuskers or Bag Balm -they're about as "non-lotion" as you can get and still receive the benefit of smoother hands. Don't worry, we're not looking for "baby's butt soft" here (though this can be achieved if you want), just tolerably un-rough, OK? (TIP: In preparation for your romantic weekend getaway or your highly anticipated sleepover, the night before: Drench your hands with lotion or hand cream, then put a clean pair of socks over them and go to sleep. Next day? There's a baby's butt at the end of each arm.)

Always be sure that your fingernails are short and clean. Dirt under fingernails is something that most people find *max disgusting*, so buy a nailbrush if you don't already have one. Keep one on the sink and one in the shower.

Consider getting a manicure and/or a pedicure. Many people find men's hands to be <u>very</u> <u>sexy</u>. (Feet? Not so much – which is why I'm suggesting a pedicure.) Your hands are probably sexy, too, but we need to see them through the gunk and dry skin. So why not make yours look great? Besides, you'll probably get pampered for an hour or so by a hottie. So what was the downside to this?

YOUR FEET

The first time someone sees your feet, even at the beach, it's sort of personal – especially if you don't live in Bora Bora. So make sure that they look good. Well, as good as they can – considering they're feet. Give them the same consideration that you give your hands. Use lotion on them if they're dry and rough.

Dr. Scholl's makes an overnight foot cream that can make you better in bed. Well, it will make your feet feel better in bed. You just put it on your feet when you get into bed and sleep with it on. ...Hey – this stuff might accidentally soften your hands, too, if you don't rush to wash it off after putting it on your feet, that is. Anyway, when feet touch other feet, soft is good. And better in bed.

Toenails. If you have **thick, yellow, fugly toenails**, then call the pharmacist or go to the doctor and get a prescription. It's probably a fungus. Toenails can be gross enough without this disgusting condition. But there's an easy fix – just like everything else I'm telling you about.

Clean under your toenails, especially if you wear dark socks. The dark lint gets under your toenails and stays there, so use the file that's in your nail clippers or use your nailbrush to get it out. Also keep your toenails short by cutting them often (straight across to avoid ingrown toenails - no rounded corners) with nail clippers – not with your leatherman or bayonet.

A weird toenail story: When I was 15, my best friend and I would go swimming at her great uncle's house – he had a great pool. He was a World War II vet and we called him Uncle Grump (because he was). He always had the old bayonet from his ARMY rifle with him, and he used it for everything that required a tool. Why? I don't know. But one day he was cutting his toenails with it (????) and he slipped. Soon gangrene showed up. Then the surgeon. Then the wheelchair. After that, we called him "Super Grump"... from a distance cause he still kept that bayonet on his lap. Geez. "And the next nominee for the coveted Darwin Award is..." So anyway, use toenail clippers, OK? (Always find the right tool for any job. Rarely will it be a bayonet.)

ATHLETE'S FOOT

If your foot itches often and you do not have a mosquito bite or poison ivy, you have athlete's foot. If you've tried lotions and creams such as Lamisil, and/or all the other over-the-counter products for this problem and your feet are still not looking and feeling good, you should see a doctor. He or she can prescribe medications that can get rid of it quickly, because if you have athlete's foot, *you must get rid of it.*

STINKY FEET

First, let me say that if you are one of those guys who laughs off your stinky foot problem, the same way you're proud of yourself for clearing a room with a *fart*, then let us welcome you to *the real world*. We're so glad you're here. Get this. Stinky feet – like bad breath - can kill plants and small animals, so you need to wake up and do *anything* in your power to get rid of yours now – to avoid your accidental death (unaccidentally plotted by anyone you live with). No joke, foot odor is a *huge turn off* to most people. That makes it a *very serious problem* for you, and if you suffer from this most unfortunate affliction – well then – here's one word for ya, Man: *LISTERINE*.

Yep, Listerine. Can you believe that? The same stuff that can get rid of your stinky mouth odor can get rid of your stinky foot odor. Go figure. Any flavor, too. Just add a half-cup of Listerine to a pan of water – cold, hot or warm – and place your feet flat in the pan for about 10 minutes. Make sure that the tops of your feet are covered. That's it. Do this as often as needed, but especially before going any place where you know your shoes will be coming off. For most guys, a foot soak in Listerine is typically good for 24 hours. Try it and see. Some guys can soak once every 2 or 3 days. (Recycle, but be sure to use it in your mouth first.)

Either way, remember that once you've incorporated the Listerine foot soak into your life, you're going to need new shoes, boots and socks. Your old ones have that old stink built into them now. (Even after your old socks are washed and smell clean, your sweat will reactivate the stink.)

If you can't afford new shoes, then at least see about having your old ones fumigated. Yellow Pages. Shoe Repair. Ask if they can 'deodorize' your stinky shoes. Otherwise, go shoe shopping. I'm sure any girl between the ages of 1 and 98 will be happy to shoe shop with you. Because putting stinky shoes on stink-free feet will make your Listerine soak kind of pointless, won't it?

Following are a couple of suggestions for dealing with your chronic foot odor (although for some guys the Listerine eventually stops the odor all together):
*   Buy some shoe liners with charcoal or any other material that addresses foot odor.
*   Always wear socks with your shoes or boots, since the socks will absorb the sweat, which causes the foot odor. (Look for the socks that help prevent foot odor.)
*   Try talking to a dermatologist or even a holistic healer. *Sometimes*

natural remedies – essential oils like patchouli or sandalwood - or nutritional changes can help with foot odor.

* If you wear dress shoes, and odor is an issue, cedar shoe trees will not only hold the shape of your shoes, but they can help eliminate the shoe odor. You can get them in a nice shoe store or in the men's shoe section of most department stores.

* Start wearing open shoes. Sandals. Einstein did that.

Really. Sandals. TEVAs, Doc Martins or Birkenstocks. You can wear sandals like these year round. In the winter just wear socks with them. If your feet don't sweat they won't smell.

What? You think sandals are goofy? Oh sure. You're going to tell me that you can't climb outside of your strict *fashion* comfort zone to try a pair of ultra-comfortable granola shoes that could finally eliminate the most horrible, where did everybody go? make-you-stay-single-forever, why me? clear-the-room-in-3-seconds-flat, stinky feet syndrome? Yes you can. (And if/when the sandals start to stink - it's time for new ones.)

Of course, the sandals are fine for you to wear to work if you teach philosophy at University, but probably not if you are an ironworker. Probably not wise to wear snow machining, or playing tennis either. Use your common sense, but try it when you can. Go to REI or Sports Authority to find socks that are climate appropriate and give the open shoes a try. Your life will have a wonderful, new, stink-free meaning.

h. The Low Down
Fact: Your butt has a serious design flaw. Sorry. Unlike the canine, feline, bovine and other "ine" butt models, yours does not automatically slam shut after each use.

Nope. Yours is high-maintenance issue. Like a gun, you must clean it after you fire it. We're now talking about the lower third of your torso, so since there doesn't seem to be a classy or polite way to address the issues connected to this area, please forgive me for being direct instead. You're probably used to this from me by now.

Seriously uncomfortable subject coming right up.
Surprisingly, one common, and *very personal* complaint that people share about their guys, is butt stripes on the underwear. (I know. Gross

topic but it must be addressed – I warned you.) Can you believe that? And we are not talking about 7-year-olds. This would imply that many guys simply don't know (or care) about how to effectively wipe their butts. Yes – it's a bad design, but you own it *so deal with it.*

Look at it this way, when you blow your nose, you are sure that no evidence of the "blow" remains on your face. Right? OK. So with regard to *your* butt, you should know that it is really important for you to give *it* the same clean-up effort that you give your nose. Not necessarily because people will see the *yuck,* but because not being clean back there can cause major pain *if you happen to get hemorrhoids.* Also, if you don't keep really clean back there, *you could happen to get hemorrhoids.* Or serious butt itch. Diaper rash. Either way – pain. And since you aren't a poodle, you can't put your legs in the air and scoot your butt across the floor, letting the carpet deal with the itch for you. (Bummer. There might be major entertainment value in *that.*)

Beyond the pain issue, there's always a chance that someone might see your underwear at the end of the night. Hopefully, not the ambulance team or paramedics like your mom may have warned when you were a kid. Remember that? Moms had this thing about telling you to be sure you changed your underwear every day because you might get into an accident, and then the doctors and nurses would see that your lazy or spacey mother did not make you wear clean shorts.

Wow. Those moms might have gotten better results if they had suggested a scenario that actually sounded appealing to you. Anyway, here's the solution if you can't complete the job with your Charmin: Buy some individually wrapped Wet Wipes and always keep one in your pocket. (Or install a bidet. Ten million Frenchman can't be wrong.) The accidental stripes are a big problem, so after a few passes with the Charmin, bring out your trusty, anti-crusty, Wet Wipe. (At the very least, wet a paper towel.) Are we clear on this matter? If so, AT EASE.

Making your adjustments. Just like you shouldn't pick your nose where people might catch you doing it, you should keep your hands away from your crotch, no matter what. This means that you need to make the necessary physical adjustments in the restroom, before you come out. In other words, still maneuvering your package around, or zipping up as you are walking out of the restroom, not only tells people that you don't wash your hands after you make a deposit, but it also makes you look like a classless and clueless idiot. So adjust your boys in the bathroom – *before you wash your hands* and come out.

> **Scratching your crotch.** Never do this even if there is only a snowball's chance in Tahiti that someone will see you do it. If a constant itch is present, and you're sure your comical roommate hasn't put itch powder in your shorts, then you have a problem. If avoiding the doctor's office is your ultimate goal, then visit a drug store and look around or ask the pharmacist about a possible over-the-counter remedy. Cruex, Lamisil, Lotrimin, and Micatin are all OTC products for various 'guy itches'. **(FYI - www.shopinprivate. com, will help you avoid the embarrassment of buying this type of stuff in a store. They sell everything from hemorrhoid cream to hair loss products to condoms in size** EXTRA SMALL.**)**

Get this: There once was a guy who clearly had jock itch or crabs or diaper rash or *something*. Whatever the cause of this creepy and itchy situation, he kept his fingers glued to his zipper. Wait, did he think no one noticed him scratching and poking and wriggling around in an effort to stop the itch? Geez. Anyway, it kind of became a pathetic little joke behind his back. Nobody would sit where he sat and everybody wondered what kind of bugs he had – and where he had gotten them.

So why am I telling you this? Because I want you to know that if you have an itchy crotch, and you scratch it, people will definitely notice. Just like picking your nose while in your vehicle. *You are not invisible. We can see you in there.* Anyhow, this itchy condition will not go away on its own. You *must* call the pharmacist or go see the doc. There's usually an easy fix. Otherwise, your itchy crotch will drive you crazy. And your friends will put you in a class all by yourself – literally. Only you won't know it.

> **Practicing unsafe sex.** Don't bother practicing. You'll never get good at it. But if you've had unprotected sex - and an itch, a drip or any other oddity has started to occur down there, don't mess around here. Go get checked. Sexually transmitted bugs won't go away without medicine – and they can really make you nuts. Also, pull out your little black book and start making the dreaded phone calls to anyone with whom you may have exchanged fluids. Suggest they go get checked. Bummer for you – but ya gotta do it. Uh, charm? Re-read that earlier section on MASTERING THE APOLOGY.

If you aren't circumcised, you're probably aware of some extra steps you may need to take to keep healthy. (Like never put anything away wet). Circumcised or not, every guy should know to keep very clean, and wash and *dry completely*. This will keep the painful problems that uncircumcised guys often deal with - under control. If you have a son who is uncircumcised, be sure to teach him the maintenance routine so that he doesn't end up suffering from the painful skin conditions that you may have experienced as a kid.

Tips from Chapter 7: Your Personal Hygiene And Body Maintenance

1• **Shower *every day*, scrubbing *all of you*.** Your hair, face (mustache/beard), ears, hands, torso, arms, underarms, legs, genitals, butt, feet, fingernails, toenails.

2• **Make sure that you smell good.** There are several ways to make this happen. There's liquid body wash for the shower, scented deodorants and body spray for use after the shower, and of course, there's aftershave and there's cologne. **ONE SQUIRT ONLY.** We'll smell it! *Trust me!* (And don't use them all at once.)

3• **Take care of your hair no matter how much you have or don't.** Either way, long or short, thick or see-through, keep it clean. If you are losing your hair, that's OK. Do not let this small fact mess with your self-confidence or your self-worth. Guys intentionally shave their heads these days, you know. Why? Are they losing it anyhow? Maybe. And maybe they are just into looking *tough*. So which would you be? *We-don't-know*. And unless you tell us, <u>we never will</u>. (Google "men's hair loss" and learn about your options.)

4• **Update your hair style.** If you have a bi-level, then I hope you have a bass boat and a beer-belly to go with it, Bubba. Cheers! Feesh Own! Seriously guys, if you want respect, positive attention, and the pointing and giggling to stop, then go to a salon and let a stylist there make you look good. Try whatever they do to you for one month – gel and all. If you can't stand it after thirty days, go back to whatever you had before. (Then be prepared for everyone to tell you how good it looked before you changed it back.)

5• **Dandruff – if you have it, we shouldn't know it.** Try Selsun Blue, Head & Shoulders or the top secret and industrial strength remedy you'll find on page 130.

6• **Wash your face in the morning *and before bed*.** The skin on your face needs to look good, so take care of it. Try some L'Oreal, Nivea or Neutrogena skin care products for men to solve your *too oily* or *too dry* problem. If bumps are an issue on your face, then visit: <u>www.proactiv.com</u>. Or a dermatologist.

7• **Keep your lips soft by using Chapstick or Carmex often.** It fits right into your pocket. Gee. It's almost like they planned it that way...

8• **Keep your nose clean.** But not with a cloth handkerchief, Grandpa. Whatever you get out of your nose does not belong in your pocket, capisce?

9• **Your tan or lack of it.** I'm with Goldilocks on this one. Too much tan is very scary, but totally pale could creep us out, too. You need to be *just right*... with just a little color. You can achieve it with self-tanning lotions or rare naps on a sun bed. If you decide you will risk your life with a trip to the beach once in a while, leave the oil in the car. Use some sun screen.

10• **Have your eyes checked every year.** If you wear glasses, keep them clean. Wear safety glasses whenever there's a chance that whatever you're doing could end up in your eye.

11• **Clean your ears, nose, eyes, teeth with something other than a finger.** Q-Tips, Kleenex and toothpicks come to mind, but *never in public.*

12• **Go to the dentist to get your mouth healthy and clean, even if you must get a loan to do it.** Then have the dentist show you how to keep it like that forever. Brush your teeth when you wake up and brush before you go to bed. Floss once a day. (If you'd like to wake up with great breath, get some OxyFresh™ Products. *And have a great morning...*)

13• **Be sure your hands are clean, soft and smooth instead of dirty, cracked and dry.** Keep them clean by using **germ-X** or **Purell Hand Sanitizer** frequently – if you can't get to the soap and water.

14• **Use body lotion if your skin is dry.** Gold Bond Medicated Lotion can help with severely dry, scaly, itchy skin. Or get a massage and let the massage person make a few recommendations for your head to toe skin care and maintenance.

15• **For various 'body' issues, a neighborhood pharmacist can often help you.** They aren't doctors but they can answer your questions – or give you directions to a doctor.

16• **Take care of your feet**. Keep them *clean and soft*. (No one you are sleeping with will call you a wimp if you have soft feet...) Get rid of **foot odor** by soaking your feet with Listerine. Try Lotrimin AF, or ask a pharmacist or a doctor for help if you have **athlete's foot**.

17• **Keep the lower third of your torso healthy *and clean*.** Keep a Wet Wipe in your pocket to avoid racing striped shorts. If that doesn't work, then buy yourself some dark underwear. Or some *Depends*.

CHAPTER 8

Your Body and Health (Open Wide And Say "Aaaah")

I don't get it. What is with YOU *and doctors? Females will spend 25 of their waking hours focused on their bodies, trying to keep them healthy and looking good. You, on the other hand, will pay 10 times* less *attention to your skeletal system than you do to your stereo system(s). He-lllo!!!*

a. Your Posture – Stand Up and Be *Taller*

Unless you have a physical affliction that prevents you from holding your head up and standing or sitting up straight, you need to wake up – and smell your lost inches.

How's your posture? Do you stand and sit up tall? Most people don't even think about their posture until someone with really bad posture appears. Then watch everybody straighten up real quick.

Good posture is a great physical quality, and it can make you appear taller – and more confident. For whatever reason, everyone seems to think that tall is impressive. Did you know that the majority of U.S. presidents have been above-average height? (Harry Truman was an exception. But he dropped two nuclear bombs, so I'm sure no one mentioned his height.) Pretty amazing to think that we voters believe the tall guys are going to make better leaders. But again, whether you're tall or not, you can look taller by:
1. Standing straight and holding your head up.
2. Bringing your shoulders back.
3. Holding your stomach in.
Start paying attention to those points.

How about when you're seated? Do you sit up straight? Your back should be against the back of your chair. If you stare at a computer screen throughout your day, be sure it's at your eye level so that your neck isn't constantly bent. (Set your monitor up on top of the Yellow Pages or on that stack of manuals you don't read.)

THE WALL TEST

OK pal – up against the wall. Here's a test to determine if you're a slouch or not: stand with your heels, butt, shoulders and the back of your head against a wall. Good. This is you standing straight and tall. Now step away from the wall and relax.

Did you lose anything? Can you still see out of the window? If the view from your window suddenly has turned to nothing but sky, then you have baaaad posture. Yep, if you are noticeably taller when you're up against the wall than you are when you stand on your own, you need a book. Any book. (Not this one – you're reading it.) Go and get a different book now, please.

Now set that book flat on your head, unopened. Yes, this is what girls used to do – *they still should*. Anyway, connect with your inner 007 and place the book on your head. Just do it so you'll at least know what your straight back feels like. Place the *book* (no floppy magazines) up there and balance it. You'll get it. Balance is the key. Keep the book balanced on your head as you walk around the house, doing whatever you normally do. This will improve your posture. (Hint: You can do this while your mouth is taped shut. See page 138. For best results, close your blinds.)

This exercise will feel totally stiff, but that's because it's exaggerated while the book is on your head. In reality, it's just training your body to stand tall and move smoothly. (Great posture is mental. It's your brain that you need to rely on to remind you stand or sit up straight.) What you are doing with the book on your head is a good exercise, and if you say it hurts, then you'll need to decide whether you need to see a doctor or chiropractor about your back issue or simply admit that you've slumped since diapers and you just want to whine about needing to straighten up.

You may simply need an encouraging example of what you are trying to achieve and you can get it by watching any James Bond film. No matter which version of Bond you're seeing, you are looking at perfect posture. I think they plan it that way. The 3 prerequisites for any good 007: Charm, style and good posture. (Kudos to the moms of Sean, Roger, Timothy, Pierce, Daniel and that one other guy – George.)

Go and have your spine checked out. Especially if you have had - or are having - back troubles. Many people see a chiropractor on a regular basis, but they usually have had injuries or pain issues that led them there. You guys can and should have your spine checked regularly, to keep your back healthy and free of nagging issues. Please put this on your 'to do' list. **Visit www.bhpw.com** and learn more about your spine

— and how to preserve it. (Among lots of other great tips on your spine and it's connections.)

ATTENTION MEGA-TALL GUYS:
I'm just going to venture a guess here, but you probably don't like to stand or sit up really straight do you? Why? There's no way you can hide the fact that *you are above the rest of us*, so why not accept it and be proud? Please! - just hold your head high, because being different is not a bad thing, and almost any short guy would *pay* to be you. Also remember this: Slumping makes you look like a *high* guy with a *low* IQ – so *don't slump*.

b. Your Weight and Build – Are You Flabulous?
Imagine you are a magazine model. Would we find your photos in "Muscle & Fitness" *or uh,* "Pigs In A Blanket?" Either way, keep in mind that the hottie of your dreams may be allergic to fat. (At least to you – covered in it.)

Can you see your fly? If not, then you may be suffering from a chronic condition commonly found in men that involves severe swelling of the abdomen – typically caused by excessive consumption of *anything*. But it is totally treatable, and once treated most studies have shown a successful return of clear and normal vision with regard to the fly by slightly bending the neck. Also, many men have reported a sharp increase in sexual activity with an actual other person. Go figure.

You are in complete control of how toned – or not – your body is. So if you are not happy with the way your body looks or feels, then change it. Join a gym or buy a Bow-Flex. (Don't worry about being self-conscious in a gym. Everybody is. Remember, there's nobody here but us chickens.) Or order those workout DVDs from Billy Blanks, the Body Boot Camp dude. If you are committed to change, then any of these suggestions can practically guarantee your success in losing weight or building muscle, or both. (FYI: If you can't afford to join a club, call your local Parks and Rec people. Many of their rec centers have public weight rooms.)

GET FIT
Personal Trainers: You don't think that all of those Hollywood tough guys just woke up one day that hard and tight, do you? No way. They have all answered to personal trainers, nutritionists, and whip-crackin', butt-kickin', body buildin' Drill Sergeants. And you can, too.

Enlist a personal trainer at the gym (possibly on staff there) to help you get in shape. Call and ask the club about fees for this service. At some clubs, it may be included in your monthly dues. If not, try to figure out a way to afford it, or you can ask the employees there to create and help implement a workout routine for you. They won't assist you in each workout or push you to the extreme like a PT will, but they are always there to help you and answer your questions – and lift the bar off your neck.

Either way, you'll just need to make a pact with yourself and take control of your mind. *(You know that mind of yours can make you do **anything**.)* If you can get your mind on your side, then the sky's the limit with your body, and soon the only six-pack in your life won't be in your fridge, but right there where your beer belly *used to be*. Making a bet with a buddy is also a great motivator.

Eat less, walk more – That's French. Well, this is a rule that the men and women in Paris seem to unintentionally live by. Have you seen those guys? Have you seen those women? I think 'fat' is not in their vocabulary. It sure isn't in their butts. And most people in Paris do not exercise for the sake of exercise. They do it subconsciously because it's a normal fact of getting through each day. They take stairs because elevators in much of France are rare – and small and slow.

Most people in France use the metros in the cities, so they walk to and from them. Their daily routines just *naturally cause exercise*. They walk or bike from Point A to Point B, but they do not make a production of the fact that they are exercising. And they stay slim and generally look as good - or better - than many people who devote *years* of their lives to the really 'un-fun' *exercises*.

FLABULOUS
LOSE WEIGHT NOW — HERE'S HOW: If you discover that you can control your mind, but you still can't control your wallet or your schedule (geez), then following are a couple of the simplest and most pain-free solutions to lose weight:

1. CUT ALL OF YOUR MEAL PORTIONS IN HALF.

It's OK. You can keep on eating whatever you eat now. You do not need to <u>diet</u> or stop eating the foods that you love to eat, you simply need to start cutting your usual portions IN HALF. That's it. YOU WILL LOSE WEIGHT simply by eating HALF of what you are eating now. TRY IT. If you want to look better, feel better, and weigh LESS, then do it. Cut your burger in half and give half away. Put away your Jethro bowl and eat a SMALL bowl of Lucky Charms. Eat two pieces of chicken instead of 4. You will survive and you will lose weight. Really. It's fool-proof.

2. DON'T EAT OR DRINK ANYTHING AFTER 6 P.M.

(It'll take your body about a week to get used to less food and no food at night. Drink lots of water to keep you full.)

Beyond cutting all of your portions in half, walking more and eating NOTHING after 6pm, to lose your extra weight and get seriously healthy, you should start eating healthier foods. (Thanks for bearing with me now while I pretend to be your mother…) Fresh fruits, vegetables, chicken and fish. The easy foods that are bagged, canned or frozen are convenient and cheap, but they don't have the same health benefits that fresh foods have. Typically they are loaded with preservatives, too, which *aren't good for you*. They can make you fat and *keep* you fat. They're *preservatives* alright. They'll *preserve* <u>your</u> <u>fat</u>.

However, since cost and time are a factor for most of us, the good news is that microwavable meals have come a long way, Baby. So if you are serious about wanting to lose weight but can't really afford the fresh stuff, then try a Lean Cuisine or a Healthy Choice for lunch or dinner, or both. They're not bad and you can lose weight with them.

There are many decent-tasting, low-calorie, low-fat freezer meals available these days, including Weight Watchers brand. Check out your market's health food or nutrition section for a selection of healthier microwave foods. (Yes, it's true. Microwave food may not be the best way to go, but *hey*, we're comparing to <u>the drive-thru</u>, OK?)

WEIGHT LOSS TIPS:

• **Cut your regular meal portions** *in half.* You won't starve – I promise.

• **Graze throughout the day. Eat 6 _small_ meals, not 2 or 3 large ones.** (Remember to use your head in choosing your food items. Don't build your meals out of ice cream, potato chips and root beer.) By eating more often, your body will work more frequently, hence more efficiently, to process your food. Less down time.

• **Always eat breakfast.** Something hot or warm works best to get your body up and running.

• **Brush your teeth right after you eat.** The taste of toothpaste in your mouth will make the idea of food less appealing. (Try brushing then drinking a glass of O.J. and you'll see what I mean. Crest and Minute Maid don't like each other.)

• **Each a.m., take a high-speed, 30-minute walk before going to work.** Get up a half hour earlier. Make this a <u>priority</u>. You'll feel *great* all day, because walking will benefit your mind, too.

• **Make time to use your feet instead of your vehicle once in a while.** Plan your walk times and walk often.

• **Don't park close to the door.** Take the parking spot that is as far away from your destination's entrance as possible.

• **Eat your meals at the dinner table and not in front of the TV.** Focus on every bite of your food – not on a TV show, and you'll actually notice when you are full.

• **Serve your food in the kitchen from the stove,** not from big bowls and platters on your table. The last thing you need after cleaning your plate is a pile of baked potatoes or a mac and cheese casserole staring at you, saying "eat me."

• **REPEAT. Don't EAT or drink anything — but water — after 6 p.m.** Seriously. For successful weight loss and easy maintenance to keep it off – then follow that last tip. That's it. Do not eat or drink anything other than water after 6 p.m. Go ahead, give it 1 month. I dare ya.

WEIGHT WATCHERS

If you are a really big guy, consider calling them. Their methods are clinically proven to work. Almost two years ago my buddy, Paul, started using the Weight Watchers plan and 90 lost pounds later, none of it has come back. Recently, a clinical study followed 8 people as they each attempted to lose 100 pounds or more. They all succeeded and 6 of them used Weight Watchers.

Jenny McCarthy, model, actress and 1994 Playmate of the Year (like I needed to tell you who she is...), was bummed to discover - immediately after giving birth to her baby boy - that he in fact, did not pop out weighing 60 pounds. So she decided to join Weight Watchers.

"I tried a few times, unsuccessfully, to lose weight. It wasn't until I joined Weight Watchers that I was finally able to do it. I went to meetings — and my son came with me."   -Jenny McCarthy

There are many Weight Watchers locations to help you in most cities. Just like AA. Serious help for a serious problem. Go. There are nice people there to help you, and soon you will see your fly again.

Just like the gym, the dance or yoga classes, everyone else there wants to improve, just like you do. So the people with brains will not judge you for being there. (Don't worry about the people without brains.)

Is There a Chemist in the House?
Good. Here's your ticket to a Nobel Prize in Chemistry or Physiology & Medicine:
You know that there are hundreds of diet pills on the market that offer to suppress appetites, right? But what if there were a pill that would temporarily zap the sense of taste? (You know, the way Lamisil unintentionally can?) I mean, what's worse, **not eating** or **not tasting**? If a pill could be created that would temporarily suppress the sense of taste, then think of how our American masses would **skinny down and healthy up**. Because essentially, if we could not taste our food, we'd only be eating to feed our body machine - **not** because we need to wrap our lips around a Twinkie.

A pill that could zap our sense of taste would mean that the useless high fat, high calorie junk we eat would have no appeal. It's true. People would only be eating to live. Not because they can't keep their hands out of the Cheesy Poofs. Right? Get this: If you have chocolate in your mouth and you can't taste it, it feels like lard. And any fried food – when you can't taste it – feels like bumpy, crunchy grease in your mouth.

Within a short time (perhaps a month) without tasting what we eat, we could actually change our minds about what we decide to eat once we can taste our foods again. Because after tasting the equivalent of cardboard and/or hand lotion for a month, it seems obvious that a piece of wheat toast with no butter, or a salad without the extra dressing, would taste great. And think of how fat-free, healthy and HARD your body would become. There would be no need for adding salt or other things that jam up your arteries and tick off your heart, either.

Obesity has been linked to: hypertension, coronary heart disease, adult onset diabetes, stroke, gall bladder disease, osteoarthritis, sleep apnea, respiratory problems, endometrial, breast, prostate and colon cancers, dyslipidemia, steatohepatitis, insulin resistance, breathlessness, asthma, hyperuricaemia, reproductive hormone abnormalities, impaired fertility and lower back pain. (You may have noticed that Erectile Dysfunction is not listed here. But don't start partying over that fact. Many of these conditions require medications with a nasty little side effect. I'll bet you can guess what it is.)

c. Get Healthy or Suffer More and Die Sooner
Pay very close attention to your heart and to the things that touch your bike seat when you're on it.

(Why would I spend the next few dozen pages talking about your HEALTH? Because if you don't feel good – then you can't be… charming? Plus, you'll whine non-stop and suck the life out of the rest of us.)

If you're under 20, you believe you're invincible, we all know that. But you're not. And just like the rest of your gender, you need to focus on prevention. *Health issues will not go away just because you ignore them.* Have your prostate checked yearly if you are over 40. (But be warned. When the doctor puts on that single glove, it's not because he's about to pull muffins out of the oven.)

YOU CAN IGNORE IT BUT IT WON'T GO AWAY…
Guys are always blowing off health problems. My uncle has lived with a chronic pain issue for about 300 years. He's afraid of surgery. He's afraid it will hurt. He-lllo! He's in so much pain at any minute of any day that his stock reply to anything is "OW." I can't imagine that surgery, which could end his pain, could possibly be worse than the pain he's suffered - non-stop - since the beginning of time.

AVOID THAT DEADLY DISEASE CALLED "DENIAL."
If you have something odd going on in your body, see a doctor or a homeopathic practitioner. You probably have medical insurance and don't even know it. But even if you don't, make an appointment anyway. Ask about payment plans or search out a clinic that can offer a <u>sliding fee scale</u>. Most health issues are fixable – especially if you catch them early. **(Cancer would have much less power over humans if people would just pay closer attention to their bodies and get checked more *regularly*.)**

THE DOCTOR VS. THE PHARMACIST. We will declare a T.K.O. here, but only because you refuse to go to the doctor. No matter how irritating, painful or disgusting your symptoms or condition may be, a pharmacist may be able to hook you up with an easy, over-the-counter fix. Since we know you have a severe allergy to medically trained professionals, try visiting the drug store. (And as I told you before, a pharmacist does not have a box full of one latex glove.) If it so happens that you are stunningly close to death, a pharmacist is also qualified to call an ambulance for you.

ACHES AND PAINS. If you have the standard muscle soreness that occurs from a hard workout, helping a buddy move, or trying to play basketball like a 16-year-old, then try ThermaCare Heat Wraps, Icy Hot's *Maximum Strength Patches* or *Pro-Therapy*. These remedies will help put you in a better mood.

If you suffer from a serious, chronic pain issue, a real industrial strength pain, then research CERAGEM on the Internet and locate a CERAGEM center close to you. First let me tell you that they are FREE. Next, let me say that if you have pain, and your only options are surgery or swimming out to sea, then what do you have to lose by trying a CERAGEM therapy session? Go to www.ceragem.com and learn about this incredible therapy.

Mangosteen, acai, goji. Have some JUICE. For turning your borderline *anything* health condition into a better state of physical and mental well-being, get your hands on some of these juices. Google them. These *all natural* juices have about the highest concentration of antioxidants in the known world and they specifically zero in on **inflammation**. Think about it. Practically everything that's wrong on the planet is due to inflammation. A few ounces of any of these juices each day, will be ssssso much cheaper than surgery (or a funeral), so try them for a month or two — then talk to me about your chronic case of *whatever*... Author Kevin Trudeau writes in his book, **Natural Cures *They* Don't Want You to Know About**, "I have seen firsthand, illnesses and diseases simply vanish within a few months of drinking these juices." He's referring to Xango®, Goji®, and Noni® juices. Try some.

SIMPLE TIPS FOR MAINTAINING YOUR OVERALL HEALTH

There are many simple ways to get on a healthier path. Here are some suggestions, especially for those of you who live in that "drive-thru" line. (Yes, I am your mother again.)

1. Improve your diet – eat better foods. Limit your fried and fat foods, and eat more vegetables, fruits, fish, chicken and nuts. Eat more salad.

2. Work out. Get trim and stay that way.

3. Take a vitamin. Go to GNC and do some research on what you need. If that's too much work, too expensive or too taxing on your brain, then go to the grocery store and buy some *Men's One-A-Day Vitamins*.

4. If you are a soda-holic, try drinking water instead. If you can't bring your taste buds to do plain water, then drink Propel Fitness Water or Fruit 2o. They are flavored waters, but are still better for you than soda. Can't do that either? Good grief. Then drink Caffeine-Free Diet Coke. (Consider buying a juicer.)

5. Exercise for *at least* 30 minutes, *at least* every other day. A fast 30-minute walk can classify as exercise. (Exercise will not only give you a flatter stomach, but it improves your circulation, which can also give you thicker hair. Hmmm. Tighter bod, more hair... would there be a negative side to this? I'm not seeing it.)

6. Find a good doctor. Ask someone you know for the name of his or hers. Get yearly physicals – even if you have no insurance. Make payments if you must. It's important.

7. READ FOOD LABELS! There are some ingredients that you may want to avoid. For example, a certain sugar substitute claims to be a great alternative to sugar, but other sources claim that it's more like sugar on steroids. A fat builder or enabler. Those other sources say that this substitute actually likes to build fat factories in your body and then keep it's product — FAT — right there where it was developed. In you.

8. DO NOT IGNORE ACHES AND PAINS. When something's not right, call your doctor, your homeopath, your Shaman or your Aunt Esmeralda and then go get checked out.

<u>Never wait</u> **to go get checked!** Why is it that guys hate to get checked by a doctor? You always seem to wait until Death has called for directions to your house before you even consider a visit to the doctor. What's up with that? Don't you know that no matter what the problem may be, the longer you wait, the more money and flesh it's going cost you?

A good friend of mine was having back problems but kept avoiding the doctor. After about a year, my friend's legs started to get slightly numb and started to burn. After about a year and a half, certain muscles started to get numb, too. Namely, the sphincter. You know what that means, don't you? Depends. That's right – diapers for adults with issues. This person had issues all right – in the form of <u>13</u> out-of-commission vertebrae. Ten hours of surgery fixed **her**.

Yes – her. Surprise, surprise. She had driven a dump truck and other types of heavy equipment on the North Slope of Alaska for years, and the bouncing and vibration had taken its toll on her back. Ten hours of surgery and 4 months off work (<u>because she waited too long to see a doctor and get checked</u>) finally fixed her. Sort of. Anyway, she isn't back to perfect health and she never will be, because waiting too long prevented her full recovery and also required dozens of steel plates in her back. But at least she can still walk. And she doesn't require a diaper – anymore.

Then there's my old buddy, The Bag Man. He's another friend who waited to go get checked when he started having severe stomach cramps and seeing blood in the toilet. He would not go to the doctor. When the pain became so bad (that took almost two months) that he couldn't stand up straight or leave the house, he didn't even put up a fight when we all stuffed him into the little clown car and zipped him straight to the hospital. Yep. Doctor Central - where the guys in lab coats and PJs rushed him directly into the Operating Room, and life as he knew it changed forever.

Now he dumps from a hole in his side into an attached plastic bag. He never even knows when he dumps. (Hence the attached bag.) Oh sure, the bag stays hidden under his clothes, but accidents do happen. This could have been avoided, you know. With a trip to the Doc as soon as he starting feeling the cramps and seeing red in the can.

So if you let *your* health problems go this far before *you* go get checked, I don't feel sorry for you. Just don't forget to empty your bag. And check it for leaks. Also clear a spot on your shelf for your shiny new "You Blew It" award, because that could definitely have been avoided.

Here's the grossest *Go Get Checked* story. (Prepare to hurl.) The air was filled with the nastiest, most disgustingly putrid smell imaginable outside of my doctor's office one day. As I stepped out of the car, the smell was so strong that I had to look down real quick to be sure I wasn't standing in a septic tank. Geez. *What a stink.*

There seemed to be a serious sewer leak nearby. I noticed that the windows of my little doctor's office were wide open, which was incredible, since the outside air was almost unbearably *bad*. Anyway, I soon discovered that the smell was actually coming from *inside* the office. My goodness. What in this whole wide universe could create this most horrifyingly *rotten* smell? You'll never guess.

An abscessed **scrotum**. Yep. An abscessed (way infected) nut sack. Yo! A man had waited two YEARS to go get checked. Meanwhile, this flaming infection of his scrotum grew. The gunk (a.k.a.: pus) inside his sack had been there for TWO YEARS and his testicles were swollen to the size of grapefruit (guess he hadn't seen his pants in a while – hopefully he was Scottish). My doctor lanced it for him, and that's what smelled. Two-year-old *pus*. And this procedure had been done *hours* before I'd even arrived. I'm not sure what final treatment was required for this guy, but chances are, the lancing procedure was just the beginning...

Good grief! This scrotum infection must have actually started in his *brain.* Please tell me what possesses a guy whose balls painfully swell up like balloons to *not* seek medical help. The human body clearly can come up with some pretty freaky stuff. (Especially when there is no gray matter directing its actions.) Go get checked.

FYI: Any abscess may come and go. You may wake up one day to discover that your painful *whatever* that was swollen the night before, is not swollen anymore. But that may only mean that you've got some time to go get checked before it starts to kill you again. If your skin is red and feels hot when you touch it - this probably means there's an *infection.* And your body typically can't heal infections like that on its own, so whether it's a tooth, a nut or a cut on your finger, if it's swollen, red and painful, go get checked.

Graveyards are full of *people* who waited to go get checked. Now they don't have to worry about it. But I bet if they were given a second chance, they would probably go get a medical checkup anytime their cousin in Toledo *sneezed*.

If you have medical and dental insurance, <u>use them</u>. Guys are notorious for ignoring and wasting these GOLDEN ASSETS. If you aren't sure if you have health insurance, find out. Ask your boss or human resources person about it. Hire a private investigator. Do whatever it takes to figure this out, and if you have benefits, use them.

There are hoards of guys out there who would do anything to have your medical, vision and dental coverage, and access to the medical treatment that you have. Please do not take it for granted – use your benefits. If you have no insurance, many healthcare offices can set up a payment plan for you. Hospitals, too. So *what's your excuse?* Go.

Pay attention to your body and the way you feel each day. Don't wait for aches, pains or sore spots to become gaping holes or lost limbs before you go and get checked. Whether the barrier between you and getting healthy is *money* OR *fear* – we both know that you can overcome each, so come up with a way to get yourself in to be checked out.

Dr. Stinkenstein: Here's a suggestion for your health (but mostly for the health of anyone who lives with you): If you suffer from Stinkus Buttus Maximus, also known as: **nasty gas**, try some Beano or Gas-X. Or see a doctor and ask what you can do about your ACTION PACKED BUTT.

Depression.

Are you suffering from depression? (*Who isn't.*) Well, I have good news and bad news. **The bad news** is that you will need to get off the couch to schedule an appointment – and if you really *are* depressed, then getting off the couch will be the toughest part. **The good news** is that the way you are feeling is completely beatable and is as temporary as you want it to be. There are many answers to solve it. But you'll need to actually participate in fixing it by dragging yourself to the telephone to schedule with a doctor or homeopath.

If there is no way on Earth that you will do that, then start by making a different call. Here's the number: (yes, you can remain totally anonymous.) 1-800-273-TALK (8255). I told them to be expecting you

– and don't hang up if a guy answers. Talk to him because he's probably been where you are. Besides, do you really think he's gonna know who you are? And the majority of callers are *GUYS*, so *that* proves that you are not alone.

Prozac can help. One option if you are depressed may be medication. There are plenty of FDA approved drugs to zap your depression (call it frequent or constant rotten moods), and also several natural remedies that could help, too. Come on! You would rather sit around dreaming of how to get dead – than get real help and get rid of your bummed and hopeless outlook? *Oh, please.*

It's highly unlikely that you will require brain surgery, so you can put that worry to rest. So what else would hold you back? That severe case of *happiness* you feel each day? Right. Get off your ass and call the TALK number I just gave you, or tell someone you trust that you think you are dealing with depression. There are many sources of help for you out there so prepare to crawl out of your cave and let them start helping you. Why suffer alone?

Still making excuses about your health (physical or mental)?

OK. Then hear this: *When the plane is going down, you'll do ANYTHING for a parachute.* On a more dramatic note, they say there are no atheists in a foxhole. *(Now's your chance to avoid going down.)*

You get the message, right? Change your ways now. Imagine that this is YOUR LAST CHANCE. Why wait for your 1st glimpse of the Grim Reaper, or until you are suddenly being pulled toward the light?

Tips from Chapter 8: Your Body And Health

1• **Stand tall.** Use a wall to straighten you up. Use a book to show you how to walk tall.

2• **Get into shape.** Buy a Bow-Flex, join a gym or hookup with Billy Blanks and his blubber burnin' Boot Camp DVDs. Start working out 3 or 4 times a week.

3• **Eat less. Walk more.** Take a 1/2-hour walk every day.

4• **To lose weight, cut your meal portions in half.** *All of them.* Eat only half of what you eat now. No – you won't die if you do this. You won't starve either. But YOU WILL lose weight, and you'll look and feel GREAT.

5• **Eat foods that are good for you.** Limit your junk food. Drink lots of water, and READ FOOD LABELS. Avoid fats, too. **Remember that fresh foods are waaay more beneficial to your body than processed.**

6• **Eat breakfast, then several small meals throughout the day.**

7• **Brush your teeth after you eat.** If your teeth are clean and your mouth tastes like toothpaste, then you won't be so tempted to put more food in it.

8• **DO NOT EAT AFTER 6:00pm.** (7pm at the latest.)

9• **Do not eat in front of the TV.**

10• **Do not serve your food from large bowls and platters on the table.** Serve your food from the stove, that way you won't sit and think about how you are going to finish the left-overs off, too.

11• **Join Weight Watchers if you are overweight.** (You won't do that? Then eat at Subway. Try Jarod's diet there. It could work for you, too.)

12• **Don't deny that you have a health problem if it looks like you may.** Don't avoid the doctor if you discover a funky body issue.

The results of any health problem could be a very simple fix — if you go to the doctor... or death — if you don't. (DENIAL is not a cure for anything and can often be *fatal*.)

13• **Get yearly physicals.** And maintain your overall good health.

14• **Take a complete, men's multi-vitamin every day.**

15• **If you hate waking up each day, hate going to work, hate getting off work, hate watching TV, hate not watching TV, hate what I'm telling you right now... ya just might be depressed.** But THAT is fixable, too, so step away from the cliff and make that phone call I suggested about 3 pages ago (page 167).

HOT HEALTH TIP:
Buy a book called:

"The Doctor's Book Of Home Remedies For Men"

from Prevention Magazine and Men's Health Magazine.

It covers everything from warts to premature ejaculation, and it's a very easy read — with 2,000 TIPS

Attention all arrogant doctors and healthcare providers (you know who you are): get attached to the medical records on your clipboards. If YOU are a doctor or healthcare provider, and you allowed yourself to be taught in medical school how not to form attachments to your patients and their families, then perhaps you landed in the wrong field.

SECRET: No self-preservation is necessary here. Re-invent yourself. Show your human side. You are a customer service provider. A really well paid customer service provider, providing a very important service, but still a customer service provider. Don't forget that when it's time for you to meet your maker, the fact that you died with the most toys... Range Rovers, Rolexes and real estate, will probably only get you a seat in the back of the bus. (Unless you have also collected patients-turned-friends along the way.)

CHAPTER 9

Your Home, Car, Job, Pets (And Other Routine Stuff)

OK, guys. These are the daily facts of your life, so they can really affect how much you love or hate waking up each day. If any of these things in your house are dragging you down, then you should be thinking about a remodel.

Before we get into your home life, let me say that if by chance you are shopping for a new place to live, raise your standards. Find 3 places and pick the nicest of the 3, even if it costs you a little more. Remember that your home is where you will be spending most of your off work time. You'll want a nice place where you – and other people — will want to hang out. (Especially if you are currently single and are shopping for a hot roommate. Just beware that if you meet someone and things get serious, you may still end up looking for a better place with them, but where you live when the two of you meet, can determine if there will ever actually be *'the two of you'*.)

a. Play Well With the People Who Live With You
Whether we're talking about your best friend, the love of your life or your child, there are a few things you should know to ensure your success as a roommate or co-cave dweller — no matter who your roommates may be.

BE HANDY, MAN
First, let me tell you that being a little bit handy around the house will be a great thing no matter what. So if you aren't comfy with a hammer or wrench, buy a book that will show you how to fix stuff. Try "Do it Yourself Home Improvement: A Step by Step Guide" by Cassell, Parham and Coleman.

If you know how to mow the lawn, prune the trees and whack the weeds, then you will always be, uh, popular? If you can fix a drain, replace a kitchen sink and install a garage door opener, then you will also probably always be gainfully employed. Because if you can do those things, or learn to do them, it means you have a brain between your ears. (Even if you do take it out and play with it once in a while, at least it's clear that you know how to properly re-install it).

> **"You don't want to have to be the man and the woman in the relationship. I always say you want a man who can fix the toilet."**
> **-Pamela Anderson**

So just in case Ms. Anderson decides to park her Porsche in your garage, ya better know how to fix the toilet (and disconnect he garage door opener).

BE A GREAT ROOMMATE
You should show great respect to the person or people you live with whether you sleep with them or not. And you should respect their habits *and* things as well. On the other hand, if something that they do is driving you crazy, you need to figure out whether it's worth the battle (or the cold war) that bringing it up might cause. If it's worth it to bring up, then be very diplomatic when you do. Think before you speak and <u>think about</u>

<u>the response that your words might provoke</u>. If it isn't worth bringing up, then get over it or get out.

Tips for getting along with your roommate:

• Remember to clean as you go when creating your masterpieces in the kitchen. It's easy. I know you want to eat your prize-winning creation of a sandwich *now*, but hold off for the single minute it will take to put the mustard and mayonnaise back into the fridge and clean off the counter with a Clorox wipe. (Prepare your sandwiches on a paper towel – then there won't be a mess on the counter when you're finished.)

• If you always get mayonnaise on your knuckles when you put the knife in the jar as you prepare your sandwich, wipe off your hands with a paper towel. Gunked-up hands cause greasy prints on the cabinet doors and the refrigerator handle, and will tell your roommates that they are living with a baby monkey.

• If you use the last of something, or you notice that something is getting low, either replace it or call the proper authorities. Keep a grocery list on the refrigerator. If you use the last of *someone else's* something, replace it ASAP, OK? And just like in the bathroom, leave the place like you found it – or better.

• Always put things back where you found them so that when someone else needs that item (tape, scissors, flashlight) it will be where they would usually look for it.

• Don't be a mooch who constantly asks for stuff (or favors) from your roommates, either. Pull your own weight. Pay your bills. Clean up after yourself, your pet and your visitors. If your roommate has a complaint, try to resolve it quickly. If you regularly butt heads with this person, then move out or kick the roommate out. Life's too short to live with a drag. Even if the drag is *you*.

• **NEVER invade your roommate's closet, CD case, vehicle, food supply or bank account unless you are instructed to do so by that roommate.**

• If you snore, find a way to stop, or you might die. Maybe from a chronic case of *sleep apnea*, and maybe from a chronic case of your bed mate holding a pillow over your face till you're dead. Seriously. If you snore, you may have a bigger health problem, so don't ignore it. (Noboby else can.) Go get checked. Your sleep partner will probably even make your appointment and drive you to it.

IF YOU HAVE A ROOMMATE WHO CALLS YOU 'DAD'

There is no job more important than being "Dad". *You can't swing a dead cat around here and not hit a 'bad daddy' with it. They're everywhere. So set yourself apart and get a clue. Understand that* **you** *have created that little angel* *or monster – so invest some time and effort into making it a success. (Even if you're on* <u>welfare or state aid</u>, *you can still be a great dad to your kids.)*

> "My father used to play with my brother and me in the yard. My mother would come out and say, "You're tearing up the grass." And my Dad would say "We're not raising grass. We're raising boys."   -Harmon Killebrew

I'm not a dad, but if you are one – I can promise you this: When you're almost dead, you are not going to be looking back on your life and saying, "Gee, I wish I'd spent more time at the office". Or "Gosh, I should have been a better *employee/golfer/beer drinker.*"

If you are a daddy, then let me point something out to you. NOTHING you will ever do in your work life or career will compare to the significance of what you do with your child. You may be a financial advisor to millionaires, you may be a heart surgeon, you may perform the mechanical inspections on 747s or mass transit systems, but like I just said – your job as a dad takes priority over *any* job you have *or ever will have.*

Stop *screaming* at your kids. The dads (and moms) you see in the grocery store or the amusement park, or the *mirror* – who yell and scream at their kids – are LOSERS. When a kid is out of control, doesn't listen, or doesn't understand or care about whatever you are saying, screaming won't make the message any clearer to them. Your approach isn't working. So re-group and find a new quieter, more focused way to communicate with them. Try a book called, "Why Good Parents Have Bad Kids: How to Make Sure That Your Child Grows Up Right" by Kent Hayes, and "How to Raise Kids You Want To Keep" by Jerry Day.

Dads (and moms) who treat their kid(s) like it is nothing more than an annoying pain in the butt are simply telling the rest of us that they only have a kid because once when they had sex, they were too stupid to use a condom.

KNOW YOUR KIDS
Spend time getting to know your kids – everyday. Since you now know that raising your son or daughter is your single most important job *ever*, and the #1 reason for you to get out of bed each morning throughout your life, let me add this: If you have been coasting along,

putting minimal effort into being Dad, then you need to re-think your choices. It's not too late. I'm no expert on fatherhood, but I can tell you that loving your children – and proving that in <u>everything</u> you do - is the first requirement for turning your creations into happy and successful full grown humans.

Focus on your kids' lives. When they're young, talk to them. When they're teens, listen to them. <u>PAY</u> <u>ATTENTION</u> <u>TO</u> <u>YOUR</u> <u>KIDS</u>. Read to your kids while they're small. This will build trust and friendship. With teens, talk to them when you're in the car. There's not much eye contact and teens usually aren't into eye contact. At any age, talk to them at bedtime because typically, before they go to sleep, they are likely to open up and talk to you, so be there.

Raising any child without love is sort of like planting a garden without water – or running a motor without oil. One simply gives you NO results, and the other gives you a *ruined product*.

Again, whether it was intentional or not, you created your little off-spring, so instead of treating him/her like you wish they weren't there, invest your love and time in them. Complete the project you started and you may end up with a re-production that you can actually be proud to have your name on.

STEP-DAD
If you happen to be a 'step-dad', be a great one. Put some effort into your step-kids' happiness and well-being. Even if they don't seem to care about you, they will. You set the stage since you're the adult, so when you do the right thing they'll see it and learn. And their mom will see that you *rock*.

b. Is Your Address in Distress?
Where and how you live tells the rest of us who you are – it's another one of your personal billboards, you know, like your clothes and your car or truck.

(This is some ultra-basic information for you regarding how you live, and though I'm not meaning to insult your intelligence, remember that all guys are not created equal. Some are just learning to use bed sheets and some are just learning to flush. Peace, man.)

Even if you live in a beat-up trailer or a dumpy old apartment, it can still be a great place if you fix it up a little and keep it clean and picked up. A <u>clean house</u> (condo, apartment, trailer, ice-fishing shack, yurt, whatever) is important for many reasons, but here are two:

First. If your place is clean, and well kept, then everyone who walks in will see that taking care of your world is a priority for you – which might mean that you are a responsible, capable and stable guy. All good stuff.

Second. You will feel better every day when you are living in a tidy place. Why? Because walking into a clean space usually makes you feel good. For instance, if you travel, how do you feel when you first walk into your hotel room or when you first get into your rental car? Typically you always will find these two places clean – with everything in its spot. Coming into clean, orderly places usually creates a positive feeling for people. (Yeah, because they know it's vacation and they won't have to do *jack* but sleep there and order room service.)

CLEAN YOUR HOUSE – It's good for your CHI (look it up)

Having your place cleaned up and your stuff put away makes for a more productive and happy you. If you have weekends off, then Thursday after work is a great time to clean the house and do your laundry. You'll come home for the weekend on Friday after work and your house will be clean. Right on. Or you could designate Saturday mornings or Sunday nights. Whenever. Just find 3 or 4 hours someplace in your week to tidy up your house (and car).

> **No time to clean house? Then hire someone else to do it. Grab the Yellow Pages and look under "House Cleaning" or "Maid Services." Estimates are usually free, and they may even do your laundry, too.**

Here's a list of cleaning supplies you should have on hand:
1. A broom (get a Swiffer)
2. A mop (get a Swiffer)
3. A vacuum cleaner
4. 409
5. Windex
6. Paper towels (lots of them)
7. Lysol Tub & Tile Cleaner
8. Clorox Wet Wipes
9. A Clorox disposable toilet wand
10. Febreze Fabric Spray
11. Cheer, Tide or Gain detergent
12. Bounce Dryer Sheets
13. Dish/Dishwasher Soap

(There are *green* alternatives to many of these products.)

Here's a simple plan for your cleaning time:
1. Put on some music that will energize you and jazz you up.
2. Gather your dirty clothes, sheets, etc. to wash. Start the washer then add the detergent <u>before you add your laundry so that it will dissolve first</u>. Make sure the washer settings for your load size and temperature are correct. *(To avoid making pink or gray clothes, be sure to separate your colored clothes from your whites – especially socks.)*
3. Pick up any dirty dishes around the place and clean the kitchen while the first load of laundry is washing.
4. Clean the bathroom from the mirror to the floors to the tub/shower to every inch of the toilet.
5. Sweep up the floors and vacuum the carpets. If you don't want to mop your non-carpeted floors, spray them with 409 and wipe them up with paper towels or your dirty bathroom towels. (Does the idea of cleaning your floors with your used bathroom towels gross you out? Then your floors are waaaay too dirty. Get them clean with paper towels this time, and then never let them get this dirty again, OK?) Be sure to clean in the corners and the top of the baseboards, too.

You can get rid of the soap scum in your tub or shower and your shower doors by spraying them with products like Lysol Tub & Tile Cleaner (Scrubbing Bubbles) or Simple Green. In the future, try drying the shower doors after you shower – then they'll stay clean. If you have a shower curtain, replace it when needed. They get pretty scummy, too. (Leaving your shower door or your curtain open a little after your shower, will allow air to circulate in there, and that'll help reduce mold.)

Use Clorox Disinfecting Wipes on your toilet. <u>Every inch of your toilet</u>. Behind your toilet. Beside your toilet. Above your toilet. All around your toilet. There should be no pee, old or new, anywhere near your toilet. (Maybe you should just stop using your toilet.) Pay attention and improve your aim. Go practice at the Peeing Range, or aim for the Cheerios – like your mom probably showed you when you were 3.

When your washing machine stops, place the clean clothes in the dryer with a Bounce sheet and start washing the next load with the dirty towels you used on the floors. (Use lots of detergent.) Then go tidy up the bedroom and living room. This usually just means dusting and vacuuming and picking up your newspapers, magazines, coats, shoes and so on. Get some Pledge wipes to dust your tables – they're easy. (I once caught my boyfriend dusting my tables with the throw pillows from my couch… *Geeeeez. What do you even call that?*)

YOUR BED SHEETS

Here's more common sense, guys. Always have sheets on your bed. *Clean sheets.* Why some guys sleep on a bare mattress with a blanket is a mystery. Maybe it's because they hate washing sheets. So buy another set or two. Life is better with clean sheets. If you have two or more sets, then you won't need to do so much laundry. Also, I know you make your bed each day, so keep doing that, too. At the end of the day, a bed that's been made up and clean is very inviting, and you will get a great night's sleep in it, too.

A DISGUSTING KITCHEN OR BATHROOM will tell everyone you are a pig. Old food dripped, spilled or smeared, (and bodily fluids that are no longer in your body, classified as "Bio-waste") shouldn't be loose in your house. Your fridge and stove, sink, tub and toilet should all look like you never use them. Again, keep a bottle of Clorox Disinfectant Wipes on your kitchen and bathroom counters. Use them often. Wipe up spills or drips on your stove, in your fridge or on the floor – when they happen. If you drip something on the counter, or down the front of the cabinet door – wipe it up now. Why wait until later when it dries *or gets fly babies in it?*

DECORATE YOUR PLACE. (Sure you can use spare Harley parts for this if you want, but a visit to Pier 1 will create more appeal...) After you've cleaned from wall to wall and from ceiling to floor, you may want to ask a friend (someone with a home that looks great) to help you decorate. Really. If you have no 'stuff' around your place, and it looks boring, spice it up. Put some pictures on your walls. Get some colored throw pillows for your couch (but don't dust with them.) Buy some trashcans for your bathroom and kitchen, too. (Why do guys never have trashcans? What's up with the cardboard boxes? I know guys that use plastic leaf bags in their kitchens and bathrooms until some female brings real trashcans over. *Can someone please explain?*)

You could go to K-mart or Target and pick up some things to make your domain look nice to other people. You can do it. If you have plenty of cash on hand, and you don't want to do the decorating yourself or have any of your friends do it, call an interior decorator. (Yellow Pages again. You should be pretty familiar with them by now.) Then sit back and watch everyone who walks in say, "Wow. This place looks gggggggggreat."

If you notice that your house doesn't have a nice smell when you walk in, find whatever stinks and throw it away or clean it and spray it with Febreze. (Not your cat, though.)

c. Things to Feed to Your Shopping Cart

Listed below are a few items that want to be on your grocery list. Consider keeping them on hand. They'll help you (and your place) look, smell and function - really well.

- *Your Grocery List* -

For your body:
- ✔ Carmex or Chapstick (lip fixer)
- ✔ Glide Dental Floss (it's slick and won't shred between your teeth)
- ✔ Crest or Colgate Tartar Control/Whitening Toothpaste
- ✔ A power toothbrush (try a Sonicare, an OralB or a Crest Spinbrush)
- ✔ Shampoo and conditioner (L'Oreal, TRESemme, Nexus)
- ✔ **germ-X** or Purell Hand Sanitizer
- ✔ Wet Wipes (individually wrapped hand wipes)
- ✔ Dr. Scholl's Pedicare Essentials Ultra Overnight Foot Crème
- ✔ Altoids, LifeSavers or TicTacs
- ✔ Old Spice High Endurance Body Wash or Gillette Hydrator Body Wash
- ✔ Olay Moisturinse (in-shower *lotion*)
- ✔ Deodorant or Anti-perspirant (find one with a great scent)
- ✔ Cologne or Body Spray
- ✔ Aveeno Lotion – lightly scented formula (or Cornhuskers or Bag Balm)
- ✔ Q-Tips (for every angle in your ear and for your dry nose issues)
- ✔ A fingernail brush (or two for your sink and shower)
- ✔ Neosporin and Band-Aids
- ✔ Men's One-A-Day vitamins
- ✔ Nyquil (to help you sleep if you have a cold – don't wait till you have one)
- ✔ Rolaids or Pepto Bismal (for your upset stomach – don't wait till it hurts)
- ✔ Propel Fitness Water or Fruit 2o (if you can't handle plain water)
- ✔ Beano or Gas-X (for the Stinkasaurus that lives in that cave called *your butt*.)

Some of the following items are repeated from your cleaning supply list.
- ✔ Clorox Disinfectant Wipes (for your kitchen and bathroom)
- ✔ ✿ 409 (spray cleaner)
- ✔ ✿ Windex or Windex Wipes (for your mirrors and windows)
- ✔ Glade Air Freshener (bathroom spray)
- ✔ ✿ Lysol Tub & Tile Cleaner (w/Scrubbing Bubbles)
- ✔ ✿ Palmolive Dish/Dishwasher Detergent
- ✔ Febreze (fabric spray for stinky sofas, chairs, carpets and curtains.)
- ✔ ✿ Cheer, Tide or Gain (laundry detergent)
- ✔ Bounce (dryer sheets)
- ✔ Dryel Home Dry Cleaning Kit (if you have 'dry clean only' clothes)
- ✔ A comedy CD or cassette – or 10 (for stress-free driving)
- ✔ A *dirty* clothes hamper
- ✔ Armor All Leather Wipes (for your shoes, belts – and car)
- ✔ Waste baskets/trashcans (tall for the kitchen, small for the bathroom)

WARNING: There are many toxins listed above, so look for the ✿
to find the greener items that are available from Seventh Generation,
Bi-O-Kleen and Green Works. (Even Clorox is cleaning up their toxic act.)

d. A Little Green Looks Good on You

The Earth is calling. It needs your help. And whether you drive a Suburu or a Suburban, you need to answer it's call and start thinkin' like a tree hugger.

We are mess makers. There's only so much real estate on this planet, and since you probably don't have a new spot picked out for yourself on Mars, perhaps you should start taking up a little less space. Imagine how big your pile would be if every single bit of trash you have ever created was stacked up for you to see. Think about it. How many wrappers, cans, containers, coffee cups and *pieces of paper* have you tossed in the trash (or left behind for someone else to toss) in your life? Would your pile fit in your house? Your yard? Your city block? Probably not. So please consider the mess that you leave behind and see how much you can reduce or eliminate as you go through each day. *Please start recycling now.*

e. It's Not What You Drive. It's Whether There Are Petrified Curly Fries Under the Seat.

If some cute teenage girl has written, 'wash me,' in the dirt on your ride, then you know you are looking like a <u>pig</u> *on display - in a rolling pigpen.*

Whatever you drive, <u>**keep it clean**</u>. The rules about your clean house also apply for your car or truck. But this one is a much more obvious statement about you, because you can't just close the curtains around your vehicle and invisibly sneak it down the road.

There's no excuse for not putting some effort into keeping your ride clean. So here are a few suggestions for you and yours:
1. Wash it often or take it to be washed. Cleaned inside, too.
2. Be sure that your windows are always clean – inside and out.
3. Keep the interior of your ride free of junk and food debris. Remember that the dropped chips under your seat can outlast your paint job.
4. Hang an air freshener somewhere in the interior.
5. Keep an umbrella in your car/truck. You know … for your mom or anybody else who will melt if they get wet.

Your vehicle represents *YOU*. What you drive is like part of your appearance or image. It doesn't matter how old it is, just make sure it's clean – inside and out – and it looks like you take care of it. If you drive a totally beat, oil-burning rust-bucket, consider getting something in better condition. New or used, there are easy payment plans available, you know. *Just like at the dentist.* ☺

f. Fur, Feathers, Fins. Is There a Pet in Your Life?
Whether you have a dog, a cat, a parrot or a piranha, keep your pet happy and healthy. Because the way you treat your pets tells us everything about <u>you</u>.

Granted, many animals have nasty habits. Some animals shed. Some drool. Some bite. They frequently stink. They chew your shoes and they all poop. But none of them know how to use the toilet. Regardless, if you have one, bad habits or not… ya gotta love it.

If you have pets, make sure you take great care of them. Because if you don't have the time, energy or borderline mental illness that it takes to be a great pet owner, then you shouldn't be one.

If you have a dog, let it be part of the family – in the house. Why have a dog that lives on a chain, in a 'dog run' or in the yard – outside? (If you ignore your *not-allowed-in-the-house* dog, and it could talk, it would probably yell this at you: "Myyyyyyyyy liiiiiiiiiife suuuuuuuuuucks!!!!")

Pet poop in the house? If you have pets that poop in the house, whether they do it in their cages, in their litter boxes or in your Nike's, be sure to clean up the mess as soon as it's made. Especially the litter box. Get rid of the stink before it infiltrates your house. But remember that urine seeps into any surface that will absorb it, like your carpet and carpet pad, your bedspread or your favorite shirt. So if urine is the issue, you need to ask your vet or the guys at PetSmart how to solve this problem. And keep some <u>pet odor eliminator spray</u> under the sink. If your house stinks, you're probably used to the nasty smell and don't notice it so much. But your visitors sure will.

With the litter box, make sure you rope off the area with police tape or something to ensure that it is isolated and away from anything that you can't wipe up with a Clorox Wet Wipe or 409. If you have a dog *and* a cat, keep the litter box where only you and your cat can get to it. Otherwise, I can explain why your dog's breath singes your nose hair.

Food and water. <u>Always</u> be sure that your pets have <u>fresh</u> water (as a rule, they're thirsty more often than you are.) Also, certain foods for humans are actually toxic to animals, so feed them their special 'Purina *Whatever* Chow' or their IAMS, and give them *pet treats only*. Not brownies. Ask the vet if you don't believe me. Make sure your pets stay healthy by taking them for regular checkups, or when anything seems unusual or wrong. Spend the money and keep them healthy. Remember, they can't tell you about their aches and pains.

YOUR DOG

You and your dog are best friends – so prove it. Speaking of their aches and pains, imagine yourself – on all fours – jumping in and out of the back of your truck. Your dog's bones and joints are similar to yours, so as your dog gets older or heavier, help it in and out of high spots, OK? If you think this is bull, then *you* try riding in the back of your truck for an hour or so. It's hard and it vibrates and it hurts, so put something big and soft back there for your dog to sit or lay down on. Lay two empty tires down in the bed of your truck with a sheet of plywood over them and a blanket on top. Make sure you can clip your dog's leash into the truck bed, too, so that there's no risk of it falling out.

TRAIN YOUR DOG

Here's the ultimate proof of a single digit IQ: a guy screaming at his dog. At the top of his lungs. Geez. It's so much easier than that to get your dog to do what you want it to do. Call PetSmart. They offer classes for **you** (and your dog.) You don't train your dog *by kicking it or yelling at it,* but by rewarding its good behavior. Ask it to do something, and when it does, give it a Snausage or a Scooby Snack.

If your canine thinks he's the lead dog, and you can't convince it to listen to you, then get a book called "Dog-Friendly Dog Training" or "Great Owners, Great Dogs". Because if you are constantly yelling at it, then that nasty tone is all it will ever hear from you and eventually it will stop listening – just like a teenager.

Be a responsible pet owner and teach your dog good manners. In public, keep your dog on a leash and be sure he/she is cool around people and around other dogs. Have a happy dog that everyone likes. *Again,* if you can't get your dog to listen to you and do as you tell it to, then take it to obedience classes. They work really well, and all of a sudden, you've got a well-behaved dog buddy that you, and everyone else, will actually like to have around. What a concept. WOOF.

WALKING OR HIKING WITH YOUR DOG

When you are out with your dog, be sure you pick up after it, and keep it off other people's property. Do not leave your dog's crap behind for some other dog or human to step in. No excuses here. Keep plastic bags in your pocket, then just turn the plastic bag inside out over your hand and pick up the poop. Clean up the poop in your yard, too, otherwise it may come into your house via some crappy paws. So pick up the poop and toss it in your trash outside. Use a shovel to pick it up if you're grossed out. Or call the bomb squad. I don't care. Just get rid of it so your dog doesn't step in it. Or roll in it. Or eat it. They do that you know.

If stinky dog breath is an unbearable issue, then have your dog's teeth cleaned by the vet once in a while (start a 'dog breath' fund now, because it can cost big bucks to have this done). And buy some Greenies® (don't give them Greenies® every day. Check with your vet.). They are green chew bones that come in all sizes and contain a *make my dog's breath stop smelling like butt* ingredient.

MAKE YOUR PET A PRIORITY – Or give it to someone who will.

Cesar Milan says that the only difference between a good dog and a bad dog — *is the owner.* We know he's right, don't we? Be nice to your dog. They come happy from the factory, so you don't have to do much to keep them that way. • *Pay attention to your pets* • *water and feed them* • *play with them* • *give them access to a 'pee and poop zone'* • *give them a comfy place to sleep.*

If you have a dog that you don't really have time for, or you aren't into anymore, then you should probably rethink the whole pet ownership thing. Besides cramping your style, <u>you</u> having a bad or sad animal isn't charming. Take it to a shelter where it can be adopted by someone who really wants it. Either make it part of the family, or let it be adopted by someone who will love it. People who go looking for pets at an animal shelter are typically going to take great care of it.

If you have friends who have pets, be sure they take great care of their critters, too.

Could you be classified as an animaniac? If so, that's not a bad thing. But if you are looking for a mate, be sure to get that animal-lover bit of information about yourself on the table quickly when you meet someone new. Because life can become a real bummer when you meet the love of your life, only to discover that the person hates, is allergic to, or wants to hunt down and kill anything with fur, feathers or fins.

By the way, hunters, if you are out to kill something, I hope it's because your freezer is empty. Because if you hunt *just to kill*, you aren't charming or cool (or even oxygen-worthy to some people). I'm sorry, but Buddy! Find another hobby and lose the camouflage. The only charming killer is Bond, James Bond, and he only kills *bad people*. (I recently saw a trophy room complete with all the standard African kills, including a ferocious antelope and a giraffe. Hmmm. It takes a tough guy to shoot a giraffe (do they even run?). The phrase 'dick with feet' comes to mind. Now THAT would be a *trophy*. SORRY.)

> "I ask people why they have deer heads on their walls. They always say because it's such a beautiful animal. Wow. I think my mother's attractive, but I have photographs of her."   -Ellen DeGeneres

(Oh stop. She's funny. She has her own TV show & she's probably gettin' more of what you want than you are.)

g. What's in YOUR Wallet?
Did you know that the average American spends about 20% more each year than he or she earns? Yep. Buy now, pay later. Waaaay later. With lots of interest.

Money (or lack of it) is the #1 reason that battles occur in ANY romantic relationship, so be careful here. Being in debt and having collection agencies after you is completely un-charming. That's because the stress of owing big bucks zaps your spirit and makes life suck. Learn to manage your finances well. If you need help, call a credit counselor.

CREDIT CARDS WILL KILL YOU
"CHARGE IT". *No don't.* Most of us are in debt up to our eyeballs and completely over-extended. If this is *not you*, right on! Keep up the great money management. However, if you *are* in the "I owe, I owe, so off to work I go" boat with the rest of us, then hear this: the Yellow Pages have free credit counselors. They can help you budget your money and get your debts paid off. Also, software programs like MS Money or Quicken can shed light on that mysterious money hole called 'your finances', and

they're easy to use. You'll be surprised at how quickly you can be debt-free once you're focused on where your green is going. So get out of your debt hole – and stay out. Soon you will start *loving life*.

Maybe you have just a few credit cards with balances. In that case, focus on paying off one card at a time. Put every dime that you can spare toward that one card each month until it's paid off. Then use the cash you would have put on the card that is now paid off, and combine it with your regular payment amount to another credit card balance. Stay focused and repeat this until you have paid off all of them. Start now.

Get an airline mileage credit card to pay your monthly bills and then pay that card off each month. Use it when you pay your phone bills, cable bills, other utilities, groceries, gas and so on (things you currently pay with cash or a check). But do not carry a balance on these cards, because many of the airline mileage cards have high interest rates. Again, pay it off each month. Only charge on this card what you can afford to pay in cash each month. Then use that cash to pay off the card monthly. The miles will build up quickly, and soon you'll be on your way to Machu Pichu – especially if you are out of debt.

Don't apply for – or accept - any new credit cards – even if you always are getting pre-approvals in the mail (– shred those). If you receive by mail any new credit cards that you did not order, call them to cancel that card immediately. Otherwise it could show up as a debt on your credit report and screw with your credit score.

Pay off the cards you have and use your mileage card for your routine expenses from now on. If you opt not to get one of those, then make a habit of paying off any cards you do have – each month. This is absolutely vital to your *overall* success, because as I said before, you can't be charming if you are bogged down with worries about the money that you owe.

I know, paying off credit cards and debt may mean no treats for you for a while, but that's OK. When you get the urge to go and spend money, hop on the Bow-Flex or go to the gym. Not only will you be *financially free* soon, but you'll also have a rock-hard six-pack where your old beer belly used to be. Here are two books that could help with your debt:

"Rich Dad's Advisors®: The ABC's of Getting Out of Debt: Turn Bad Debt into Good Debt and Bad Credit into Good Credit" by Garrett Sutton. **"Managing Debt For Dummies"** by John Ventura and Mary Reed. (Don't be offended that I would recommend a "Dummies" book for you. If you are wanting out of debt, you are no dummy. You're *brilliant*.)

h. You'd Better Take Your Job and *Love It*

Do you live to work or work to live? Let's just imagine that you work a regular 40-hour workweek. Now guess how many hours this means you might work in your lifetime? I'll tell you.

There are between 60,000 and 100,000 hours in your work life. Depending on what age you decide to start and stop working, and how much time you spend sick – or at the beach. With this said, can you see the importance of finding a job or career that you like? Granted, most people don't stay at one job for the entire 30 or 40 years they spend working, but even so, that's a lot of work. So given that you spend so much time investing in your wallet, don't you think it makes sense to be happy while you're doing it?

Again, we're creating charm here, and that means we need to remove every single barrier that might be preventing it. Things that are making you unhappy must go, so if you are unhappy at your job then you really need to start looking for a new one. Remember that you were looking for a job when you found the one you have now, so simply start looking again. Don't be afraid to jump out there. But follow this advice, Tarzan: Don't let go of your current vine until you have a tight grip on the next one.

No matter what your job is, <u>be sure you are the best employee that your boss has ever hired</u>. Take pride in your work – even if you're mopping floors, because *if you are the best at what you do*, especially if you don't like doing it, then you probably won't be stuck doing <u>that</u> for long. The best workers get promoted. (Even Steven Spielberg started at the bottom of the film director food chain.)

Also, just about any boss will be happy to give a good employee more responsibility. Perform well and prove to your boss – and to yourself – exactly what great things you can accomplish.

Everyone you meet is a possible ticket to a better place, so put a smile on your face and go charm them all. Have you heard the saying, "It's not **what** you know. It's who you know?" Well, it's true more often than not, so go out and make a good first impression everywhere. You may meet a guy who has a cousin who has a sister-in-law whose husband is a mechanic who has a friend who lives next door to a lady whose bookkeeper has her nails done by a woman whose son has the <u>perfect</u> job for you. Ya know what I'm sayin'? Connect.

YOUR RÉSUMÉ

Begin your new job search by putting a great résumé together (Google "résumés" for samples). I repeat, make sure you find your new job before quitting your current job, and give your current employer at least two weeks notice. Your new employer should accept and appreciate the delay if you explain that you need to give notice, because it shows you'll probably do the same for him or her if you leave. Very important. Don't ever leave a job under bad circumstances. Leave in such a way that the employer would hire you back in a heartbeat if you asked. (Like you should do with ALL of your relationships — work or personal.)

If you don't have a degree and want one, but can't take the time – or the pay cut – to get it, find an online university. You can participate in classes online at your convenience. Trade schools are everywhere, too. If you have to drive 50 miles to attend night classes a couple of nights a week, do it. (Wear your seatbelt.)

Are you clueless about what you want to do? Then look in the Yellow Pages under "Employment" and make an appointment with an Employment Agency. It can't hurt, but it could send you in a whole new direction and ultimately land you in a very cool place. You never know what you may discover. But I'll tell you one thing for sure: Charm will help you get whatever you want, so you are taking the right step by starting here.

Also, it's never too late to learn something new, so if in the back of your mind you've always thought about becoming a professional chef, find out how you can do that. Do another Google search for "cooking schools".

If you are between jobs, get out there now and take the best of the first 3 job options you find. The time you are wasting by not working is going to bite you later – financially AND psychologically, so go do something until something better pops up.

I'm serious about that. Your self-worth is at stake here, and it doesn't matter who you're hanging out with, or that your friends and family are supportive. You must do *something* in order for you to maintain or develop your self-respect – even if it's volunteering, taking a paper route or flipping burgers.

🏆 **You should seriously consider volunteering. No - not as a beer sampler at Hooters… Since you aren't getting a paycheck while you're unemployed anyway – why not volunteer some of your time to help people who need help? (The people you help will probably start to worship you and that's a great boost to your unemployed ego.) I can tell you that if I were considering hiring you for a job, and I learned that you volunteered while you were between jobs – I'd probably snatch your butt right off the street so fast your head would spin. That's because volunteering says that YOU ARE NOT LAZY. And that you want to help people. Both major pluses for you, and for your future employers.**

Besides, when you get out there and meet people as a volunteer, you'll have a better chance of meeting someone who can offer you a better job and get you to where you want to be. **So use your charm to impress everyone you meet.**

THE JOB INTERVIEW

Whether you are interviewing for the position of a counterperson at Auto Zone, or a position in the marketing department at Chase Bank in Manhattan, do your research on the company. Check out the company website. Learn about their past performance and learn about their future plans. Get all the info you can so that you can carry on an informed conversation with your interviewer. Before the interview, you may also call and ask your contact there for more details about the position.

Be prepared to answer any question. "What do you know about our company?", "Why do you want to work here?", "Why should we hire you (what experience or talent do you feel you can bring to this company, org, project, etc.)?" are a few questions you may be asked. So be sure you have analyzed your own background for your past experiences to tie in with the position in which you've applied. (Remember that your answers must tell the interviewer how the company will benefit by hiring you – NOT how you will benefit by getting the job. "I need the money", "I've always wanted to work in show business", "because it's a really high paying job" and "I love fast food" are all BAD answers.)

You must tell your interviewer *what you can do for them and* <u>*why*</u> <u>*they should want you*</u> **on their team**. Try giving answers more along the line of these: "Most of my experience till now has been in installing car stereos, so selling them for you will be easy considering that I know your products so well." **OR**, "My background in landscaping has helped me learn about the variety of shrubs and trees that grow well in our climate here, and the care required to keep them healthy. I feel that knowledge could really benefit your greenhouse customers. " **OR**, "You know, even though I don't have any formal computer training, I got my first computer when I was 10, and I've been taking apart and rebuilding my own systems since then. I have a vast knowledge of the various product lines. Also, I've set up, maintained and upgraded systems for just about everyone I know over the years. I have several reference letters from small business owners. Why don't you let me show you what I can do?" **OR**, "Since I have no experience in this area, I can promise you that I always put a lot of energy and passion into whatever I do. I am a very quick learner and I would be happy to work here for a day – without pay – just so that you can see how quickly I will learn your system and pick things up."

Hey! Working a day without getting paid will not kill you, and if it's a good job, and you really want it, then make this offer. If you don't have a job, you aren't gonna get paid for that day anyway. Work a day for free and prove how great you are.

Be sure to tell your interviewer that you pride yourself in your abilities but also in your finesse with other employees. Then make sure it's true. A guy who can work well with others will remove that major 'pain in the butt factor' from the equation and that's a really good thing. Personality problems between workers is always a royal pain for employers.

Always ask your employers for a reference letter. Many of your future employers will base their decisions about hiring you on what your past employers have to say about you. (That's another reason for you to always leave a job on good terms.) If when you receive your letter, something stated in it doesn't seem to make you look good, or something is left out, then make a copy of it and go ask for your former boss to modify it. (You already have the original letter from them. He/she will write a new, better letter for you or they won't. Either way, you have the first letter someplace safe, so what do you have to lose? If you think that you were great at underwater basket weaving, but the letter doesn't mention it, ask them if they would mind adding that fact. The worst that can happen is they will say "No. – You actually sucked at that.")

Turn your cell phone off. And never drink alcohol while in a job interview. These statements may seem obvious, but I must warn anyway. No matter what, no cell and no booze (regardless of how pushy with the drinks your potential new boss may be – unless he insists you get drunk with him before he'll hire you. Good luck with that.) If you are invited to lunch, dinner or a BBQ by someone who may want to hire you, leave your phone in the car and DO NOT drink alcohol. The use of your cell by answering it, checking your voicemail, making a call, or texting will all tell your potential new boss that something is more important to you than getting this job. Drink booze and sure enough, you're gonna start whining about your ex, your last *creep* of a boss, or start bragging about how Lulu, your gorgeous little pot belly pig, recently won the blue ribbon at the county fair. All bad moves, *Homer* – so no cell or alcohol.

Refer back to **"What Are You Wearing?"** for info about how to dress for a job interview. Over dressed is better than under-dressed but unless you are interviewing for the DJ job at a dance club, leave your *bling* at home. Also, re-read **"Manner Up"**, to be certain you are ready for lunch at the top of Trump Tower. **And after any interview, send your interviewer a card saying "THANKS". Whether you made a good impression or not, this will make you look better. Think of it as the cherry on top.**

To be safe, Google "Successful Job Interview Tips" or go straight to monster.com or collegegrad.com. They'll help make sure you are prepared for (and ace) your next job interview.

THE MILITARY IS A JOB OPTION

For many, joining the military (don't forget the National Guard and Coast Guard are in this category) is a *great* option. And for you guys who feel that you are stuck in a place where good work options don't exist, it may be your best chance for a successful future. Sure, you could consider moving to a different community, but you still would be on your own in finding a good job, a good place to live, yada, yada, yada. And I realize that the military may not be for everyone, but no matter how you feel about it, don't slam this book shut. Just listen.

If you can get into the military, the opportunities can be limitless and you'll probably end up learning a trade that you can use forever. See for yourself by stopping into a recruiting office. They'll ask you several questions – maybe they'll have you fill out some forms, too, and then they'll try to determine, given your life experiences so far, what interests you and what types of jobs would fit you best. (I think the age limit was recently raised, plus the military will now let your tattoos in, too.)

They'll discuss many jobs with you. From electronics, navigation, weaponry and mechanics, to aviation, computer technology and the medical field. The list is very long. After hearing what your options could be, you still have made no commitment to join. So unless you are convinced quickly that this is exactly what you want, and you decide to join right then and there, you'll walk out of there the same free, civilian guy that walked in.

But be warned, you can't slide into one of these places with a "what's in it for me?" attitude because they'll probably turn you around and boot your arrogant little ass right back out the door. (Especially the Marines. They are a tough business for tough guys and you're probably going to end up explaining what you can do for *them* and why *they* should let *you* in.)

The Peace Corps. If you are a good candidate, the P.C. can offer you many opportunities and it can pull things out of you that you probably didn't even know were there. This is a good thing, so call them and find out what the program is about and if you can get in. Visit their website at www.peacecorps.gov, then definitely check out www.soyouwanna.com. It's no walk in the park, but if there's an amazing guy living inside you, this group will pull him out.

Anyway, get on it, Bud. Go and do something, or make some changes now so that you can begin the next fantastic phase of your life – just to avoid looking back at the years gone by (when you are 80) and asking, "Damn, what was that and where did it go?"

> Speaking of your work, here's an extra bit of advice: It's always a good idea to avoid a sexual relationship with anyone who is connected to your place of work. Your boss, your employee, partner, mail clerk or delivery person. Why? Because if the relationship doesn't work out, then your life at work will turn messy, embarrassing and can even create the need for you to pathetically beg for a transfer or hire an attorney. A potential law-suit? Who needs that? All because you let Junior in your pants run the show again? (Junior needs a leash.)

What you do for a living, and how well you do it, pretty much defines a big part of who you are as a person. For this reason, it's hugely important that you have a job that you enjoy and makes you feel good. If you are currently in a position that doesn't make you happy, see what you can do to improve it. Talk with your supervisor, partners, co-workers or anyone you could rely on to help improve your situation. Leaving a job is not always necessary if you are simply looking for more of a challenge or a change.

> "Don't gain the world and lose your soul. Wisdom is better than silver or gold."   -Bob Marley

EFFORT AND PRIDE

You can be enormously successful at everything you do if you put effort into it and take pride in the results, whether we are talking about your job or business, your education or your family and personal life.

Basically all that is required is that you not be lazy, and that you complete every task with a high enough standard that you'll be proud to put your name on it. Example: if you are painting a red wall white and the first coat only gives you a pink wall, then you can say "that's good enough" or you can put another coat of paint on it and get it *white* (or you could use a primer to begin with.) Simple? Easy? Fun? No. The right thing to do? Yes. You can be known as the king of half-ass, or the go-to guy who will always do any job well.

IF YOU ARE AN EMPLOYER

Believe this or not: Ruling with an iron fist is *OUT*. Those days are gone. These days, if you want to get (and keep) good employees, you need to keep a positive focus on your workplace and the people in it. If you have happy employees, you will have very happy customers. Your 'people' will do your job for you. So your only concern should be that you are doing as much as you can to make your employees happy at work. Seriously. Negativity breeds more negativity, but a great attitude will create other great attitudes, and that's what you want in your business.

I'll use **GO DADDY** as a perfect example of a positive workplace. The people there go above and beyond to take care of their clients. When you call them, it sounds like there's a party going on in the background. One day I asked the guy on the phone there if they were taking calls while playing volleyball on a beach. He laughed and said that they were actually not near a beach, but if they were, the boss would probably have them set up on it. He explained that their boss was always coming up with fun ways to keep his people motivated and happy. Obviously it works.

That's what it takes to get the world on your side. A positive attitude, and the belief that you can get whatever you want - as long as you help others get what they want first.

> If, as an employer, you need to cut a few corners cost-wise, don't start with the issues that will take away from your employees. Start with yourself. If your people know that you are taking better care of them than you are yourself, they'll value you and do all they can to see that you won't have to sacrifice either. Think of it this way: as a boss, you shouldn't think of your people as 'employees', 'staff members', or 'team members'. They are your REPRESENTATIVES - and even if they are on "your team", you need to realize that first and foremost, <u>they represent you</u>. With this in mind keep 'em happy and they'll represent you well.

IF YOU ARE A CREEP OF A BOSS

To put it bluntly, if you – as the boss - act like an ass at work, your employees will act like asses there, too. YOU won't see it - but your customers/clients will. YOU set the tone for your workers. Get over the idea that it is *"YOU – against THEM."* Please! They are on your payroll so if you don't trust them, then get rid of them. Don't hide behind copy machines and water coolers, thinking you're gonna catch one of them screwing off. Good grief, Boss. — *Paranoia will destroy ya.*

Accept that once you say "you're hired" to someone, it means that you will trust them to work for you. If you do not trust a job applicant, *do not hire them*. Once they are on your team, let them see that you are relying on them to play a position for you and you want to help them play it successfully. Try the person for 3 months (probation). If they don't cut it, let 'em go. Don't be the psycho boss who hides around corners, hoping to hear his employees 'diss' him.

If you have to keep reminding your people that YOU ARE THE BOSS or that YOU ARE IN CHARGE, then guess what. You're *not*. (For a laugh watch "The Office". American or BBC version. Maybe get a clue, too.)

A logical rule to follow with regard to your employees is "be slow to hire and quick to fire". Don't keep a lazy, rude or otherwise putz of an employee around to spoil the rest of your crew. Flush out the toxins — even if they ARE related to your wife.

Read any book by Dale Carnegie. You'll get a *real* clue and you'll discover how to be a great leader. Soon your employees will tell their hard-working friends — and everyone else — that working for YOU, is the best job in town.

Tips from Chapter 9: Your Home, Car, Job, Pets

1• **Make sure you live in a *good place*.** Move if you must. You spend too much time there to not like where you are.

2• **If you are a do-it-yourselfer around the house, be sure you do it yourself *correctly*.** Duct tape is great, but it won't fix everything. Get some Time-Life How-To books. Or visit Lowe's or Home Depot and check out their '*How To*' section... not the Disney Store for the "Mickey Mouse" section.

3• **If you don't live alone, be respectful of your roommates.** (And if you snore, remember this, Cowboy: guys have been shot in their sleep by their irritated, sleep deprived bunk-mates.)

4• **If you have kids in your house – make *them* your priority.** They are the ultimate investment.

5• **Keep your house clean.** Not just tidy, but really *clean*, OK? Your kitchen and bath should be spotless. (No dried pee on the toilet or its base. Or on the floor or walls around the toilet. _No dried or dripped pee anywhere in your zip code._)

6• **Decorate your place.** Make it look nice. If you can't do this without recruiting an army of friends with better taste than yours, go for it. If you won't do that, then at least show some imagination and use your old motherboards and CDs to create some funky wall art.

7• **Keep a Grocery List.** Get one with a magnet on the back for your fridge. It will ensure that you don't run out of whatever it takes for you to survive the flu, a craving for Cap'N Crunch, the disaster you left in the bathroom, or the invasion of your needy pals.

8• **Keep your car or truck clean.** Inside and out. Place an air-freshener and an umbrella in it, too. (Use Armor All on the tires and they'll look brand new. From the sides, anyway.)

9• **Take great care of your pets.** Keep them happy, healthy and treat them like they are members of your family. Make sure they always have food and fresh water.

10• **Don't force your dog to live outside.** A dog at the end of a chain, in a cage or confined to the porch is pointless. So if you have it only to notify you of intruders, then get an alarm system. (It won't drool or clock out when it smells a T-Bone, either.)

11• **Get out of debt so you won't have money issues on your mind all the time.** Free credit counselors are out there just for *you*. FREE.

12• **Get an airline mileage credit card to pay the monthly bills that you usually pay with cash or checks.** You'll get the airline miles and you'll only need to write 1 check to pay the card off each month. Bon voyage.

13• **If you hate your job then find a different one.** You spend too much time at work to hate it - so start shopping for a new one *now*. What are you waiting for? A raise? (Make some bread. It'll *raise*.) Making more money is probably not going to make you like your job, so move on.

14• **Put together a great résumé.** Even if your work history is limited you can still create an impressive looking résumé.

15• **Learn a new trade if you aren't happy in your current field.** Go to night school or an online university.

16• **If you currently aren't working, then find 3 job openings and take the best one.** You need to have a job to have healthy self-esteem.

17• **VOLUNTEERING while you are between jobs will hugely improve your resume.** This will tell your future employers that you WANT to work.

18• **Ace your next job interview.** Learn all you can about the company you want to work for, then Google "Great Job Interviews".

19• **Consider the military** if good job options are limited or non-existent where you live. The Peace Corps may want you, too.

20• **If you are an employer, read a book or two by Dale Carnegie.** He can show you how to be an awesome leader, and a great and successful boss. This can definitely increase your profits.

CHAPTER 10

Your Relationship Résumé
Your history and references.

If you had an actual 'Relationship Résumé' with reference letters from your past partners for your potential partners to read, would yours be stamped with "Great guy – Sorry to see him go," *or* "Not eligible for rehire - Call 911 if he shows up."?

Behave well in your relationships, just as you do at your job. Because even if you are currently in a forever relationship, you can't be certain that it will actually last *forever*. Someday you may need to go shopping for a new one and your past could end up playing a big part in your future. Simply be great and give every relationship your absolute best.

a. Just Dive In
If you are afraid to get 'too serious' with someone you are already pretty much 'too serious' with, and you can't just say, "OK, I want to be all yours," then put your wishy-washy self back in the **"CLEARLY SINGLE"** *line until you wake up and figure out why.*

If you are in a good relationship that you don't want to end, but you can't seem to completely commit, then this story may sound familiar to you:

MY MISTAKENLY UNMARRIED COUSIN
OR ... A STORY OF AVOIDANCE

My visiting 24-year-old unmarried cousin and I hiked a mountain one day. His trip and this hike had been arranged weeks before, and oddly, every mom, aunt and grandmother related to either of us, or who had ever passed us in traffic, knew we had it planned. So I had been instructed by all of them to pump him for information during our outing and find out why there had been no wedding bells. He had, after all, been glued to the same amazing girl, his high school sweetheart and constant roommate *for 8 years.*

When we got to the top of our target mountain, I explained that his *still single status* was an extremely distressing, hand wringing, family crisis to the relatives.

It was quickly revealed that the culprit of his avoidance of the pulpit (ha!) was his parents' dysfunctional marriage. Yep. Watching his mom and dad's unhappy marriage for all those years had spooked him completely out of the merge lane. (This was news to me. I thought his folks were perfect.)

Anyway, apparently he was paranoid about becoming half of a similarly unhappy couple. He had completely bricked his mind off to marriage, because though on the surface his parents were great, at home they had separate bedrooms, dens and TVs, separate friends and separate bad attitudes about their separate lives.

Wow. Poor guy. He was certain that *this scary union between his unhappily married parents* was his destiny too. Grief! Sentenced to a miserable life of torture and all of the other benefits of marriage. But who knew? And who could blame him for heading for the hills instead of the altar?

Soon we got off the topic of his parents and on to the topic of his own chickypoo. We discussed his 8-year partner, who at the moment was back home towing the line and paying the bills so that he could be off someplace far away hopping around on mountain tops and eating PBJs. (Gee, what a bitch. I can clearly see why he'd be avoiding marriage with *her*.)

He said they had the proverbial, "We've been together since high school – and you know me better than anyone – and you know I'll do anything for you – even if I whine about it sometimes, because you make me crazy – but I can't imagine you not in my life – because look at all we've been through together – and you still make me laugh" kind of relationship.

After my cousin thoughtfully described his relationship with this partner to me, he had a giant revelation. He realized that the two of them had a chronically great relationship. Check this out, they treated each other with love and respect, they had fun, but most important, they'd built a really nice life together – in all the same rooms.

How could he worry about his wonderful, "I'm so comfy when you're around – because you bring me things from the fridge when we're watching a movie – and you smell good – and sometimes we fight and I really hate that – because you can be so bossy – but you do my laundry sometimes – and you let/make me jump you when I get a woody – and when I'm sick, you bring me Nyquil® – and I can pollute the room with my butt and you don't move out or stab me in the forehead with a pen" chickypoo?

How could he think that his warm, intelligent, loving, funny roommate/sidekick would physically and emotionally turn into (presto!) his unhappily married mom, just because she speaks those two words, "I do?" And even *more* far fetched was the idea that HE would actually become his unhappily married dad and hence complete the creation of the world's second most-unhappy couple?

Hmmm. His parents are two of my favorite people in the world, and if they were miserable together, then I'll just say they hid their *alleged misery* with superb skill. (Though actually, I'm inclined to believe that my cousin is just whacked. Nonetheless, we must pretend that we believe him for the sake of the story.) Some couples can fool us all – and they do. But why would you do that? Fix your relationship and actually make it what you are pretending it is!

Anyway, for all those 8 years, while their friends were getting engaged, then getting married and having babies, my cousin and his over-achieving sweetie had to stay out of the couples' pool. Because my cousin was afraid that somehow, because this *was* the couples' pool, the minute that he got wet, he would have a fatal, allergic reaction to the water, and after it ate all the skin from his bones, one-eighth of an inch at a time, he'd catch a cold and die.

But, alas, a change had actually occurred up there on old Revelation Mountain and my mistakenly unmarried cousin's view had changed dramatically. He finally *got* that *his marriage* could be fantastic. So we continued to talk for a while, and I called him a bonehead a lot, and soon the sun started to set, so we skipped down the hillside, through all the little daisies, petting the bunnies and the deer along the way.

We knew then that there was, indeed, new hope for the future and that happily ever after would probably occur after all. Soon after, the long-overdue wedding bells rang throughout the land and the unappeasable were appeased and there was finally peace in the valley.

The moral to my story is this: Your relationship is exactly what <u>you</u> want it to be. Period. Our unhappily married parents don't create little clones of their bad relationships and then deem them <u>our</u> legacy. Neither do our brothers, sisters, aunts or uncles. *You make your relationship whatever it is – and if you don't like it, then you can make changes.* Just don't go through each day, week, month and year living with a debilitating fear of getting into the "couples' pool."

YOU AND YOUR MATE RULE <u>YOUR</u> <u>ENTIRE</u> <u>WORLD</u>. You *can make a change* in a two-person relationship – you do own 50% of the stock, you know. Besides, you and millions of your neighbors with very differing opinions go to the polls and VOTE on all kinds of issues all the time with the expectation that you can actually change the world! And he-lllo! *You do!*

I repeat. Yours is a *two-person relationship.* You can *change* it. Negotiate this change by talking with your partner and explaining how important a specific change is to you. Bargain and volunteer a trade – a change for a change. Start with just 1 change each. Example: Your mate wants you to do the dishes more often, you want your mate to stop hogging the computer or T.V. ... so make a deal that you will do the dishes every other day/night, and then <u>you</u> get to have access to the box of your choice.

> One tiny change in any environment can make a HUGE difference – like night and day. You want proof of this? Walk into a dark room and turn on a light.

b. Always Treat Your Mate Like You Are on Your First Date

If you've got a good thing going, then keep it going by always treating your mate like you are on your 1st date. What? Too much work? You'd rather be lazy? You can't give up the farting, burping and nose-picking? If this is what you're thinking… then you actually need to stay single forever - so close this book, roll over, and go back to sleep.

Let's talk about that attitude of yours. The one which makes you think you don't really need to put much effort into your relationship because you think that if it ends, you will be JUST FINE. Oh yeah. **Don't make me laugh…** We all know that in reality, you will shrivel up like a Shar-Pei puppy, then plant your pathetic and pitiful shriveled little self next to the door and HOWL - for 61 days.

If you are in a great relationship that you would like to keep, right on. Then all you need to do to keep this relationship happy and healthy is pay attention to what your partner says and does. Yep. *Always pay attention to your partner. It's the best and easiest way to maintain a great relationship. Simply care enough to pay close attention and really listen to what your partner wants and needs. Not only will you keep your relationship strong and solid, but you will also get everything you want from your partner.*

Be generous. It's contagious. If you give in and make little sacrifices in your relationship, your mate is going to see it and appreciate it. This will set a good example – and cause them to do it for you. Try it for 30 days. Give in without any fuss or production. Just say, "If that's important to you, we'll do it." To do it won't hurt you, I promise, and the points you will score are huge. Go beyond the old '50/50 give and take' standard. Create a 100/100 relationship. To do this, you may need to give 200% at first, but it will evolve into something great.

FYI – A great relationship comes about when the two of you have become considerate enough of each other that you will always put the other person's wants and needs ahead of your own. What? That sounds nuts? OK, but it happens when you care about your partner's happiness *more than you care about your own*, and believe it or not, that should be the goal in every romantic relationship — and it is totally do-able. This is obviously meant to create a healthy and giving relationship between two people with hearts and brains. Not a relationship with one person cracking the whip and the other one hiding under the bed.

Also be sure to show that you really appreciate when your partner gives in for you. Make sure to say "thank you" and show real appreciation.

LOVE, LOVE, LOVE

If you love your partner, then say "I love you" often. Don't expect that your partner knows it. Hearing you say it is like getting a great little gift, *and it will definitely strengthen your bond.* Speaking of love...

"WHAT ARE YOU THINKING?"

This dreaded question, *"What are you thinking?"* – will typically plague a relationship in the first 6 – 12 months, but in some cases can go on indefinitely. And not only can it make your blood run cold, it can cause you to break out in hives. But don't worry. You can answer it easily, once we have put you in touch with *your feminine side*.

OK, we all know that the urge to ask, *"What are you thinking?"*, would never even develop in the male brain because the male brain could not care less about what another human is thinking. He may wonder what his dog is thinking from time to time, but not another human. Oddly, CAT scans performed on *female brains* will often reveal a very prominent mass shaped like this:

WAYT?

So instead of denying the fact that this *"What are you thinking?"*, condition could develop in your mate's head or surface in your relationship, why don't we just prepare you for its arrival instead? (And avoid the risk of exposing you to yet another needless case of silent treatment – or severe head trauma...)

When your mate asks you this question (and you are not in a life threatening situation with limited options), they typically are looking for an answer that has something to do with *THEM*. Something *deep*. So give them that. Here are some examples of your responses; first – the bad answer (the one that you would normally give), followed by the good answer (the response that *you should actually give*).

Bad answer: "I'm trying to figure out what's up with this friggin' hard drive."
Good answer: "I was just thinking about how glad I am that we met."
Bad answer: "Boring, technical stuff – nothing to do with you."

Good answer: "Just thinking of how smart, talented, cute, sexy, beautiful, (insert their favorite adjective here) you are."
Bad answer: "Something you wouldn't understand and could care less about."
Good answer: "Wondering how I ever got lucky enough to have you."

If your mate is feeling especially relentless, beware that any of these 'good' responses may prompt them to then ask you... "Really? *WHY?*" So start planning your answer (or escape route) for that now. And be prepared to spend a decade or 2 on the subject... Sorry – it's a girl thing.

> "Women may be able to fake orgasms. But men can fake whole relationships."   -Sharon Stone

IF YOU ARE A BITCHY GUY...

then clue-in, Pal. Snap out of it and appreciate your *great partner,* if you have one, and lighten up. Figure out which battles are worth the fight and then *drop the rest.* Guys can be bigger, naggier nags than women any day. Sorry if this sounds sexist, but dealing with a naggy guy is just not right. So if you are one, the least you can do is warn us by dressing the part. Curlers in your hair, white gunk on your face, a beat-up old robe and fuzzy slippers would be a good start.

Talk things over. Be patient and understanding. The nagging won't work, but a mature, adult conversation about whatever is bugging you probably will.

Also remember that when your mate gets mad at you, don't retaliate and get mad in return. Calmly and nicely deal with their issue, then if you have one of your own, deal with it later. (Would you have brought up an issue if they hadn't brought theirs up? *That's what I thought.*)

> If you are constantly blowing off complaints or requests from your partner as "nagging," you're making a big mistake. Simple things like putting your dirty dishes in the sink or dishwasher, or hanging up your coat may seem small to you, but obviously it's not to your mate. If they are so bothered by an issue that you keep hearing about it, then you'd better address it, because evidently it's waaaay more than a zit – it's a tumor.

(Take the same approach to avoid nagging from your partner as you now know to do when you feel the urge to be the nag. Get your mate to talk to you about the issue then deal with whatever it may be - like grown-up, intelligent people. <u>You</u> <u>can</u> <u>do</u> <u>it</u>.)

DUCT TAPE DOES NOT WORK ON RELATIONSHIPS...

Doesn't the idea of dealing with the emotional complications of an intimate relationship appeal to you like nails on a blackboard? OK. So avoid it. Here's how: Understand that the main reason people leave relationships is *not* because of the BIG issues. You know, like one-half of the couple comes home and explains, "Oh by the way, Sugarplum ... I drained the savings account today and bought a Bugatti." They leave relationships because of the *little issues*. Lots and lots and lots of little issues – like the dishes and the coat.

I realize that for someone to leave you over this seemingly insignificant stuff sounds absurd, but when you think about it, why shouldn't they? *Asking for something simple from the person who claims to love you, and not getting it, will cause gradual but severe damage in the form of resentment.* Very deep resentment. Envision great big nails in the coffin of your relationship. But those nails are completely *avoidable!* (No – not with a titanium coffin.) All you need to do is answer the requests.

DO NOT ROLL YOUR EYES

In an argument or heated discussion with your mate, **never roll your eyes** in response to some absurd (in your *opinion*) thing they have just said. If you do this, you may unwittingly cause yourself to break out in a serious case of *head injury again*.

This is another tip that could prove vital to your survival. Think whatever you want during an argument – but *rolling your eyes* as your partner talks, vents, rants or cries about something that appears to be upsetting *(ya think?)* to them, could end <u>badly</u> for you. This behavior could cause your mate to completely lose trust in you and decide that they want... how should I put this?... a guy who is a bit less of an insensitive ass?... for a partner.

Seriously, during any distressing episode, you need to care about calming things down and getting the problem resolved, or at least *act* like you care about getting it resolved. Eye rolling is a definite indicator that not only do you **not care** that your mate is upset, but that you may think their issue is <u>stupid</u>. So if you have been in the habit of rolling your eyes (an action that is typically combined with a defensive *"what-ever"* or "*give me a break*" type of verbalization from you), then we need to get you to a treatment facility immediately – before the condition escalates into partial blindness – or getting your eyes gouged out. (Isn't there a National Center for Eye-Rolling Control in Atlanta?)

AVOID THE SUITCASES

Believe me when I offer this *SERIOUS* warning: Do everything in your power to solve any 'little' problems that exist in your relationship. Your mate may try repeatedly to resolve a problem that's important to them, but there is a limit. If you've been asked 84 times to close a drawer or to not leave your shoes in the middle of the floor, the person asking *will stop* asking at some point. But this is not a good thing. Nope. This is when you need to be *very* afraid. Here's why:

> It's normal for people to have their feelings hurt when they are ignored, especially when they're ignored while asking for something from the person they love. Over time, your partner will get sick of having requests ignored by you and will start thinking about opting out of that relationship with you. First, being ignored hurts, and then the hurt becomes pissed. Then the pissed becomes "I gotta go -- Bye."

(Granted, there are probably other things driving your mate to inch toward the door, but eventually there will be a pushy little final straw that will shove your soon-to-be-ex out through it.)

At that point, the energy that was wasted in asking your lazy butt to do this favor is being expended on packing suitcases. Because in the mind of your mate, there is grass waaaay greener than you out there waiting *someplace.* Even if they aren't looking for greener grass, it doesn't matter. They know for sure that they're done with *your* dead, brown grass. So prepare yourself for your new existence on the dark side of the moon, because once you're alone, that is where you'll think you are.

When those suitcases appear, don't think it's because you've won a trip to Cancun. Not even. Once they show up, you're doomed. So don't wait day after day or month after month, ignoring the 'nags' and thinking that the issue, whatever it is, isn't *that* bad and will go away. (*It'll go away all right*, then, bummer for you, Dude.)

Chances are that what prompts you to finally pull your head out of your butt will be the sound of a slamming door. And then? Too late. Life as you know it has just ended forever – via that slamming door. But HEY! The issue did go away. You win! The problem is gone – it went out the door. Now let's see how long you last before you become a dried up little puddle on your un-mopped floor.

Here's how to avoid this event: Don't try to win the little battles. Obviously you've already had many chances to try and win, but the issue is not gone – and your mind now has officially classified it as 'nagging.' Your strategy clearly does not work. And since you have not won, just give in. If it's not going to put you in the hospital or cost you thousands of dollars, then why not just give them what they want and make them happy – *even if it's totally stupid to you?*

Remember that a great partner – that would be you – can choose to accept something even if he doesn't understand it. Let your common sense direct you here. You try the 'giving in' thing for one month. If the only difference you see in that month, is your partner basking in the sun while you feed them bon-bons and peel their grapes — then you have my permission to give that R-ship it's walking papers. At least you'll know that you tried.

Beware of the deadly battles that money issues can cause, too. But if your only problems are money, you're not terminal. You're pretty normal. Look in the Yellow Pages for that credit counselor I mentioned before.

CAREER VS. PERSONAL LIFE

What's your priority – your job or your love? Do you put your job or career ahead of your love? Why? Because your boss pays you and your mate doesn't? Hmmm. Maybe you don't get why your boss makes you do certain things a certain way throughout your day. But you do whatever your boss tells you anyway without arguing, right? If you will basically do whatever your boss asks all day without questioning or arguing, but you ignore your mate's wishes or you argue about what your mate wants, then you need to ask yourself, "What the HECK am I thinking?"

Why would you put your boss in a higher place of importance than the person you love? We all seem to save our bad attitudes for when we get home from work. But when you stop and think about it, why do we do this? Our home life is the ONE THING we should work on maintaining *for the rest of our lives.* Do we feel that way about our jobs? I don't think so. I hope not! Put it this way, who would you rather live without – your boss/job or your mate? (If the answer is not 'your mate', then write yourself out of this script now, and skip ahead to "Dating" and, uh, let me add… *good luck with that.*)

> **I'm not saying you should stop caring about performing at your job. I'm saying that you need to <u>start performing</u> in your personal life. Any workaholic will tell you that if your home life sucks, your career is probably rockin'.** OK, my response to that would be, 'what idiot (who actually <u>has</u> a personal life) would place his career above whatever is waiting for him at home?' The career will change, and inevitably it will end, but hopefully - if you will pull your head out - your mate/family will be with you until the lights go out.

If you have the misguided belief that your personal life will wait – in some kind of suspended animation – until you are ready to finally clock out, then I hope your heart (and theirs) will do the same. If you feel that making all the money, and grabbing all the success *now* is your priority, because you believe that there's plenty of time for the wife and family when you finish that *one project*, or worse, when you retire, then at least take your vitamins. I can guarantee you that the things you are missing out on now, will not feel the same to you, your family, your body or your mind, once you feel your work on the job is finally done (and realizing this after it's too late will suck with mass amounts of *gusto*.)

COMPETITION WITH YOUR MATE

Don't create a battle of wills between the two of you. Two of my good friends did this constantly. She'd go to the fridge for a soda and he'd ask "Would you get one for me, too?" She'd say "No. Get up and get it yourself." Hmmm. Lovely. (Don't worry, he wasn't abused. He was equally jerk-like to her.) They are both married to other people now.

Remember that you and your mate are not competing for successes. You should both want for the other to get everything they want. If you feel that when your partner gets their way, you are losing something, then you have a serious relationship problem. And that problem is the two people in it. So change your ways. (Or change your partner.)

That behavior is very immature and will never give you the great relationship that you both could *and should* have. If you are already in this negative type of twosome, then sit down and discuss how to rid yourselves of this ridiculous, competitive dynamic. Be generous instead. Do nice things for each other – not because you want or expect something in return, but because you love and respect your mate and, it's the type of giving person you want to be.

> Jagged Little Reality Pill:
> If you are half of a couple that is clearly unhappy – moping around and complaining about your partner and your life each day – **then you are looking stupid, lazy and as irritating as Hell**. You know why? Because it's obvious to us that you would rather **whine** about the fact that your life reeeelly sucks than make whatever changes are needed to make it **not suck** - a.k.a.: better. So start improving your relationship **and your life**, then start talking about **how good you and your mate have it and how happy you are together**.

Once you decide to keep the peace, start putting your dirty dishes in the dishwasher and hanging up your coat. If the problem is that you just always *forget*, ask for help remembering. That's easy. Just say that you forget, and you only need a *calm* reminder to get into the habit. **(There is a clear and obvious difference between wanting to do something but forgetting, and not wanting to do something because you think it's stupid.)**

Just give in! Make a trade if you have an issue of your own that you would like to see change. You can bargain your way into a fantastic, healthy partnership. Then you can be one of those awesome guys with an awesome partner, in an awesome relationship. (And now you'll irritate us for a whole new reason.)

Again, if you are the nag, stop nagging. Sit down with your mate and explain how important your issues are to you, and that you don't want to be viewed as a nag. You just need to know that you are important enough to this person that your concerns are addressed. Offer a trade. Offer to start doing or stop doing something that's important to them, and then ask how you can help create the change. But always be supportive and encouraging, not mean, sarcastic or demanding.

> "I hate to be a failure. I hate and regret the failure of my marriages. I would gladly give my millions for just one lasting marital success."   -J. Paul Getty

Wow – all that money and not enough mental fortitude to know that it doesn't take millions to make a marriage work. ('Work' being the key word here.)

THIS JUST IN! **GODZILLA IS ON THE BEACH!**
If your mate has been bugging you to go to couple's counseling,
then you need to be **praying** that it isn't too late for you to say,
"YES!"........... "YES!" "YES!" "YES!" "YES!"

DO NOT HESITATE. Go. A request to seek counseling from your
mate will often have a clear message behind it. Here's an example
of one of those messages: "You take me for granted now. But
there is this guy at my work who doesn't. He's really nice to me.
He thinks I'm funny and smart and cute and perfect. He listens to
everything I say. He treats me like royalty. He takes great care
of himself and he cares about what I think of him. He's not glued
to his TV, his computer screen, his buddies, his job or his beer.
I'm thinking of <u>leaving you</u> and moving to a little grass shack on
a beach in Fiji <u>with him</u>. If you think I should go with him, **then
please don't come to counseling with me."** ...
TAPE **THAT** TO YOUR BIG, FLAT, HI-DEFINITION TV.

YOUR VISITS TO A COUPLE'S COUNSELOR will be so much
easier, more comfortable, more inspiring -- **less excruciating,
less expensive and less requiring of anti-depressant medication**
than your lonely visits to the shrink. That would be the shrink
<u>you</u> will need to see right after that plane to Fiji blows sand in
your face as you chase it down the runway, waving your arms and
yelling, "I'll go to counseling, I'll go to counseling!" That is a place
you do not want to be. Trust me – you would rather be sucked out
of a Learjet window, at 30,000 feet.
(READ THAT AGAIN. IT'S CALLED A "VITAL RELATIONSHIP SURVIVAL CLUE"
AND YOU JUST GOT IT FOR A MEASLY $19.95.)

MY DAD'S GREAT ADVICE:
     He used to tell me to always be sure and give my best effort to *every*
relationship. You should try this, because I've literally heard busloads
of you guys sadly admit that you could have done waaaay more to keep
and maintain the relationship you lost with the love of your life. (A.k.a.:
the mother of your kids – a.k.a.: the co-owner of your boat, your dog,
your 401K and your NASCAR memorabilia.)

     **There are many reasons that guys don't put out more effort (mostly
laziness — and the mistaken belief that the mate will never leave).**
But the end result is always the same. In your case, that would be YOU,
wishing that you had another chance to go for relationship counseling
with the love you lost. Instead, you wasted your chance by *not making the*

effort – and now it's too late, and there you sit, alone, crying in your beer, your wine or your Butterfinger Blizzard.

There is an EXCELLENT book on relationships called "His Needs, Her Needs" by W.F. Harley, Jr., Ph.D. My girlfriend bought a used copy and when she opened it, she discovered that some poor guy had made sad little notes thru-out the book about his dead relationship. His recurring notes included "Casey asked me to do this but I didn't" and "This would have been so easy for me to do but I didn't even want to try". How sad is *that?* Please pass the tissue.

Avoid that! Here's how - a list of relationship Do's and Don'ts which can help you remain un-pathetic. Please note that these are serious rules for *serious* relationships – especially since you've decided that it's a good thing and that you *do* want to keep it going:

Here is a hard fact. When a girl leaves a guy, and she is asked why she left him, she can talk for 3 days about how much the last year with him has sucked. She'll point out 365 issues that finally made her go. But when the guy is asked about their break-up, he'll almost always say, "I don't know what happened! Everything **seemed** OK to me..." So. Are you guys seriously trying to make me believe that you didn't notice when she got pissed at you for **doing or not doing** whatever she had asked you to **do or not do** - for an entire year or longer? **PUH-LEEEZE!**

1. Edit "You *always* ..." and "You *never* ..." out of your discussions (or arguments). It's a complete exaggeration.
2. Talk about the changes that you'd like to see in your relationship.
3. Listen to, and respect, all of your mate's concerns or complaints.
4. Don't be lazy – instead help your mate out with *everything*. Don't wait to be asked.
5. Be supportive and understanding of your mate's job or career issues.
6. Fight your urge to be jealous or suspicious. Trust your mate – *or leave.*
7. Control your temper – take a walk – then calmly talk things out.
8. Give compliments and show your appreciation to your mate.
9. Accept and get along with your mate's family and friends.
10. Never start a fight, whine or pout to your mate *in public.* (You are an intelligent adult – so act like one.)
11. Don't criticize or put your mate down. Offer suggestions instead.
12. If you *love* your mate, then say so. Say it often – *with feeling.*

13. Voice your concerns or issues so that you can get them resolved.
14. Don't hold your issues inside to fester – calmly discuss them.
15. If faced with an issue between your mate and your best friend or your mother – be loyal to your mate (if you want to keep them.)
16. Remember that your mate is your absolute best friend.
17. Never put your job, friends or family ahead of your mate.
18. Get into the funny stuff together. Find movies, books, CDs – and things that will make you laugh.
19. Give in often – you'll set a good example for your mate.
20. When you head for the fridge, ask if your mate wants something, too, since you're up anyway.
21. Pick up after yourself.
22. Leave the bathroom and kitchen cleaner than you found them.
23. Keep your promises – or DON'T MAKE THEM.
24. Always tell the truth – without hiding or leaving anything out.
25. Get a credit counselor if money issues are causing problems.
26. Take *tears* seriously. Soften your approach if crying shows up.
27. Don't yell and shout – control your voice and your emotions.
28. Don't make empty threats like, "That's it, I'm outta here," if you're not.
29. Don't nag or whine about things. *Talk* about issues, don't nag.
30. Don't be a sarcastic smart-ass when your mate is upset. Show that you care and that you *respect* how they feel.
31. NEVER make *any* hurtful or immature comment like "screw you" or "give me a break!" Be *understanding* and listen to what your mate says.
32. Don't tell your mate that *they make you feel* this way or that way. **You are in total charge of your feelings.**
33. Never allow yourself into a situation that you know will upset your mate.
34. Don't tune everything else out when you read the paper or watch TV.
35. **Always treat your mate like you are on your 1st date. (Regarding your *farts*: Unless you want to be single, you need to consider what your partner *is really thinking of you* each time you probably let one fly.)**

"People stay married because they want to. Not because the doors are locked."   -Paul Newman

Stay positive and figure out whether your relationship is really what you want. If you decide that it is, then you should never give it rope to hang itself, but you should do everything you can to keep the rope away from it. **If you and your partner feel that your relationship has become more negative than positive, call a counselor. Or call it <u>toast</u>.**

WHEN TO PULL THE PLUG

If you feel your special someone isn't so special anymore, and you are constantly ticked off or bitching at each other, you've tried everything — including counseling — without success, then skip ahead to "Dating." Get out of your dead-end, unhappy relationship <u>now</u>. Otherwise, you are both going to end up *screwed*. Forever.

AUTOPSY YOUR DEAD RELATIONSHIPS. Before you start chasing the next 'love of your life', figure out what has been the common problem in all of your past relationships. Beware that unless you make plans to fix yourself, you will be taking <u>your half</u> of the problems in your current R-ship with you to the next. You will end up bouncing from bad R-ship to bad R-ship — always wondering what was wrong with everyone else. But eventually your history might slap you in the face and prove that YOU are the real problem, the common denominator, so figure that out now. Then you may continue the quest for your perfect partner. Or whatever.

Figure out what (about yourself) is preventing your relationship success. You are your greatest investment. And you are fixable, my friend. We all are. But you'll need to invest a little time, energy and effort into finding out what you are doing (or not doing) that is bad for your love life. There are millions of people with awesome relationships out there – so you know they're possible, but they only happen between awesome people, so make sure you are one of *those*.

KEEP YOUR PANTS ON

Keep yourself out of situations that, if discovered, could get you into hot water with your mate. **Here's an example:** I once knew a very cool guy who told his mate that he would never put himself in any situation that might cause problems between them. (He understood human nature and simply catered to its sometimes *needy* needs.) So one night he went to a bachelor party. The bachelor and all the other guests were close friends of his. (Like since Cub Scouts and Little League close.) Anyway, soon after he arrived, the strippers showed up, and among other things, they started stripping *everyone*. So this charming guy quietly grabbed his coat and split.

Now I realize that you might want to think that he should have stayed there and had fun. Maybe you believe that he could have stayed and simply said, "No," to the strippers-turned-hookers and that leaving was dumb because he could have just stayed and simply lied about whatever might have happened. Or maybe he could have imagined that no one would ever find out. Yeah. *Sure thing, Pal.*

But the next day, after someone *had* found out, and the story broke about all of these guys playing hide the salami with the strippers-turned-hookers, guess what… he hadn't been there and his partner knew it – because he'd gone home, told his partner that the party was a snore, and they had gone out to a movie.

Brilliant. Not only did he avoid being tempted by the idea of easy sex with someone else, but he managed to keep himself out of the tabloids that hit the newsstands the next day. The other 'un-single' Boy Scouts and Little Leaguers weren't so brilliant.

So always consider how your mate will feel about where you are and what you are doing. For instance, it's probably a good idea to avoid giving a hot co-worker a ride home. Tempting? Yes. You like the idea of being the hero to a hottie. But why create any questions? And here's the bigger question: what happens if the hottie makes a move on you? (Sure it could happen — you're reading this book, aren't you?) If that occurs, then your life will jump from 0 to 60 right now, and you probably are not prepared for such velocity without warning and a little preparation.

STRIPPERS

To many guys, having strippers at a bachelor party is as American as, uh … *cherry* pie. However, many future wives see this, at best, as immature. At worst, they see it as proof that their guy is not ready for that serious commitment called 'marriage'.

Here is a little advice, (in case you must involve strippers in a bachelor party) which could ensure you will survive it with minimal embarrassment, injuries or paternity suits. Take it to a strip club. Don't invite the strippers to your place, your buddy's place or the motel by the Interstate. You and your crew/posse are much less likely to be *recorded* doing anything wrong if you are in a 'public' club. (But there's no guarantee either way so be prepared to explain your actions to the press, then go ahead and smile for the recording device.)

> **Remember this: Your little head has a much lower IQ than your large one (believe it or not), so you should always avoid letting it make any important decisions for you. Think of it as that psycho little lab rat that will always choose the cocaine over the food. Dead soon.**

Bottom line. Someone's always going to find out when you've done something that you should not have done. The only way for you to keep a secret – *for sure* – is to be the ONLY person who knows it. This means that if you decide to break the rules, nobody else can be involved – get it? People talk, so if you are at the scene of a crime, you'll get nailed for it sooner or later. **I hate to tell you this, but what happens in Vegas, *NEVER* stays in Vegas.** *Sorry.*

c. SORRY Seems to Be Your Hardest Word

Guys, for some reason, would rather be hung by one testicle out of a low-flying hot-air balloon than admit they have done anything wrong - or that they need to utter those two horrifying words, "I'm sorry."

Do you puff up like a blowfish when you need to say you are sorry for something you did or said, or forgot to do or say? Can someone please tell me why that is? Anyone? Anyone? Oh. I know. Because you are a guy.

There. *It's that simple.* Guys will go out and waste loads of precious time, energy and money in hopes that the situation they've created (the one that warrants the apology) will fix itself or be forgotten, rather than just look at the person or people they have screwed up with and say, "I'm sorry." My goodness. What happens in the womb that creates this odd affliction suffered only by the male of our species? There must be something, because girls, *for the most part*, can apologize for anything. Heck, we'll jump out there and apologize for things we didn't even do just to resolve a problem and clear the air.

So do us all a favor here. Try imagining that you've done something wrong right now. Nothing major. Something small and easily fixed. On second thought, imagine something huge and not so easily fixed. Then think about it for a while. Think about how you *will* get caught and inevitably be questioned about it. Now think about the response of your 'victim' when you deny it or blow it off. Yeah, you recognize this response, don't you?

Now imagine the response as you say you are really sorry. See? Oh, wait. You can't imagine that one because you've never seen it. Hmmm. Those two responses are as different as a Ford and a Chevy.

(Remember that in a fight, the guy who is the most beat up usually gets the tea and sympathy. And lots of attention afterward. So if you've done something wrong, and you say you are sorry about it, then offering that real apology is suddenly going to get you some good spotlight. I know. It's another one to scratch your head about.)

Here's the key: The person that you owe the apology to, is looking for **ONE THING** *from you. It isn't a birdhouse, a bicycle or a pizza. It's those two words, "I'm sorry."* Period. So don't run out and buy flowers or a trampoline. Of course, you can run out and buy those things if you think they'll help. Just do that <u>after</u> you say, "I am sorry". Be sure you say it like you really mean it. Just saying the word "*Sorry*" sounds like a half-assed attempt. Put the "I'm" in front of it. Capisce?

No matter what the issue, by immediately saying you are sorry, you are on your way to fixing it. As I've told you before, confessing and apologizing will tell everyone you are a totally standup kinda guy. You can do it, and you usually will not be killed for being honest and admitting to doing whatever you've done.

HOW TO APOLOGIZE

Stand up straight, take a deep breath, look your victim in the eye and say, "I'm sorry." Then be prepared for any response these two words from you may bring on (probably shock), and then simply help clean up the mess you've made. If your victim doesn't accept your apology, be sorry anyway, beg forgiveness and *wait*.

Don't jump into the boxing ring just because the person won't accept your heart-felt apology immediately. Stay calm and let the person rant if that's what it takes. Remember, you started this mess. You are simply fixing it now, so hang in there. You're cool. Hopefully your victim will get over it, because you've done the one thing that will help them get this problem resolved. *You have said you are sorry.*

Once you realize that saying you're sorry isn't life threatening, you'll automatically start doing it whenever needed – no matter what. And trust me when I say that you will have moved yourself into a totally 'new guy' category and your 'victims' will see you in a more *screw-up and disaster-free* light.

If you are the person who deserves an apology from someone, don't hold a grudge. Be forgiving and accept the apology. If the culprit *doesn't* apologize, but you feel you need one to clear the air, then ask for an apology. Get it resolved and get on with life. Just say, "you know I'm upset about … and I hope you care enough to say you're sorry and mean it." (Be careful not to say, "you owe me an apology!" Too hostile and demanding. It doesn't always go over well and can even start a war.)

d. Jealousy Ends in L-O-U-S-Y.
And lousy is the only way it will allow you to feel if you allow it in. Keep this big 'ole green-eyed monster at bay, because no matter what form it takes, or who brings it into your world, when jealousy shows up – you are in trouble.

You cannot control another human being.
I'll repeat that often because it's your strongest DOSE OF REALITY. People will do whatever they want to do, and just because you decide to worry and be suspicious about someone fooling around on you, doesn't mean that they will or won't do it. It does mean, however, that you'll experience mass amounts of pointless anxiety, which will cause you a more stressful and – most likely – a shorter, more irritating life.

> JEALOUSY HAS NOTHING TO DO WITH TRUST
> You must realize that **it's not a matter of trust** when it comes to worrying about your partner cheating on you — or whatever it is that you are worried about. It's a matter of realizing, that no matter what, you don't have control of that person. To say that you trust your partner is nice, but in reality, it doesn't matter if you trust them or not. You CAN'T control them … so simply **chill**.

It is what it is. (Which probably isn't what you're thinking it is) and you will only suffer if you let yourself worry about it. When it comes to your jealousy, you have 2 choices. You can stay single and never worry about being cheated on, or you can stay in your R-ship and never worry about being cheated on. The outcome will be the same, and your jealousy won't change what happens.

But you can be a great guy – which might make your partner see that cheating on you would be stupid and foolish. And since you know you can't do anything about your partner's choices or actions, *stop worrying.* You can do it. It's called <u>mind control</u>, and it's YOU controlling your mind. Push those nasty little thoughts of your partner cheating (and all of the make-you-boil details) *out of your mind.* Simply be a great partner and don't be suspicious or insecure.

Here's an example of what I mean: After my guy and I had been together for only about 8 months, he was transferred to a job in another city – a two-hour flight away. Again, he was a NEW boyfriend. So sure, I could have imagined that whenever he called me before bed each night, he had some other warm body snuggled up next to him. But what fun would imagining *that* scenario be? Yuck. My brain and I made a pact never to go there.

Anyhow, he and I did not know each other all that well yet, but we did know we wanted to pursue our relationship, even if it meant long distance for a while. So he stayed in the city of his job during the work week and then came home on weekends. Get this: He was a supervisor for a major airline and his responsibilities came in the form of counter agents, fleet and food service people, cargo people and *flight attendants.* All ages, shapes, sizes, fingers with rings, fingers without rings - with differing degrees of commitment to their rings.

Well, this guy is a peach who can charm the skin off a snake. So I realized that I would have zero input with regard to his activities, as he would with mine. We could worry about some hot, sexy someone coming on to our mate, and the possibility that either of us would go for it, or we could relax and accept that no matter how much we worried, we still would do whatever we wanted and there was absolutely nothing either of us could do to prevent it.

It simply made sense for us to relax and accept that if we wanted this relationship, we would have to trust and respect it. Which we did – and it paid off. That new location was temporary for him and soon my snake charming peach moved back, and we were both very happy to be back together. Our patience and trust paid off.

Here's my point <u>again</u>. *Worrying and being jealous and suspicious will not prevent someone from cheating on you.* There is absolutely NOTHING you can do to guarantee that someone will not cheat on you. No marriage license, chastity belt or Superglue can guarantee it, so how can you? Get over it. Don't torture your partner with accusing questions and other forms of miserable distrust and jealousy. That will only hurt your relationship and make you look bad. Not to mention the added expense of all the jugs of Mylanta or Pepto B that you'll need for those ulcers you're causing yourself.

IF <u>YOU</u> ARE JEALOUS

Talk about it. Tell your partner, and ask for help to get over it. It's likely that they want to be understanding and helpful – *so don't push your partner away by fighting to prove that they aren't trustworthy!* Ask for help getting over your fears. Most people don't enter into relationships so they can cheat, so right away you should realize that your fears are most likely *wrong*.

In my opinion, the only way that you can even come close to ensuring that your partner will be faithful to you, is by being the absolute best partner that anyone could ask for. If *you* do everything in your power to make sure YOU are the best you can be for your partner, then you have done your job and they'll have no reason to look for anyone else. (And why would they want to screw up a relationship with *incredible you*?)

DON'T PLAY HEAD GAMES WITH YOURSELF

You can't win. Sometimes your brain lies to you. Your mind can create twisted little scenarios that will make you believe things that aren't real. Like the images it can conjure up to convince you that you're partner is cheating. When this starts to happen, you've got to shut down the process before you go nuts. Shake your head! Snap out of it! You can do it! Stop it immediately by reminding yourself that you are giving power to that whacked little section of your brain that likes to inflict needless pain and suffering on the rest of your body. Don't be sitting around thinking of what might be happening behind your back – because chances are... **nothing is.**

On the other hand, if you do all you can to be the best for your partner and they end up cheating on you anyway, then guess what. **You don't want that partner.** There are issues there - way beyond your expertise. But don't die over this. You're a great catch – so if you wind up back on the market, someone terrific will probably come right along and snatch you up quick, you charming guy. So let the cheater go.

IF YOUR PARTNER IS JEALOUS

If your partner is the one with the jealousy issues, be patient. It could be that this person has a past that involves infidelity. Maybe someone fooled around on them, maybe they fooled around on someone. Either way, they are distrustful. So try to understand, and reassure your partner instead of fighting about it and getting mad and defensive. (Even though your first response when accused of something you haven't done may be to punch the wall and storm out of the room.)

Don't get angry at your partner if they are jealous or insecure. The patience and understanding you show can help the insecurities go away. If you get angry when your partner is jealous, then they will never stop being jealous, and then you're really screwed. Be understanding and explain (I know – again) that you have done nothing – and are doing nothing – wrong. Typically, a partner will eventually believe the truth and the pattern will change. But you must remain patient, sweet and calm, because defensive responses will only make matters worse, *and create more doubt.*

Ask what your partner needs from you to help get over the problem. This could require a lot of self-discipline, but if you are happy with everything else in the relationship - it's worth it. Stay calm and let them spew for as long as it takes, even if you are being accused of something horrible or just plain ridiculous. *(Counseling can help make this issue go away.)*

The secret to ending your partner's jealousy and suspicion is your willingness to help them end their worries – no matter what it takes. If there is a certain circumstance – something that you know has created this issue for your mate – then address it and explain it. Even if it means admitting that you screwed up and used bad judgment by allowing the situation to occur.

Again, in this process, do not reply or try to defend yourself while your mate rants. After they have blown it all out, calmly explain how you feel. Let your partner know that no one else matters to you. (And then be patient as you see they don't believe you. Sorry, but this may take some time...)

If reading the last few paragraphs has pissed you off, and you're thinking, "Screw that, I'm not putting up with any jealousy crap," then don't. You may not be the type of guy who can handle (and help) a jealous partner. Go to the chapter on *dating* and find a partner who isn't jealous. But be warned, most everyone can be pushed to jealousy at some point. Practically no one is *completely* immune.

As far as jealousy or envy *outside* of your intimate relationship is concerned, say if your co-worker or your best friend seems to have everything that *you* want – or is the way <u>you</u> want to be – don't waste time being jealous or envious of *them*. Use that energy to figure out how you can achieve that success or status (or whatever tempting thing *they have* that *you want*) on your own and get it. You can do it. Just focus on *your goals* and not on <u>that</u> person or his or her stuff. Get your own.

> I have a guy friend who is jealous of any other guy who gets attention. It's really mental. If a group of us start to talk about another guy's great personality, hot looks or amazing bowling score – this guy starts to yawn or cough or turn up the stereo. This disturbing behavior just makes him look like a self-absorbed, insecure spotlight hog.
>
> So if you find yourself hearing about a guy that everyone else seems to think is so fantastic, do your image a favor and say "Wow – he sounds pretty cool" and leave it at that. Otherwise we'll all know that the other guy has probably flushed more charm down his toilet than you will produce in your entire lifetime.

If someone is clearly jealous of you, be generous with that person. Share credit when you can. Give him or her compliments in front of others. Try to boost their ego. (But if they become psycho toward you, run *away*.)

When it comes to competing with other guys, relax. You do not need to win every time. Be generous and pass the ball to your competitive team member once in a while. If you can do this, then you always will be the winner. (If this makes no sense, ask a girl to explain it to you.)

e. Cutting Strings – or Doing the 'Dumping' Deed

If you decide after dating someone a few times, or for a few months, that you are not into this person anymore, you must cut the ties quickly.

Not ending a relationship after you have lost interest in someone will cause stress for you both. You must end it, but do it nicely – with care. Even though you may dread breaking the bad news, bite the bullet and do it anyway – gently. In person, or at least by phone. You cannot drop this bomb via e-mail or voicemail or text message. Geez! You must do it live – there is no way around that.

You can't run away because they will find you. Do not think that your actions – like not calling or not showing up – will cause this person to figure out on their own that you are outta there simply because you've dropped off the scope. It ain't gonna happen, and I'll tell you why. *Because they don't want it to.*

Heads up! The person getting dumped wants to believe that you are still interested. And they'll keep on hoping it and believing it until the big red buzzer on the wall sounds, the strobe lights start to flash and the trap door in the floor suddenly opens up and drops them into the "You've Just Been Dumped" section of Hell.

It's a total bummer. And usually there is no way around the nastiness that attaches itself to a breakup, so just do it and get it over with. Then you both can move on. But I'll warn you: What goes around comes around. With this in mind, treat your 'dumpee' like you'd hope to be treated if you were the one getting dumped.

It's OK to tell your dumper that you aren't into them because they won't shut off their cell phone while you're together. You <u>can</u> also say that you've got to go because they won't shut up about their last boyfriend. But you <u>can't</u> say that you are ending the relationship because they have freckles or boney fingers or eyes that bug out. That's mean. *If the reason you are leaving isn't something that they can control or change, then keep your mouth shut about it.* Simply say you've lost interest.

If the reason you want to shake off your mate is something that they can – and should – fix, like they spend half of your time together texting, or on the computer, or they eat like a pig, then politely tell them what it is so they can fix it. Most people want to improve themselves. (The fact that you are reading this book is proof of that.) So be nice and diplomatic and tell them why they are being dumped – if they can change it.

Hey! Maybe you'll get lucky and discover that the feelings are mutual. But if not, don't try to offer excuses. Just apologize and go. If this person goes crazy and won't accept the dump and starts to harass you or throw darts at you – just leave. If they try to boil your bunny or chase you with an ax, call the cops.

ARE YOU A SUCKER?

Do you have an "S" stamped across your forehead? (You should have that surgically removed...) Have you been taken advantage of or cheated on in past relationships? If you have given the Sun, the Moon and the stars to someone – or everyone – only to get a scrambled egg in return, you probably need help choosing your partners. As you enter into a new relationship, look back and think about the relationships of your past.

If you have a record of picking losers or psychos that treat you badly or make you crazy, rely on your friends, family, neighbor or mailman to help you screen your future partners. Listen to the advice of the people who know you and care about you. Ask your dog. (But not your mom – she'll vote 'em all off the island). You could also consider checking out www.eharmony.com or www.match.com and let Dr. Neil Clark Warren or Dr. Phil screen the psychos for you. Because there _are_ 29 different dimensions of compatibility, you know. If you need more choices for an online dating site (then please keep reading this book) go to the online dating Mother-ship — www.edatingcentral.com. There you can take your pick of a dozen or so dating spots.

Imagine this: Your dream lover could be online at this moment - completing a profile at eharmony.com – sitting on a sofa – typing on a laptop – in a house – only 3 blocks away from your house. Drinking a beer. Watching the game. Waiting for a pizza. **Wearing spike heels.**

f. Accepting That <u>You</u> <u>Are</u> <u>Dumped</u>

*If you are dumped and you make a scene about it, chances of your 'dumper' wanting you back are thong bikini slim. (This could be painful, but you should know that **I am on your side**. Remember, what you'll read next is here to help make your future easier and less excruciating.)*

Getting dumped sucks for sure, but if you can take it like a grown-up, you will save yourself a lot of embarrassment and heartache. So once it's official, and you've heard those two words, "it's over," don't roll around in your self-pity puddle for days, weeks or months. No way. **Allowing yourself more than a few hours of "woe is me" only will make you pathetic, so do not park your bus there.** We know that the pathetic version of you is not what will bring your dumper rushing back to your door. But **strong, confident and <u>in control</u>** might. Keep reading.

Box up the reminders. After your hour or 2 of "I wanna die" or "I can't go on," get your broken-hearted butt up and start packing ALL of the deceased relationship's belongings and paraphernalia. The photos, movie stubs, books, CDs, trolls with green hair and anything else that reminds you of the dumper. *Now.* No reminders whatsoever. It's self-preservation time. (Yes, you may sob like Nathan Lane while you do it.)

Box them up nicely – do not break things – and put them under the bed, in the spare room or in the back of the closet until the dumper calls for them. You must do this to save your heart the added pain of constantly seeing all of these reminders. Don't forget the refrigerator magnets and the 3 cans of Vienna sausages in the cabinet.

LEAVE YOUR DUMPER ALONE!
Imagine what advice our old friend, Dr. Seuss, might offer…
Don't call to say I miss you so
Don't call to say the plant won't grow
Don't call to say your heart won't beat
Don't call to say the fish won't eat
Don't call to say the car won't start
Don't call to say 'you got the part!'
No matter what you have to say,
DON'T CALL THE DUMPER ANYWAY!

Because they don't care. Call the crisis center instead. (I'm sorry, but you must leave the dumper alone!! This is vital to your future. I'll tell you why in a moment – so hold that thought... See 'YOUR ANSWER' coming up soon.) Talk to your buddies or your parents or your 3rd grade teacher, but do not call or follow your dumper. *DO NOT.*

I'll offer you three very important suggestions:
1. Do not call the dumper – especially don't call and hang up when someone answers.
2. Do not visit the dumper.
3. Do not spy on or stalk the dumper.

No matter what! Leave the dumper alone!

If you know about real estate, you'll get this: *location, location, location.* Meaning your **location** and your dumper's **location** should under no circumstances be the same **location**. EVER. Avoid seeing your dumper, or being seen by your dumper. I'll tell you why soon.

Do not drive by the dumper's house or sit outside of their work. Stalking is illegal. But even worse than *that* is it's typically *a huge turnoff* to the person you are stalking. Now I ask, what would be worse – going to jail or cementing the 'done' deal? I know. You do not want to cement the done deal. You are in an "I'll do anything" state, so you would even risk going to jail.

That's because your judgment is so clouded by "my life sucks" that the least of your worries is jail. But stalking or chasing your dumper will do bigger damage than landing you behind bars. It will push your dumper away and it can really turn off everyone who knows you. Do you really want to create this giant turn off? The answer would be 'NO'.

> When you get dumped, you must accept that your dumper has stated that <u>the two of you are **done**</u>. This means that no matter how hard the reason for the breakup is for you to understand, you have to take a deep breath and accept it. Your dumper wants it that way, so your harassing, sobbing, demanding or whacko phone calls, e-mails, greeting cards or daisies will not help.

Do not dare stoop to the lowest of low levels and blame your 'anger' for making you do something whacked like sending black roses or dead rats. Geez. This will only bring on really bad things for you like restraining orders and arrests and big guys in white coats – plus mega doses of *bad juju*.

Also, DO NOT think that an *accidental meeting* with your dumper is a great idea. Guess again. This is *worse* than knocking on their door. They will probably be watching out for you, and if you happen to be where they *always are* each day at 1 pm, then you are sssso busted. Do everything in your power to avoid any possible chance of *bumping into* or crossing the path of your dumper. But hang on because there is something else that might work.

You are at a severe disadvantage - it totally sucks, and I am so sorry that you are in this place. But <u>you must honor the dumper's wishes</u>. Making a fuss will not help, no matter how much you cry and scream and die over it. It's all been tried before and it doesn't work. Why would someone want you back just because you're pathetic? **I don't see that happening. So don't be pathetic.**

YOUR ANSWER: Your best strategy now is to lie low and think of what Atticus Finch would do (you watched the movie, right? See page 101). If you can pull through this nightmare with dignity, then everyone – including the dumper – will appreciate your willpower and maturity. Seriously. Breakups are hard. When you get dumped, suddenly everything in your world seems surreal. It *blows*. So you need to prove to your dumper that *you are strong*. If you stay away from this person who has broken your heart – no calls, flowers, kitties, rodents or *anything* – then 1 of 2 things could happen:

1. You'll get stronger each day, and your mission to NOT call the dumper will get easier as the days pass. Stay busy.

Or *(and this is your ace in the hole)*

2. By staying away, the dumper may start to wonder where you are, and why you haven't tried to call. Curiosity about where you are may cause your dumper to miss you and want to see you. Hmmm. Who do you think will have the upper hand then? (This second scenario happens very often, so heed my advice and force yourself to stay away, OK?)

If the dumper does have a change of heart and wants you back, remain strong and don't puddle up on the floor. Be honest about your feelings but don't become a peeing puppy. Stay reserved, be nice and wait for them to tell you how they feel (or make you an offer). Then you should take a day, or at least a few hours, to think about it. You must remember that you have had your heart sucked out through a tiny hole in your chest, and even though it has been returned to you, you still have the right to be distrustful of <u>the sucker</u>. Because they may do this to you again, you know.

If the dumper doesn't call you, then we're simply back to #1, and you are getting stronger and the days are getting easier. Just be sure that you have boxed up every single possible reminder of this person. Check your car or truck for any reminders there, too, like CDs and bobble-head bulldogs. **Get every reminder out of your sight.**

> **FEAR OF COMMITMENT IS ACTUALLY A RARE CONDITION** But fear of commitment **with** you may not be. Sorry. I must make a sad but obvious point here. People are rarely AFRAID OF COMMITMENT. If you think your mate is afraid to commit, understand that they may simply be afraid of commitment - **with you**. No offense. There is someone out there for you, but it clearly isn't the person you have been having that constant "why won't you commit?" battle with. (This applies to the person that you won't commit to also. If you don't want to be serious and long term there... move on and let your mate find someone who will.)

One thing is certain. You have survived the nightmare that everyone dreads, and this means you have added some serious qualifications and character to your Relationship Résumé. This is a good thing. Rest assured that this was not your last relationship.

g. "Will You Marry Me?" Presenting a good proposal
In the history of YOUR LIFE, has there ever been a scarier question for you to have to ask someone? I doubt it. Especially if you aren't absolutely certain that the person you're asking will say 'YES'…

Do you know that the first question your fiancée will be asked by her friends once they know she is engaged is, "How did he propose?!?!" So do her a favor, and give her something good to tell them. (FYI – the next question will be "Let me see your ring!" So start saving *today* for it.)

Once you know 'she's the one', you may secretly hope that she will be the one to ask you. Perhaps you're hoping the two of you will simply reach the unspoken but mutually understood conclusion that you will be married soon. Hmmm. That could happen, it does quite often, but if it does, then you have robbed her of your 'proposal', and a very important moment in her life. THAT would not be a great way to begin your married life together. You hear stories all the time about when he 'popped the question', so most women do hope for their own special moment, too. Be sure to give yours one.

If you're thinking of proposing - then here are a few thoughts on making it pain-free – and getting you successfully to the altar. (NOTE: remember that your first priority once you know you want to get married should be a little dose of Viagra for your bank account, because once you get your 'YES', then the next step will be the purchase of the ring, the wedding, the honeymoon, or a Volkswagon bug - and your wallet will need to be UP for that action – so open that savings account now.)

Most guys hold their breath as they squeeze out those 4 words, "will you marry me", but there are a couple of ways to be sure, before you ask, that your target will actually want to hear you ask them – and possibly even say 'YES'.

Since you can't actually 'pre-ask' this important question... you know, "ummm, if I ask you to marry me, what will you say?" – then try this: "Tell me where you would like to be this time next year. Tell me what you want happening in your life in a year." If the response includes **you**, then you have made it through the first phase of testing these spooky waters. Next, spend the following month being the absolute BEST guy you can possibly be. Do **everything** to the absolute best of your ability. Impress the heck out of her, her friends and family, and the rest of us, with your charm and your all-around **terrific-ness**.

Prior to proposing, your goal is to get to a place with your future wife where it's obvious that you both want to be together forever. When you know without question that you want to marry her, then you need to begin your investigation into *whether or not she wants to marry you*.

Then, after that one month, ask her, "You know when we were talking about where we'd each like to be in a year? What do you think about that now? Same place?" If the response is yes, plus more of YOU in the answer, then you will start to feel pretty good in these waters. Kind of like your own little hot tub. At this point, you need to start planning where and how to pop the question, because it looks like you are going to get your 'YES'. Put some thought into this next step. It may be the biggest event in your lives yet, so make it memorable, and a good story to tell your kids.

But, if that month just tells you that the temperature of your relationship has dropped to 'chill', then regroup before you go any further. Start paying attention to all of the signs she is putting up for you. It may be that you need to back off for a while and see where things go before refocusing on the 'I Do's'. (Stay on your best behavior!)

WHO WILL PICK THE RING?

After you have decided that you want to propose, keep this in mind: Many women want to pick out their own engagement rings. And when you think about it, why wouldn't they? I mean they are the ones who will wear the ring – *forever* (providing you learn something from this book and continue to be that 'BEST guy' you can be). So you may want to plan on popping the question, then going ring shopping *together*. Don't worry. If she actually wanted *you* to pick it out for her on your own and surprise her, she'll tell you that - and you still can. But at least you gave her the option. Women LOVE options…

> Sadly, often a guy will pick out a ring for his fiancée and her response once she sees it is something like this: "Oh. PAUSE Umm PAUSE thanks. PAUSE It's, PAUSE uh, PAUSE nice…"

That is not your target response. (This isn't your fault. You tried. You thought she would love it, right? So make sure she will. Consider letting *her* pick it.) You are actually hoping for a little more intense response. Like she should jump for joy and then kiss you and hug you and jump up and down and then kiss you and hug you some more. Her response should be happily *explosive*. That's why you need to either be CERTAIN that the ring you pick out for her will blow her away, or you need to let her select it herself. Remember that if all goes as planned, she will be wearing it for a very long time, so you better be sure she's gonna love it forever.

Now it's time to set the stage for asking her to marry you.
Here are a few indirect/private ways you might propose:

☽ **Have flowers delivered to work** – and ask on the card (have them delivered just before the two of you meet for lunch or after work. Be waiting for her. Also tell the florist you are proposing with the flowers.)

☽ **Buy her a purse, pack or a jacket** – get one you know she'll love – then place the ring box and a tiny card which reads, "Please marry me" inside it or its pocket. (Use one of her purses, packs or jackets if your budget's tight.)

☽ **At your favorite restaurant** – order a beautiful flower arrangement to be delivered to the restaurant and then brought out by the hostess right after your wine or champagne is delivered to your table. The card on the flowers reads, "Jessie – Will you marry me?"

◦ **Buy a favorite bakery cake** and have the baker write, "I love you. Marry me?"

◦ **On the collar of your dog or cat'.** Place the ring box in a tiny gift bag and write "Please marry my dad, so we can all live happily after" on the front of the bag (like a sign), then tape the bag to the pet's collar.

◦ **Take a photo of the two of you** — then paste a text bubble above your head in it which reads "Will you marry me?". Then gift wrap it and hand it over.

◦ **At the theater** – plant the ring box in the popcorn. (No butter.)

◦ **In an email.** Send a sweet message that ends with your proposal.

◦ **At the top of a mountain after your hike up (possibly at sunset).**

◦ **On the ski slopes.**

◦ **On a boat at sunset.**

◦ **On a roof at sunset.**

(If you both drink Champagne – then you might take some with you or have it waiting when you get to any of the spots just listed.)

These proposals are NOT PRIVATE so be sure she'll like having an audience:

◦ **At a ball game (with the help of an announcer)** — if a pro or semi-pro game, call the local radio DJ who promotes the games and ask if they will help you coordinate this.

◦ **At the bowling alley** — get the help of the announcer.

IF YOU ARE A HAM (and your target won't die of embarrassment):

◦ **Over a crowd on the sidewalk** — as the two of you part and go your different directions after a date, yell back, "Hey Chris! Will you marry me?"

Please note that yelling in public is only OK if you are proposing marriage – or if you happen to notice that a falling piano is about to land on their head.

◦ **At a beach** — **with a lifeguard on duty** — **with your (and her) friends** — ask the lifeguard to announce with his bullhorn, "Hey Nikki — Jake wants to marry you! Whaddaya say? Ya want him on one knee?"

◦ **On a plane (announced by a member of the flight crew or a flight attendant after they complete an announcement)** — "…And Jamie, Dan was wondering if you will marry him… ?"

If you are waiting to buy the ring so that she can pick it out, you can still have a great proposal. Just ask, or give a card with the flowers, popcorn, pet collar, etc., then say, "Now let's go get your *ring*."

One last issue with regard to your proposal: many guys 'accidentally' propose after sex. You guys! GEEZ! So is that how so many of you end up in the marriage from Hell? Because you let your brainless head decide? After sex? Wow. So sex makes you get married? Then sex makes you have a baby? Then makes you bitch for the next 30 years about how you're not getting any sex? Hmmm. Sounds like sex can make you lose your mind, huh? OK. So, when after sex you have the urge to propose, just try saying "I love you" instead. (It's easier to get out of in case you later discover that you really don't feel quite that committed – or that the sex wasn't quite that great.)

Bridezillas are not a myth.

They exist. But only if YOU GUYS let them. Bridensteins are real too. They are created by *Dr. Groomensteins*. A wedding and a marriage are two entirely different things. Quite often, after a female is proposed to, she loses her mind. Suddenly, it's not the thought of *being married to you* that will occupy every thought in her head from dawn till dusk, but it's planning the WEDDING. Her dress, your tux, the cake, and the 1,000 white doves the two of you will set free to fly away while Beyonce or Toby Keith sings *your song*.

So remind her that you proposed to a great girl – not a psycho. Be warned that during this time, you have the ability to create a *totally out of control monster*, or you can be supportive – within reason – and help her stay sane and remain the girl you want to spend the rest of your life with. Help her with anything she needs, but if you see that she's starting to scream at her mom, her best friend and everyone else unlucky enough to cross her path, take action. Ordering people around rudely, or having temper tantrums is unacceptable, so tell her that she needs to relax a little and not be a witch over this. This is your chance to make your voice heard forever in your relationship. If you don't speak up now then she will always be your boss and you may as well have your tongue surgically removed. **I repeat: Remind her that you proposed to a great girl — not a psycho.**

h. Is There a *WIFE* in Your Life?

What's the difference between a wife and a girlfriend? About 45 lbs. Ouch. What's the diff between a husband and a boyfriend? About 45 minutes. Hmmm. Take that. He asked, "Why buy the cow when I get the milk for free?" She said, "Why keep a pig when all I need is a little sausage?"

We've all heard the jokes. But you've got to know that your marriage will only suck if YOU let it. And although we know that those jokes are based in sad truth, they are only true if you allow them to be. Yeah, we can become pretty lazy when we aren't out there fluffing our feathers and strutting our stuff as we try to impress someone into marrying us anymore. But as you'll often read here, *your relationship is what you want it to be – as long as you actually participate in it.*

IN THE BEGINNING...

> **Typically, when the average man finds a woman and falls in love with her, that's it. He latches on. And once he marries her, he is the barnacle, she is the boat.**

Men don't leave. The typical man believes that his wife is totally <u>OK</u> just the way she is, and there is little that she will do in the life of their marriage that could make him seriously think about running away. Granted, he may do other things, but it is not likely that he will leave her or ask her for a divorce. His wife may bitch constantly, spend all the money, put him down and gain 400 pounds. She may even cheat on him. But through whatever she may do, the husband is likely to remain firmly planted next to *his wife* no matter what. *The same is not true of a woman.*

> **When a woman finds a man, she sizes him up. "Wow, he's a good one," she decides. "I wonder what alterations he will require to fit me perfectly and become my perfect man? Hmmm. No matter. I can figure it out later and then I can change him. In the meantime, I will marry him."**

What's up with that? Well, let's just say that it is rare that a woman (under the age of 40 or so) will find a guy and NOT see 1 or 2 – or 90 – things that she feels she could improve about him. (This book was written by a female who has spent a major portion of her life hearing about the various levels of *potential* that women see in men. Try the advice you are getting here and, chances are, your mate will notice as you get a bit closer to being her *perfect man*.)

You see, girls grow up mentally designing their future nests, and once they are married, they build that nest. Then, if you (her husband) want to be a part of what goes on in that nest, you should plan on getting searched at the door each day when you come home before she'll allow you in. Plus, you've got to know the secret password, which may change once in a while.

Once you're in, understand that she'll be keeping one eye on you at all times. Finally, keep in mind that if you make one wrong move, you'll probably get pecked. (Maybe you've already discovered that.) Don't misunderstand. Most women generally believe that men are absolutely *perfect*. With a few dozen minor changes, that is.

However, in the defense of all women, it seems clear that part of the reason women feel men require so much 'fixing' prior to having a successful relationship is due to another woman. *His mother.* You see, most moms teach their sons to be **their great sons,** whereas they could be teaching their sons to be **a great *partner*** – to someone else – someday. Oh well. Even if your mom raised you to be all *hers,* you can re-program yourself to be *someone else's.* (You're doing it now.)

ANOTHER ASPECT OF THE 'HAPPY MARRIAGE' DANCE:

Your wife is either happy, or she is not. If she's in the 'happy' category, it doesn't mean she won't be in the 'not happy' category once in a while. But typically, 'happy' is just that, and her happiness is pretty evident. The 'not happy' wife is pretty much always clearly 'not happy'. It's obvious and *everyone* knows it. Your friends, her friends and everyone in the neighboring states.

However, there is a catch to this 'happy/not happy' condition. Yours may be the greatest wife on Earth, and she may wear the happy face and do all the happy chores, but as she cheerfully serves up your French toast each a.m., she might actually be plotting your accidental death. Try to avoid this scenario. *(Check your brake fluid once in a while.)*

Maybe your wife feels she has done for you and done for you and done for you. She may feel she is not appreciated. Perhaps she can't believe that out of all the guys out there who had sssssso much potential, she chose *you*. With that said, please live up to your full potential in your marriage. Be the best husband you can possibly be. Read more books like this one. Because believe me when I tell you, that at this point in your life, you may not show the same great potential you once did. This fact will hurt your chances if you are tossed back out into the 'dating zone' and placed back up there on the old auction block.

> "The fact that my 15 minutes of fame has extended a little longer than 15 minutes is somewhat surprising to me and completely baffling to my wife."
>
> -Barack Obama

VITAL TIPS TO PREVENT YOUR UNTIMELY DEATH:
1. When your wife asks "does this make me look fat?" you must remember that the answer is NEVER nothin' but "**_NO_**". (This is not a lie. Nothing MAKES her look fat. She is either *fat* – or *she isn't*. But you don't need to mention *that*. We will work on her weight thing soon.) You can follow up with an opinion about whether you like the item or not, but remember that nothing *makes her look fat*.
2. If your wife asks about your past lovers, she may ask who was the best. Again, there is ONE answer here. And that answer would simply be "**_YOU_**". If she presses you for a different answer, *don't go there*. You are with HER now and that fact means that you held onto the best lover you have ever had. End of discussion. (You hope.)

PERFORM A LITTLE SELF-IMPROVEMENT ON YOURSELF

Here are a few very important suggestions that can make you a lot more popular with your wife:

1. If you are grimey and smell bad when you get home from work because you worked your tail off all day, take a shower.
2. DO NOT burp and *fart* around your wife. (First date, remember?)
3. Be sure you always have good breath and clean teeth. If your wife has been asking you to see a dentist, there must be a reason, so do it. And then do whatever the dentist tells you to do to get your mouth in great shape – and keep it that way. Try OxyFresh™ products. (Info in the back of this book.)
4. Don't walk around naked or otherwise 'revealed' unless you are built like *The Transporter*.
5. **CLOSE THE BATHROOM DOOR** when you are doing bathroom stuff. (Except at shower time - if you ARE built like *The Transporter*…) If you want to impress your wife, let her see your hot strut, not your fat gut. If it isn't sexy and appealing, close the door. Keep it private.
6. If you don't usually wear cologne, ask your wife to pick an aftershave or cologne for you to wear (one squirt) when you are with her. (If you don't involve her in this sniffy purchase, and you suddenly show up smelling good, she may think there's another nose out there that you are trying to impress.)
7. Start helping her with her coat, shopping bags and anything else that will give you an excuse to be physically close to her for a moment.

(Let her discover that you smell reeeeally good.) Don't put moves on her as you help her. Let her nose bring her to where you want her to be. *Relax*, she'll get there. If she starts to act suspicious, say... she thinks you are having an affair (why else would you start wanting to be clean and smell good?) show her this paragraph.

Hi there.

This is an urgent message to all men: you're relationship will stay shiny, new and sexy for much longer if you strickly follow tip #5. Because brushing and flossing your teeth, picking at zits, examining your hairline, cleaning your ears, and doing anything at the toilet – should all be performed *ALONE*. This means the door should be closed. Even if your wife/mate/lover says they like to see you doing any of these activities, just smile and apologize. Say you'd rather shut the door and keep it private. Trust me – this simple change in habits can completely boost the good stuff in your r-ship. Mystery is appealing and can even rekindle the !SEXY! in your comfy old relationship. Oh, wait! There is one thing that your mate should always see you doing in the bathroom: that would be cleaning it. So be sure you open the door as you begin cleaning up all of your little messes.

"3 moves you must know to keep your wife sexually satisfied"

I saw that heading on a men's magazine cover and when I read it, I realized that I have my own theory of three things that will keep your wife sexually satisfied. Actually, the three things I'm going to tell you about next will keep her *begging* you for more...

Ready? Good – pay attention:

1. There is a small opening that most men get close to all the time, but really don't understand. However, trust me when I tell you that this little opening is the one that most women are over-the-top passionate about. What they like is for you to use your hand and gently pull down on the top of it so that it's more comfortable for her when she is on top of it. It's called *the toilet*, and for some reason most women LOVE this simple move. Yours will moan with desire when you put that seat (or lid) down. I know. I don't get it either but we all have our little fetishes, right?

2. There is a little spot that will drive her nuts every time you get near it – providing you do the right thing with it, that is. Chances are good that you've been going at this spot incorrectly. That's a bummer for you because unless you do what she wants with this spot, you have probably only been irritating her. You'll know the spot – it's called *the kitchen*. That's the area that physically surrounds *the food* in

your house, and when you touch it properly – the way *she* touches it – you'll put her over the edge every time.

3. There is an amazing toy on the market – and Guys, your wife probably has one of her own hidden someplace in your house. This device creates a controllable vibrating, sucking action – which is waaay more effective than anything you can do manually. She will squeal with delight when she sees you reach for this hummer, and you can get one with rechargeable batteries or you can get the plug-in version. Either way, when she sees you flip the switch on that *vacuum cleaner*, it's going to turn HER on. Suck it up, babe, and she won't be able to leave you alone.

Here's the bottom line, Romeo. Put the toilet seat down, clean the kitchen, and vacuum the floor. These are all aspects of foreplay. Sex is much better for you both when your wife can connect with her inner *vixen*. She can't do that when she's stuck doing all the housework, and that nagging little voice in her head keeps saying "I married a pig".

Complaints in Marriages

Blaming your wife for things that you aren't happy about at home isn't fair. Your words and actions can dictate what happens around the house as much as hers, you know, so don't believe you have no control over your home life. *On the other side of this coin, don't think that YOURS is the only voice that matters.*

Understand that if your wife has a job outside of your home, and brings home half of the bacon (which she probably cooks, too), then you need to step up to the plate and take your half of the responsibilities for running the 'home show'. Whoever told you that you get to come home after work and put your feet up? Your mom, June Cleaver? Well guess what, you *Ward*-wannabe, times have changed. The cooking, the cleaning, the feeding and care of the kids, pets and plants, as well as running errands, should not fall on one person. Unless *YOU* want to do it all. (I wouldn't touch that with somebody else's 10 foot pole.)

SUGAR vs. VINEGAR

You will get more of what you want in life (and in your marriage) if you take a nice guy approach instead of the jackass or jerk approach. Be nice and caring *whenever* you communicate with your wife. Even if she acts bitchy, don't go there. Stay in your nice guy mode and she'll get nicer, too. You'll see.

If *She's All That* ... AND 3 Loaves of Bread...

You and your wife can avoid the laziness that occurs in many marriages now, but you'll need to <u>get off the couch</u> and step away from the feedbag – literally. These days, weight gain seems to be the most common complaint from men about their wives. But before we go further, let's talk about how you may have played THE major role in the fact that your wife has gained a ton or 2.

OVERWEIGHT / UNDERAPPRECIATED

Women must be appreciated. They do a helluva lot these days. If your wife doesn't think that you notice all she does, at some point she will ask herself, "Why do I even bother?" (Maybe she has already asked *you* that.) I can tell you that once that happens, she might decide to <u>go</u>. If not that, then she may decide to *grow*.

The bottom line is that if you do not acknowledge the things that your wife does for you, to make your life better, then why should she care about doing them? She tries to look good, stay fit and be nice – just for you. So you don't notice? Hmmm. So she stops looking good, she stops staying fit, and she stops being nice. Wow. Then it may appear that you have just died and gone to Hell. And it's all because you didn't have the energy or the brains to say this: <u>"HoneyBabyAngelPie! *You rock!*"</u>

Do you have any idea how much a wife and mother would be paid to run a house if the tasks she performs were listed on a resume? Think about it. Personal Assistants are very well paid. And your wife may be doing all of the house and family stuff for you - while working a regular job, too. Uh, I'm holding my tongue here, Bud.

You probably feel you are the main support system of your house - though underneath your mighty glulam self are lots of smaller beams, headers and posts. But **they** are not <u>you</u>. **They are <u>your</u> <u>wife</u>**. You really need to think about all she does for you. And typically she tries to look nice while she's doing it, too. So the least you can do is compliment her on a job well done, and tell her that <u>**you get it**</u> - and that you DO appreciate all she does. <u>**You couldn't do it all**</u>, so admit that to her.

Also, since we are on the subject of your wife's appearance, you need to notice the nail polish, the highlights in her hair, the make-up and the clothes. Think back to when you first decided she was the one you wanted, and act like that again. (I can imagine you were full of compliments and attention for her when you first got together, as you schemed on how you could make her say 'yes' to whatever you were trying to do to her.)

Maybe you feel you are unappreciated, too. Well, I can practically guarantee that if you start recognizing your wife's efforts, telling her how much you appreciate her, and how great she is, you are going to start getting the same recognition from her. This will change everything about your relationship in a VERY positive way. *Don't forget that we all like to get compliments for the things we do. And when we get a compliment, suddenly we feel a little more generous... which means you'll probably get some appreciation, too.*

OK, so the return of your positive attention is what can get the excess weight off of your wife – and cause it to stay off. You start paying good attention to her like you did in your former life and you will likely start to see that beautiful butterfly *re-emerge*. Do it! You'll see. Remember that your recognition and appreciation is what she desires as pay for her job as your 'manager'. You NEED to make a huge effort. Compliment her and she will start responding by finding ways to get more compliments.

Don't forget, you have access to the grocery list, too. Don't bitch or nag about your wife's weight issue. Be positive, encouraging, tell her that you love her, and that you think that she's beautiful, and that you want for *both of you* to be healthier. Do whatever she will allow you to do to help her. If it means you will actually have to join a gym with her, take walks, do sit-ups, join Weight Watchers or give up the Whoppers, Big Macs and Laffy Taffy together, then DO IT. **You've invested an "I do" in her. And that commitment you made to her is waaaay bigger than *her butt* is.**

Females typically need only a little encouragement and support to reach a goal. Your motivation for taking a healing step with your wife may be all it takes to plunge her into the 3-sizes-smaller zone. Nobody wants to be overweight, and if you offer to partner up with her, she's very likely to succeed. She wants you to love how she looks, and she wants to love what she sees in the mirror, too. So right there you have two people in your corner. Just be sure to take your vitamins and detach from your La-Z-Boy, because this project will require some energy and work out of you.

Almost always, weight gain can be avoided with *healthy eating habits and exercise.* In the very remote chance that your wife isn't interested in losing weight, then offer a trade. Offer a *bribe*. Whatever it takes. Just keep talking until her face lights up and she bites. Hint: If you have kids, recruit them to help you convince Mom. Bribe them, too, if you must. They're kids. They'll bite on anything but brussel sprouts. If your wife always has wanted to go to the Bahamas, then dangle that carrot. If she wants a day of shopping at T.J. Maxx, then – *you gotta go!* Maybe she wants a diamond ring. Great. Ben Bridge and Kay Jewelers offer layaway plans.

Whatever she wants, let her know you are into it, too. Stay positive. (Negativity from you can create a little fast food joint in the closet.) Also, start saving your bucks for her prize, because she will probably be snagging that carrot, and then *you*, my friend, must pay up.

Speaking of prizes, remember that *you* may not be the prize you once were, either, so look in the mirror and figure out how *you* have changed. If you look better, communicate better, and treat your wife better than you did in your first year with her, then you are about the coolest, most incredibly awesome guy in *existence*. Go clone yourself.

You in bed.

OK, now it's time to talk about that 45-minute thing and how *you* score on the mat(tress). One of the most common complaints from women about their husbands (you) is the fact that you are not as romantic or as interested in sex as you used to be. **We could say that impressing your wife in bed is no longer your priority.**

So what's up? Or better yet what's it going to take to get something up? If your wife is clearly interested in sex but you aren't, you need to figure out why and then deal with it. When a woman is turned down for sex by the man she loves, it can be more damaging to her ego than *you* being turned down is to *your* ego.

> Right or wrong, we all seem to accept that guys are routinely turned down for sex. It's always been a sad, but comical little joke in our society. It's obvious in movies, on TV, and by the water cooler at your work... And you guys handle it very well, I might add. But to a woman, being turned down by her lover can be very damaging, so if this is an issue in your marriage, you need to fix it, or at least learn how to express what you need to make the idea of sex with HER more appealing. Because no matter what, there's someone out there who would love a chance to have sex with your wife.

Maybe something about your wife is turning you off, or preventing you from wanting sex with her. Could there be something else happening in your relationship, besides the sex issue, that may be pushing you away from sex with her? Money stuff? Family stuff? Stress at work? There may be many outside influences, but if you believe it is simply *her,* then you need to ask yourself if she is really the person you want to be with. If she is, then pick up a relationship book by Dr. Phil. (Or maybe one by *Dr. Ruth.*)

Otherwise, that problem will <u>never</u> go away. *Never* is a long time. Wouldn't you rather speak up and maybe fix this – even if it's uncomfortable for a minute or a month – than keep your mouth shut and deal with that 'never' thing that I just mentioned – for the rest of your life?

Here's one approach to dealing with your lack of interest in Humpy Monkey action with your wife. Have a sit down with her and ask *her* what *she* would like from *you* to spice things up *for her.* (This is sssso not about you.) Tell her you want to do for her whatever she likes.

Then whatever she says she wants from you, do your best to provide it. Get a manual (try 'Hot Sex' by Tracey Cox). Buy a trapeze. Anything she requests, do your best. There's a strong chance that she'll tell you all is well, anyway. Yep. Just fine, Honey. In that case, be more romantic. Buy her flowers and cards, pay attention to her. Prove that no matter what she wants, you are – *presto!* – her beck-and-call guy.

Bottom line: Your compliments and positive attitude toward your wife will ultimately get you whatever YOU want from her. In bed - AND everywhere else, too.

Yes, you can do that. You got her to marry you, somehow, so we know you can impress her. That is what will improve things in the sack *for you both* – guaranteed. (But you need to look in the mirror and see how far you are from the guy she fell in love with. *Then you need to start mapping your route back to* that guy.)

Sorry, but if talking about sex with your wife makes you slightly uncomfortable, you've got to get over that. Buy a book. Do anything you can to puff up your sails, step outside of your comfort zone, and sweat like a turkey in November for the minute or two it takes to break the "sex talk" ice.

Believe this: The discomfort is worth getting back - or keeping - the sizzle under the sheets. For one thing, just the fact that you're asking how to make it better for her, will likely cause her to think to herself, "Gee, wow. I can't believe he cares… I wonder what can I do to improve sex for him?" Uh - *think of all the possibilities.*

If your way of 'seducing' your wife is by saying, "hey, ya want a little?" then guess what. You're gonna get "a little". Geez, Hubby. Put **a little** effort into this attempt and you might actually get **a lot**. She's more than an electrical outlet, and she can give you more than a little 'jolt'… but you need to learn how to ask in a way that stands a chance of <u>turning her on</u>. Try this: **Walk up behind her and wrap your arms around her waist. Rub her shoulders. Tell her that her body drives you crazy.** This isn't only about you, so take her by the hand and lead her to a place she knows will mean a few exciting **amps** for <u>both of you.</u>

Can you snuggle without getting an erection? Yeah right. If your wife likes to snuggle or cuddle, bite the bullet and do it. But remember that snuggling usually ends once the erection begins and she may not be in the mood for sex. So here's what you do: rub her back, shoulders, feet – avoid any indication (or area) that will seem like you are wanting sex. If you can hold back and not pursue sex, while you are still holding her tight, massaging her body, or anything that is not screaming "let's hump!" then soon she will probably be the one reaching for the K.Y.

One BIG barrier between couples is bad breath. I know of a couple with 8 kids, but they have not kissed in ELEVEN YEARS. She is disgusted by his nasty teeth and the chronic bad breath that the nastiness causes. Wow. Obviously you can have sex without kissing… but lemme tell ya, sex is waaay better, more intense and powerful if kissing is involved. So brush first (you must brush because mouthwash won't remove the sweaters from your teeth). Then you can start strutting your stuff and getting some great results.

For your wife, sex begins far from the bedroom.

It starts in her *brain* as she sees the romantic things that you are doing for her – without a blatant ulterior motive (like *you* wanting sex). So send her flowers at work or bring flowers home. Buy her cards from time to time, write a sweet message inside and *mail them to her*. **Ask her if she'd like to take dance lessons with you.** *Treat her like you are dating again.*

ONE COUPLE'S STORY

Let me tell you what Jim, a couple's counselor, told me. He had been counseling a couple for about 6 months when one day, the husband called and made an appointment to be seen *alone*. Hmmm. That isn't part of the couple's counseling deal, but Jim agreed to see him alone anyway. When he met with this guy, he learned that through their counseling, the guy still absolutely <u>HATED</u> his wife, and he said he didn't think he could spend even one more day married to her. OK. Jim told him to go ahead and get the divorce papers and prepare to file them – *but to wait for 30 days to file.*

Jim instructed the man to treat his wife like a queen for this last month of their marriage. Compliment her. Help her with *everything*. Be the best husband to her he could possibly be, so that when he dropped the D Bomb on her, she might be nicer to him regarding <u>their stuff</u>, in divorce court. So the guy agreed to be sweeter than honey for 30 days.

Well. What do you think? At the end of the 30 days, the couple showed up, all smoochy and kissy and happy. It was unbelievable. The guy explained to Jim (later by phone) that as he treated his soon to be ex-wife like he worshipped the ground she walked on, she started doing the same to him. Suddenly these two were treating each other with love and respect, doing *everything* they could for each other. The fake 'nice' became a 'real' nice when the guy saw that his wife was being so sweet back to him.

So do you see what can happen when you decide to change your tune? She will change hers, too. Then you'll be sounding really good together. Go for it.

"Simply stated, women leave men when they are neglected. Neglect accounts for almost <u>all</u> of the reasons that women leave and divorce men." *This comes to you from W.F. Harley, Jr., Ph.D, psychologist, and founder of Marriage Builders.* (And the author of His Needs, Her Needs – which I told you about earlier.) Visit <u>www.marriagebuilders.com</u> to learn how to fluff up your vows.

COMMUNICATION BETWEEN MEN AND WOMEN:
Here's WAR Between England and France – if women ruled:
France calls England and asks, "Why did you bomb us?"
England replies, "Oh – **I think you know.**"
(And you can be sure that France <u>does</u> know...)

WOMEN ARE BITCHES. MEN ARE DOGS

Hmmm. Well, that might be what each side says about the other during a battle. But you know why this is, don't you? Because we speak two different languages and we respond to each other in two different ways. Example: When <u>you</u> get mad or hurt, typically you want to be left alone, right? Well. When <u>women</u> get mad or hurt, typically they want to deal with the problem right *now.* (Yes, this means that you should chase her to the bathroom door, begging, as she slams it in your face and locks it. Camp out there — keep begging, and soon, life is good again. Trust me. If you just go away, ignore her and turn the game on, uh, you will be prolonging your own agony. So stick around and talk the issue out with her — through the door. *Make this effort.*)

Granted, there are exceptions, but most often, that's the way it is. So how can both sides get what we need? By learning the other's language. To make this happen quickly, bite the bullet and read or re-read "Men Are From Mars, Women Are From Venus". It will totally open your eyes. Then when you get bombed, at least you'll know why...

Great communication is the key to a great marriage. The only way for you to get good at communicating with your wife is by doing it. Talk to her. About everything. In a relationship, men and women have different definitions of support and understanding. A man may view support as a very practical thing, while a woman may see support as a completely emotional thing. When there is an issue involving YOU, you usually want someone to tell you, "Hey, don't worry about it. It's no big deal." But in a female mind, she typically wants to hear, "Wow... I can see why you're upset. This is a HUGE deal. Let's try to fix it."

RED and PURPLE. Let's say that everything in life that is GOOD to a man is *RED*. Let's say that everything in life that is GOOD to a woman is *PURPLE*. So when you go out and buy a gift for the woman in your life, well of course it must be *red*, because that's the best. Right? OK, so when your woman needs support or understanding from you... again... you are gonna be sure she gets that great *red* stuff. You love the *red* type of understanding so of course that is the only type of understanding that you would ever give to her. *Red* is the best and it always works for you and makes you feel great. So she's gonna love this *red* understanding.

Now, when you need anything from your girl, well, she would only give the best to you and - naturally – she knows that the absolute best in the world is *PURPLE*. She would NEVER give you anything less than what she would want for herself so by golly, Baby! You are gettin' some of that awesome *PURPLE*! It is the greatest and she knows you will instantly know how much she loves you when you get this fantastic *PURPLE* from her.

Wow. You both are trying really hard to make absolute certain that everything you give your mate is the perfect color. The color YOU love. But both of you have missed something major. She hates *RED* and you hate *PURPLE*. *Red* does not ever work for her. It never makes her feel better. Every time you give her *red*, thinking that it will solve the problem, it doesn't! Sometimes it even makes it worse! *What's up with her?*

On the other hand, why is it that any time you feel a certain way, or need something from her, she covers you in that obnoxious *purple*? Geez. You hate *purple* and she should know that by now. When will she ever get a clue that *purple* NEVER works for you?

So while you are thinking of the colors *red* and *purple*, imagine that your **RED** solution to anything she needs from you is 'LOGIC' or 'PRACTICALITY'. While her **PURPLE** answer to any of your requests or problems is 'EMOTIONAL' or 'CARING'. When the two of you have a fight, *you* want to forget about it. *RED*. The two of you have a fight and *she* wants to talk about it. *PURPLE*. This seems to indicate that the reason you both have trouble avoiding or solving problems, is because you are each trying to force *your color* on the other – thinking that color is best for them and they'll want it.

If you can't get the color comparison concept, then try this: You speak German and she speaks French – and until you can learn a little of each others' languages, then the threat of a cold war will always loom and there will never be peace on *your* Earth.

In most simple terms: Usually for men who are upset, make no fuss. For women, make a fuss. (Of course there are always exceptions…)

Act like an adult and be an understanding partner. Resolve arguments calmly and quickly. Don't let them fester, and definitely don't sleep on them. Go to bed *happy* by dealing with issues and resolving them before bed. Then you'll wake up happy – with all of your parts, too.

> **Your wife should be your best friend.** The two of you should respect each other and value each other's opinions. Compare your marriage to the relationship with a trusted work-associate or friend. You probably don't become a moody jackass when you make decisions with anyone at work or with your friends. So why do it with your wife? Remember that she will still be by your side when your job and all of your buddies are out of the picture. So treat her like the great investment that she is, and you'll get a fantanstic return <u>every</u> <u>day</u>.

i. Cheating Will Only Get You an "F"
(And there is much more to life than "F".)
A Charming Guy DOES NOT Cheat – Didn't You Get the Memo?
Most people will agree that if you cheat on your spouse then you are low. Slug low. On second thought, if you cheat, then a slug's butt is probably looking like a hot air balloon to you.

That's really low. But in reality, we know we are all human, and humans make stupid mistakes. Frequently. There are many reasons a guy may cheat on his wife. The first is an erection. OK, I'll bag the sarcasm. This is a complicated topic, so we'll stick with the black and white of it.

Sometimes people cheat when they do not see any hope of getting what they want at home, and they are tired of hoping. But men and women want different things at home, so they cheat for different reasons. Both sides want and need to be appreciated. Beyond that, with men, it's usually sex – or escape. For women, it's usually romance or even love (– which is very dangerous for you.)

> Dr. J. Hamilton Berry compares a man's cheating to his walking into the kitchen and finding a chocolate cake sitting on the counter. He walks in and sees it. Chocolate cake! But he isn't hungry. But it's chocolate cake! It looks gooood. It smells gooood. And even though he knows he isn't hungry, it's there – and it's chocolate cake! So he will eat a piece of that cake just because it's there and he can. Wow.

(That cake will not speak to a woman in the same way … Unless of course it actually says to her, "You are wonderful and I love you. Come here and let me rub your back".)

WHAT IS CHEATING?
Just so we're clear about *cheating*, cheating means *you* doing anything with another human that would piss your wife off. No, this is not Webster's definition, but *in your marriage, you and your wife make the rules*. To put it simply, if you have to hide it from your wife, then you may as well call it cheating.

You know what will push her buttons and you know what she will get all flamed up about, so you know when you are cheating on *your wife*. Keep that bit of information *at the front* of your mind. Cheating (to your wife) may have to do with any aspect of sex. It could involve touchy, feely, flirty stuff. It may be about discussing personal or more private matters with anyone but her. Remember, you do not have to actually engage in sexual intercourse to be *cheating*. Can you say "Mo-ni-ca?"

Don't try to justify cheating with reasons like these:
• You are unhappy at home.
• You aren't getting any at home.

- Your wife doesn't understand you. (*PLEASE*. She understands you better than anyone. *Nnnnnnext*...)

Cheating will hurt the one who's cheated on, and it will hurt the one who is doing the cheating. *Do everything in your power to avoid both sides of this issue, because the after effect of cheating is like a hangover the size of Texas.*

IF YOU HAVE ALREADY CHEATED

...then you need to prepare for what that rotten little fact – if ever revealed – may do to your future. If you have cheated *only once*, with absolutely no intention of ever cheating again, then you have 2 choices.

1. You can tell your wife about it and deal with whatever painful and possibly long-term consequences that follow — **and *suffer*.**
OR
2. You can decide to bury the fact, zip your lips — and your fly — live with your guilt, make a pact with yourself to <u>NEVER</u> tell her — or anyone else (and NEVER do it again) — **and *suffer*.**

Yeah, you're going to suffer either way. Sorry, but <u>*you*</u> cheated on her. Not me. That is the sad fact. So which is the best route for you to take? Hmmm. That's your call. Both options suck. (Either way, get your cheatin' self to the doctor and get checked for sex bugs.)

Remember one thing. *No matter what*, your wife didn't deserve this (and you're gonna hate the hurt it will cause you, too). Finding out about it is going to cause her a lot of pain. So don't tell her if your only motive is to get rid of the guilt that you are tired of carrying around with you. It's your guilt, not your wife's, so don't torture *her* with the information in hopes that *you* will feel better. She isn't suffering. You are. **And contrary to what many experts have said for years, when it comes to infidelity, it may be best to leave it that way – that is** *the cheater*, <u>**suffering alone.**</u>

Not all marriages will survive cheating, so be warned that telling your wife that you have cheated is risky. It typically will create an ugly scar on your relationship that always will be visible to your wife. She may forgive you and she may try to move on with you, but understand that you have changed the love that she felt in her heart for you. **On the other hand, by going through the excruciatingly painful ordeal of telling her, chances are pretty good that you will NEVER cheat again. And I hear that re-attachment surgery has actually worked in a couple of cases...**

ATTENTION TERMINAL CHEATERS:
You're not a wolf in sheep's clothing. You're a *snake* in <u>wolf's</u> clothing.
You're married and that means you said you would be faithful to your wife. Do you think that when you said, "I do," it meant, "I do the boss's wife" or "I do the neighbor's sheep?" No. It meant that you DO choose to be faithful and loyal to your wife - forever. That means sex with your wife *only*. Your repeated cheating indicates that you do not feel the rules apply to you. Well, guess what. *They do.*

> **If you are a chronic cheater, then you obviously have a little control freak in your pants, so quit giving it control. Get counseling, get a divorce or just get a crowbar and pry your head out.**

YOU'LL GET CAUGHT...
Remember that *you* are the only person on Earth that you can completely trust to keep *your* secret. And you even screw *that* up sometimes. So unless you are cheating on your wife all by yourself (... no, that's not *really* cheating. It's something else that might piss her off, but it's not cheating), then we know there is at least one other person who knows the secret. And if more than one person knows any secret, that secret stands a 50% chance of becoming public knowledge.

Don't kid yourself into believing that if you cheat, the person you cheat with will *never* tell. Even if they have a lot to lose, like you do, they may still end up telling the story *to someone, someday*. And let me say this again: No matter what they say on TV, what happens in Vegas, does not stay in Vegas. Why? Because it's gossip, Pal, and even you guys like to dish the dirt after a beer... or five.

Another reason you will probably get caught is that most guys are easy to read – especially by their wives. Your wife can see inside that 'complicated' mind of yours, so simply put, she'll know when you are lying. Come on. If you share the remote control, the toilet, the microwave and the common cold with her, she probably knows you very well. This means that, even if you think you have fooled her, chances are you haven't, and she is simply letting you think you have. Hmmm. Now you should start sleeping with one eye open.

If you are tempted to cheat, go get counseling **now**. Do whatever it takes to stop yourself, because cheating will wipe out *everything* that remotely resembles your self-respect. Not to mention all the other aspects of *totally screwed up* it will dump onto your life.

If you are married, then here's a a simple stock answer for anyone who comes onto you and tries to get you *into them* – "Thank you, but not without a note from my wife". That should shut 'em right down.

DON'T EVER BE THE *'OTHER GUY'*

Never let anyone talk you into an affair with them if they're married, engaged, living with someone that they share a bed with - or otherwise hooked up. Even if they tell you:

*they are 'separated'
*they are getting a divorce soon
*they promise you that the two of you will not get caught

Don't believe it. Believe the exact opposite! If you are feeling an attraction to someone else who is married, fight that urge at all costs. Screw around with anyone you want, as long as YOU ARE BOTH *SINGLE.*

If you are married (or hooked up) and you think an affair with another married (or hooked up) person will mean 'safer' sex (no risk of disease, hot new sex, and a partner who will work as hard as you not to get caught because they have as much to loose as you do)… don't count on it. That person may not *really* have a great marriage, or very much to lose, and they may actually see you as a ticket to a better ride. Not only could your affair backfire like that, but if you do get busted, then you'll have two people who will wanna chop off your pecker - your spouse *and their spouse.* (Also remember that all females are designed to get pregnant, and no matter what you think or what she tells you – it could happen.) So there ya go. Everybody must be single *first.*

IF SHE CHEATS ON YOU

Typically, for many men, cheating is mechanical. The hint of an erection occurs and the rest is history. But as mentioned before, a woman's cheating is usually brought on by an emotional attraction. Someone else may step in and provide your wife with the positive and romantic attention she's not getting at home. This can cause her to fall flat on her back. In simple terms, someone said, "Hi you" to her heart (while – let's be real – someone need only say *anything* to a penis. No offense.)

Quite often, guys can cheat, zip up and leave – never feeling the need to look back. Women, however, can become very connected to the person they've cheated with. This is very dangerous for you as a husband, because men, prior to cheating, will almost always check their heart at the door. But a woman will typically bring her heart to the party and can actually fall in love when she cheats.

If you think that your wife is cheating on you, and you want her back, then don't hire a detective or follow her, hoping to catch her in the act. That would be providing the rope to hang your marriage. Instead, let her know that you love her and you are worried about what she's doing. Let her know you aren't her problem, you are her solution. To convince her that this is true, you'll need to be strong and understanding. No anger, no pitiful puppy. Be the man she fell in love with and married. Then drop it. Let her process that information until she's ready to respond.

A written note from you could be more effective than a face to face sit down, because your written message, whether you put it in a card or in an email, will prevent any chance of your message becoming an argument, or her chance to sweet talk you or somehow convince you that you are wrong. She will also have time to process the info you've provided before talking to you. *End your note with an invitation to talk whenever she is ready.*

This will likely cause 1 of 3 things to happen.
1. She will confess to you that she is cheating and she'll leave you.
2. She'll confess and stay, and then the two of you will need to figure out how to re-group. May I suggest marriage <u>counseling</u>?
3. She'll deny it, and then you'll have to wait and see what happens next. Again, maybe some marriage counseling…?

But after you talk to her, if she *is* cheating, or if she is thinking about cheating, this little message from you about it will probably make it too real and too 'revealed' for her to want to continue it and could stop her in her tracks. Why? Because the actual *discussion* of something that *should not be discussed* can turn it cold fast. Imagine a chilling ice storm overtaking her hot, sexy, tight, hard, illicit affair - suddenly causing it to feel more like a big, fat, dirty, ugly, flabby, cold and clammy *mistake.* Yuck!

If this happens, then you should take appropriate measures to ensure she won't cheat, or almost cheat, again. This doesn't mean locking her in the basement. It means tuning into what she wants and needs from a man

– YOU – and then making sure you are the next – and the only – guy to get close to *her heart*.

j. Pregnancy, Menopause, and Red Corvettes

Life is full of changes. Sometimes things happen that you aren't prepared for – even though you think you are. But as these events in your relationship occur; babies/hot flashes/gray sideburns and gold chains around your flabby neck (ew) – try proving to yourself (and to the rest of us) that you are capable of handling it all with a great attitude.

Pregnancy

When your wife is pregnant, give her all the space she wants. Not just for her expanding waistline, but for her attitude, too. Her pregnancy needs to be a happy and healthy time, so be there for her. Emotions may be, let's say, unpredictable? So be ready for anything. Also, be understanding and be sweet. Remember, *you* created her condition. (And get ready to hear all about *that* once you get into the Delivery Room.)

Speaking of the Delivery Room... here's something for you to consider:

If your wife wants you in the Delivery Room when your child is born, you need to be absolutely, 100% certain that you can handle what you're going to see in there. Be completely honest with her about how you feel on that subject. Some guys simply are not cut out to witness childbirth, even though it is *their* baby. Sure, the birth of a child is a beautiful thing – *to some people* – but to others, it's just another unappealing bodily function or bloody surgical procedure – which ends with a baby. And watching childbirth has been known to change a guy's feelings about his wife's body. (Hey—I know that sounds mean, but I'm just reporting the facts...)

Fine. Think I'm cruel if you want, but what I'm telling you throughout this book is not coming from me alone. I'm not making it up. If the idea of watching the birth makes you queasy, then tell that to your wife (and her friends). Tell her you will stand beside her shoulder and let her yell at you for putting her there, or wait outside preparing to hand out cigars. But don't be forced into the End Zone if your gut says "don't go there".

On the other side of that coin, many guys will tell you (with a completely believable excitement and passion) that seeing the delivery of their son or daughter was the highlight of their life. So start shopping for your video camera!

Before the birth, here's a simple way for you to be the ultra charming husband/daddy: suggest to your wife that you sign up for PARENTING classes (check with a local hospital or college to find them). Really. This is a great idea whether you are trying to be charming or not. Those little bundles don't come with instructions – and **it's not a puppy in there.** Get a book called, "So You're Going To Be A Dad" by Peter Downey.

Her Mid-life Crisis

If your wife is hovering around the age of 40, get off the couch *now,* because she may be thinking about greener grass. There is something about that age range that can put a woman's nose in the air, sniffing around for that so-called greener grass I just mentioned.

You love your wife, so start paying attention to her and focus on making her happy. Think about it. *She* has probably made this effort for you *daily* since the beginning of you and her. So now it's your turn to make the effort for her – at least until she gets over the **"Oh my God. Is this really my life? I can't believe I married _you_. And why do we have all these kids?"** phase.

But once you've survived that phase, don't kick back and relax. Nope. You'd better keep up the effort anyway. Because someday, when you have become gray and wrinkly, she may need to change your diapers. And unless your marriage has been terrific for her - *that* could definitely put her nose back into the air. If that happens, then look out, because the next thing you'll know, it's off to Sunny Acres for you. *Buh bye.*

Menopause

OK, you have a wife. A female. It's important that you understand this, because at some point in your wife's life, someplace between 45 and 60, females (your wife) may start to change a little. Or a lot. Maybe she'll start to speak a language that she feels nobody on this continent can understand. This will probably piss her off. Yes, this will probably drive *you* nuts, too, but imagine it from *her* side. Nothing is worse to a woman than not being understood. *Geez! Don't you get it?*

Anyway, when this "you just don't understand!" thing starts, don't back away and run for the hills. Nope. Put on your safety goggles and go on in. Really. You need to be in there with her for this.

For instance, never come between a woman and her fan.
Support your menopausal wife and all of her new physical
requirements. For instance, do not dare mess with her FAN. If
she wants the window open when it's 10° outside, put on your
thermal underwear and crawl into your mummy bag. **Happily.** And
unless her doctor has her on medication or hormones, I'd like to
suggest that you stop at the drugstore on the way home from
work tomorrow and buy her some <u>Extra Strength **ESTROVEN**</u>.
(There's **Estroven P.M.** to help her sleep, too.) It worked for me.
And Diane. And Donna, and Krista, and Kathy, etc.

Your wife's menopausal body is restructuring (no you can't tell)
and that's possibly pissing her off, too. (Theory: Eve bit that apple and
ruined it for all women. The fact that our bodies are so self-absorbed is
evidence of that. You guys get to coast through life, standing to pee and
everything.) During menopause, women typically deal with physical
issues that would put <u>you</u> in the psych ward. *That's another reason to be
glad you're a guy.*

During this change, if your wife will allow it, go with her whenever
she sees her doctor. Ask questions. Learn what's going on and what to
expect. Buckle up and hang on because you may be in for a ride. Stick
with her. Always show your support. (No matter how many colds you
end up with...)

AGAIN – LEARN TO APOLOGIZE.
For everything...that will help make this Twilight Zone episode that is
your life right now, much easier. (Re-read the previous section, "SORRY
Seems to be Your Hardest Word.") Being able and willing to apologize
(even if you don't know what it is you must have done) is an absolute
requirement. DO NOT DEFEND YOUR ACTIONS. Just apologize. Your
excuses will not matter to her while she is in this emotional state and
will most likely make her angrier. If you can say you are sorry about
something without breaking out in a rash, cramping up, doubling over
and dying about it, then you are among a very elite group of incredibly
amazing, understanding, sweet, fearless and *maximus studlius* guys.

Besides... wives (menopausal or not) don't usually kill husbands who
apologize for making a mistake. They pet them and bake cupcakes for
them. (But beware that saying you're sorry might not apply if you cheat.
In case of cheating, many women are of the mindset that the answer to
that age-old question:

'What's the quickest way to a man's heart?' is: 'through his chest with a sharp knife'.) Just remember that menopause is typically not life-threatening, but it may require that you be an unappreciated superhero every once in a while.

Mid-Life Crisis... *coming soon to a life near yours*

And it'll probably show up in the form of a shiny, red Corvette – or one of its sporty, *low* friends. Don't let it slink into your garage. Trust me, it will eventually embarrass you. If you are looking at a few gray hairs, new flab around your middle (go to the gym), and mail offers from Geritol and AARP, then find other ways to help your brain *accept* your new condition. (Try a Jeep — not a Corvette — then get off the beaten path once in a while and use it.)

> Remember that in the young, tight **minds** of the 18-year-olds you are fantasizing about, a guy over the age of 25 is borderline disgusting. And seeing you in a Corvette is not what will impress them. Seeing you in a time machine might, but since that's not an option, find someone your own age. Believe this: hearing your bones creak - or an accidental air bubble squeak out of you - as you strain to get out of your **8 inches off the ground** bucket seat - would definitely be more readily overlooked by someone born around your decade.

There's no good sales pitch for aging (other than great discounts and a membership to AARP) – so I won't try to fool you into believing that there is anything great about it, but remember all you have read here. And that you are *smarter* now than you have ever been. YOUR ATTITUDE and how you decide to deal with your increased creases - is up to you. But here's a thought that may help as you get older: Imagine being a woman as you begin this battle with gravity. There. *Feel better?*

k. After All That ... a *DIVORCE*

The end of a marriage or long-term relationship doesn't mean your life is over, it just means that you are starting a new chapter in it. Remember that everything – especially your pain – is only temporary. You'll see.

If your heart is broken, I'm really sorry. But this is temporary and you'll simply need to rely on your positive attitude to take you in the right direction, OK? (Refer back to the first few chapters, and then read "Accepting That You're Dumped.") This dark spot is a place where many of us have been, and everyone will have advice for you.

Remember that if you've been dumped, and divorce is looming, your wife should not see you in broken-hearted mode. Be strong, but polite, if you happen to be around her. *This could make her want you back.* To most people, *solid* is appealing. *Puddles* are not.

Here's the bottom line: *you need to focus on taking care of yourself.* Oddly, one very effective way for you to do this is by *helping others.* Think about it this way: If you stay busy doing whatever you can to keep your mind off the situation, time will pass more quickly, and as we've all heard, time heals all wounds. Blah, blah, blah. I know. But no matter how badly you're feeling now, it's going to get better. And if you can force yourself to think of others instead of yourself, then your mind is on something else – something positive.

You'll suffer less during this time if you help others. Helping people that really need help will cause them to be very grateful to you. And THAT is exactly what you need right now – to be valued and appreciated. **You'll feel 100% better.** Be a great guy and help everyone you can, then watch us all start worshipping the ground you walk on.

(Of course you'll still have to face going home to an empty place, but that pain will pass. Stay busy when you're there alone. Get into a hobby that you can work on when you're there or stop at Blockbuster and get a few movies. Order NetFlix. Whatever. Just don't watch anything mushy or Chick Flicky. Stick with Action or Sci-Fi... Though once your pain has eased up, I might suggest you watch a few Chick Flicks – they could help you see the light... or at least get better at understanding females.)

Even if you do something as PC extreme as volunteering at a senior citizen home or a soup kitchen, it's all good as long as you are doing something that needs to be done *to help others.* As I've told you before: *"You can have anything you want in life if you just help others get what they want first."*

Read that book I mentioned for your ego issue (or rent the movie) called "The Ultimate Gift" by Jim Stovall. It will give you a straight shot of what selflessness looks like. And it is basically an instruction manual to teach you how you can start to think – regarding helping other people, and getting over your own issues.

If the weight of a split feels like it's simply too much for you, call a counselor or a doctor. Ask anyone you know to recommend one. If that doesn't work, call your friendly neighborhood hospital and ask for the name of a counselor or shrink. I'm serious. If you can't handle this breakup on your own, then don't try to.

Not that I'm pitching for you to use drugs, but here is a cold, hard and clinically proven fact: *Prozac can help.* Quite often, the end of a marriage or long-term relationship can cause loss of sleep, overeating, *not* eating and/or other nasty side effects. Many medications are available to help you get back to normal and help you ride out the ups and downs of this surreal roller-coaster ride. If you are reluctant to take medication, tell the doctor. You may be able to compromise and find a solution to try for just a week or two, until you're feeling a little more normal.

But do whatever you must to keep your life in order until you are not so affected by this situation, OK? It's all temporary. Trust that life will get easier, day by day – so don't quit your job and give your goldfish away. You have no idea right now what life has in store for you.

Something incredible may be just around the corner, and when you meet it face to face, you need to be in the right frame of mind to welcome it, take it home and make it a part of your great, new life. But if you are still whining about your ex, then that 'something incredible' thing that I just mentioned will not WANT to come home with you.

Don't be bitter or angry because your marriage ended. Get over it, because if you waste time thinking that you got a raw deal, even if it's true, that attitude will only ensure that you'll stay single (and ticked off about it) forever. So shake off a little of your pissed-off attitude every day. You can do it. Soon you'll be smiling again and your smile = appeal.

YOUR FRIENDS AND YOUR DIVORCE
It's hard to predict where your friends will land after your divorce. They may stay with you or they may go with your ex. (Be warned that if you were a total butt of a husband, they'll probably go with your ex.) Everyone might look at you differently now that you are single – especially the couples that were part of your group of friends. They don't know what to do for you, so they may just drop back and hide. Don't take this personally if you suddenly feel like they are avoiding you. It's normal. It sucks, but it's still normal. (People often do this whenever a serious illness appears in the friends' circle, too. It's just because they feel helpless, and although they may really want to help you, they think that they can't or they don't know how.)

Also, when friends witness something bad happen to any part of their group, they automatically consider themselves and wonder, "what if that happens to me?" I mean, if it happened to you then it could happen to them, right? That's scary as hell, so forgive your scared little friends for running and hiding. On the other hand, as for the people who actually stick around to weather this nasty storm with you, well...they are your TRUE friends.

There's a saying that goes: "A true friend walks in when everyone else walks out." If you ever have the opportunity to be a true friend to someone and you can walk in to help as all the other friends are running away, do it. This is the type of move that will really make a difference in someone's life and prove that you are a *seriously great guy*. Plus the Karma Bears will remain loyal to you and they'll cover your back in the future. Remember: You get what you give.

ATTENTION Born-Again Bachelors:
Divorce is not a "GET OUT OF HELL FREE" Card. Earth to "Can't-wait-to-be-single" guy: If this divorce is your idea, then let me warn you about something. Before you celebrate the demise of your 1st, 2nd or 15th marriage, understand that you will most likely be taking at least half of your marriage's problems with you to your next relationship. Because you may be the only common (bad) denominator in all of your hook-ups. Look into it, and fix yourself before deciding that your spouse is the <u>only</u> problem. If you don't, you'll soon discover that everyone out there has all the same problems your ex did. **Yeah right. That idea might make you feel better about yourself, but – get real, problem child.** You are the only common link! YOUR approach to your relationships needs assistance so buy a book to help you get really good at relationships. There are a few listed in the back of this book with your name on them. ☺

One final suggestion about your relationship. If your partner is constantly threatening to leave you "if you *this*" or "if you *that*", then you need to sit down and think about these threats. If you can do (or not do) whatever it is they are asking of you, then *make that change*. But if their complaints and threats are based on something that you can't do anything about, then tell them that, and then tell them to go ahead and leave. They are making impossible demands of you and there is no way you will ever be able to meet those demands. Constantly hearing about a problem or issue you can't fix is no way to live. Your mate may go, but chances are that they'll get a clue, stay, stop the threats, and actually start respecting you.

If your message gets no positive response, then you need to decide whether you want to stay with this partner and live with the bitching, or you want to split, and live without the bitching – and everything else about that partner.

Tips from Chapter 10: Your Relationship Résumé

1• **If you are afraid to get too close to someone, figure out why and deal with it.** Then get close, or stay single. Don't string them (and you) along.

2• **Remember that you and your partner are the only 2 votes in your relationship.** So it will be what ever the two of you make it. You both can make compromises that will give you each exactly what you want.

3• **Treat your mate like you're on a first date.** Always keep trying to impress your partner, even if you've been together for 80 years.

4• **Say "I love you" often.** These words (if you really mean them) are like epoxy in a relationship. But only say them if you mean them. Otherwise you'll be Superglued to something you don't want to be Superglued to...

5• **Always be prepared to answer that dreaded question: "What are you thinking?"** (The good news is that you'll score big points with your answer.)

6• **Do not classify any complaint as 'nagging'.** If you've heard one several times, then fix the complaint. Work out a compromise. And NEVER use a sarcastic or smart-ass approach *if your mate is upset*. Never say anything like "screw you" or "I hate you" either. Respect your partner – even when you're mad. Stay calm and be the solution, not the problem.

7• **Stop rolling your eyes.** Get into a treatment program. This type of response in relationships creates those obviously unhappy couples that the rest of us don't even want to park beside.

8• **Decide what is most important to you: Your mate or your job.** You don't need to put less effort into your career. Just put more into your personal relationships. *If you want your mate for life,* prove it. (Remember that someday your career will be deader than a *sea scroll.* ☺ Hopefully your personal life won't be.)

9• **Do your best to keep your relationship healthy and happy.** If things start to head south, find a good couple's counselor. If you can save it, cool. If you can't, then at least you'll know you gave it your best and really tried.

10• **If a relationship ends, figure out what you did or didn't do to contribute to its demise.** Then fix yourself so that you are better next time, otherwise, you'll notice the problems keep following you. And you'll think you are surrounded by stupid aliens.

11• **Avoid situations that might make your partner worry or feel jealous.** Like constantly working late — but not reachable on your cell phone or allowing yourself to be put into a situation that could end up with you marooned on a desert island… all alone… except for Heidi Klum.

12• **Learn to APOLOGIZE.** It's easy and you'll get major rewards for it. This issue is difficult for many guys, but do it anyway. It'll get easier the more you do it. Plus the shocked looks you'll get from the people that you apologize to will entertain you.

13• **Remember that jealousy is a put down to the person who is jealous.** It's toxic to your relationships and it's sure to kill all of your happy little life cells, so bump it.

14• **Don't feel that you must compete with other guys for attention or success.** Let the win go to others from time to time and then congratulate them. This is the ultra-charming thing to do and everyone will see that you are a cool and self-confident guy.

15• **If you decide that you and the person you have been seeing aren't a great match, end it quickly and nicely.** But be considerate of their feelings. Remember that there is always the possibility that you have completely broken their heart. It'll heal, but be nice until it does.

16• **If the love of your life decides that *you* are history, don't make a scene or refuse your walking papers.** Accept that you are dumped and go hide for a while. This may make your dumper miss you. *Stalking them won't.*

17• **"Will you marry me?"** When you are certain that you have found THE ONE, be sure you give the gift of a real marriage proposal. It may not be a big deal to you, but it could be a major or HUGE deal to them. (Also, are you qualified to pick out the ring?)

18• **If you are married, then treat your wife like the most important person in your world.** *Honor your vows.* Appreciate her. Give her love and support every day. Make her your very best friend and stay beside her no matter what. You will benefit from this — big time. Plus, if you help with the chores, she may end up with a lot of extra energy each day/night. Gee. I wonder what you could do with *that*...

19• **Sex can be perfect for you and your wife, but you must try a new position.** It's called "talking about what we want sexually". Hey, you can do this while you're *spooning*.

20• **If you are *happy* with your wife, tell her and <u>everyone else</u>.** Spread some good news about marriage. But if you are unhappy with her, don't complain to your pals. *Tell her.* Be nice, but let her know what you are unhappy about and ask how you can help change or fix it. (Find a couple's counselor. They're everywhere.)

21• **If your marriage has gained weight, take it to the gym.** There are only two of you to make the decision to get fit, so speak up.

22• **Be a giver, not a taker.** Try it for a month and you'll see your wife become more generous, too.

23• **Learn your wife's language.** Read a book called "His Needs, Her Needs" and discover how to give her what she wants – and get what you want.

24• **If you have cheated on your wife, then prepare to *suffer*.** Whether you've told her or not, you will suffer. Sorry. (But never admit you've cheated — just to make yourself feel better.) Confess to your priest or confess to your accountant. Get counseling. *Whatever.* And NEVER cheat again, because infidelity brings on the worst hangover imaginable. (And you may wake up one day to discover that you've been murdered in your sleep.)

25• **When it comes to female hormones, know that you are not equipped to battle the forces behind PMS, pregnancy or menopause.** So play dead instead and you'll survive. Be sweet and calm and supportive (it won't hurt if you're covered in chocolate), and don't forget that *you love her.*

26• **Your Mid-Life Crisis:** Don't let yours get you killed. Or arrested. You can survive it with dignity, but you'll need to avoid "Girls Gone Wild". Act your age and whatever you want will probably come to you.

27• **If your marriage is on the rocks, find a good marriage counselor.** They cost *much less* than divorce lawyers.

28• **If you are suddenly faced with divorce papers, stay calm.** But do your absolute best to work things out. Remember that splitting the assets will not be a walk in the park, but if you are a nice easy going guy throughout the process, she may cancel the divorce. That happens you know...

Don't run from your past...

Get over it!

CHAPTER 11

Getting Past Your Past

No matter what's hiding in your closet; an EX that you won't let yourself forget, a set of bad parents, or guilt over doing something you shouldn't have done... you need to get over it. Pull your brain into the here and now, stop playing with it, and start using it to MOVE ON.

a. Put Out the Old Flame

The memory of your old love can be like childbirth is for a woman. Hemorrhoids, stretch marks and all the other fun stuff that pregnancy caused is forgotten (– until she gets pregnant and does it all over again).

Old flame is a good way to phrase it. (Heartburn comes to mind. Get Rolaids.) Issues from your past can hold you back and screw with your future, so kick 'em to the curb.

YOUR BAGGAGE

Would you like some help with that baggage? If you are still hung up on someone from your past, there's no doubt it will keep you from a happy future with someone else. That's really bad, especially if you are absolutely certain there is no possibility of working things out with that person from the past. If this is the case, you need to take action to get the old relationship out of your head NOW so you can begin a new and improved chapter in your life. **And don't let that person from your past string you along. Either you are together — or you're <u>not</u>. There is no in between. Move on.**

Before you jump to fall in love again, be sure that you have cleared your heart of that last love. Trust me when I tell you that the worst pain you can inflict (even accidentally) on a new love comes in the form of an old love and its issues. Because falling in love with you, only to discover that someone else still owns 10% or more of the stock in your heart, is a nightmare for anyone. And this crippling affliction could end up costing you a chance with the best r-ship to ever come your way, too. That would be the one with this new person – not the old one. The old one clearly had problems, hence it's OVER. (Yes. I am a Rocket Scientist again.)

Perhaps you are choosing to remember a past relationship as a heavenly float through the Tunnel of Love, but your friends and the other witnesses will tell you it was a flaming railcar, bucking and barreling out of control — down the *Highway to Hell*.

I realize that when you are stuck on someone from your past it isn't always possible to just shake it off and move on. But keep in mind that your memory may subconsciously be deleting the bad parts and glamorizing an old relationship, making it much better in your mind than it ever was in reality.

You know - *you're dreaming*. This isn't unusual… not wanting to admit that in real life your relationship was not as perfect as you are choosing to remember. You are probably suffering from a severe case of "can't-have-itis" – or wanting something only because you know you can't have it.

That's why it may be a good idea for you to talk about this past thing to a close, trusted friend. If you've already tried talking to someone who knows you, then you probably need to find a bigger hammer. A counselor. A shrink. *Or anyone who parks beside you in a parking lot.* But NOT your mother. (No offense Mom, but since you probably think *that no one* so far was good enough for him anyway, how much sympathy and unbiased advice can you possibly offer? You know what I mean…)

You need to pursue a trustworthy rope that can wrap itself around your heart (actually, it's your brain that needs the rope. Your heart just wants to have fun again. Your *brain* is the one hiding under the bed, blinking at you and refusing to come out). A counselor can be your rope, talking you out of that old *stuck-in-your-head* issue and pulling you out into this *healthier* time zone.

If your past involves an Evil X' – you know, the psycho that seemed so perfect in the beginning, but then shredded everything in your closet when you wanted to break up – you need to let that go. Honest. Don't worry that every person you consider taking home now to meet the parents or the plants will eventually become the sequel to Evil X.

Every relationship is different. If you've met someone who feels like a 'maybe,' then you need to take a deep breath, and give it a shot. *You can't live in fear of Evil Xs or future Evil Xs.* If your crazy X is still lurking in the shadows – you know, still peeping at you around corners – just call the cops. A restraining order may be a good idea. (Rent "Fatal Attraction.")

Here's a suggestion to avoid future Evil Xs: To put it plain and simple, going slow is the *only* way for you to see red flags or warning signs and still have time to react to them before you're doomed. Most important to avoid a psycho Evil X is this #1 safety rule: Don't be rushing into sex with someone, especially if you haven't even considered a relationship with this person. Worse yet, if you HAVE considered a relationship with this person and you already know you don't want one, then don't have sex with that person. *(ROCKET SCIENTIST.)*

For many people, the minute they have sex with you, it's time for a serious relationship – beginning with moving in together and soon planning your yearly vacations to Wally World.

If you have sex with someone you do not know very well, then don't blame me if you get what you deserve. That would be the dreaded U-Haul in your driveway. When you see this horrifying sight, you'll know it's because you let Junior in your pants give it directions to get there.

So if you have sex too soon, and then are suddenly faced with the surreal sight of someone else's stuff moving itself into your house, it will be because you were an impatient horn dog, Mister LetTheLittleHeadDoThePlanningOfYourFuture. Don't go there, Pal. Let your common sense (located in your big head) lead you to safety — via a cold shower.

Discussing your past relationships with new ones is usually not a hot idea. Granted, new prospects may ask you questions and want to know the details of your past loves, but beware. Did your Mom ever say to you: *"If you can't say something nice about someone, then don't say anything at all?"* Well, if you want to be charming, this is a good rule to follow in every aspect of your life. If you want to say nasty things about any player in your past – or present – don't.

The person you are talking to is taking mental notes, and if you bad-mouth someone you supposedly used to love, then this can (and should) always be a warning to the listener. Mainly because it will be obvious that if you'll talk bad about that past person to this new person, then you'll probably talk bad about this new person (if and when they're not new anymore and have actually become a past person) to someone else later — or the next new person. Did you get that? Good, because there's no charm anywhere in sight there, my man.

Also, always edit the venom out of your stories, OK? *Be nice, and remember that no matter what you say about others, even Lorena Bobbitt, it's a reflection of you.* And *you* are a classy and charming guy who says good things and spreads good vibes. Of course, I realize that we shouldn't lie if asked about where we've been and that's all right. Just as long as you stay calm and unemotional and non-venomous (or mean).

If you have nothing but great things to say about any of your past relationships, that's terrific, but keep your mouth shut on that, too. (As if a new person can handle hearing about the perfect old shoes they'll have to fill if they are hoping for a real relationship with you.) Simply try to remain polite and neutral in what you say about your past. And don't begin a new relationship until you *make yourself* get over that past one.

b. So. You *Were* Raised in the Woods by Wolves

Let's talk now about bad parents. Interfering, demanding, manipulative and controlling parents. (You are warned that this is not a charming subject. It may piss you off, and it will not teach you much about being charming. But, hopefully, it will help the guys who need to hear it – so buckle up and brace yourself.)

First, let me tell you that I know the Bible, and Buddha and Barney all say that we should honor our mother and father. But mothers and fathers do some pretty 'UN-honorable' things these days, so honor yours accordingly... If they used you as an ashtray, or poked you with pointy things, then they would fall into that 'UN-honorable' category. In other words, if they did bad stuff to you — verbally or physically — then save your honor for the people who deserve it. They don't.

Here's a load of *bull:* You can choose your friends, but you are stuck with your family. *Ha!* We can choose the people we allow into our lives and I'll tell ya, if you are related to a person or a clan that isn't good for you, then move away and don't tell them where you're going. You owe *nothing to anyone who makes you feel badly...* even if they *did* supply the DNA that created you.

DO YOU HAVE ROTTEN PARENTS? (Let's just call them 'donors.')
My point for placing a strong focus here on *rotten* parents is because so many of you guys have expressed that you still are trying to live up to an absurd set of standards set by your moms and/or dads, years ago. Those standards may have been unreasonable even then, but for you to still break your neck trying to please your demanding parents – now that you are an adult, possibly with your *own* family – is **nuts**. Let's fix it, because if your parents are good people (we can hope), then they know you are an adult now and *they will let you be whoever you are, and let you do whatever you must.* They've already taught you what they know, so the rest of your lessons will come from living your life *on your own* – and changing your own diapers, bandages and opinions.

You know, in many places you must have a license for a dog or a cat. So why aren't there any requirements for having a baby? If you have the proper plumbing, then I guess you're qualified to make one. (And without a condom – you might get one.) With this said, there is a simple fact that you may need to face with regard to your parents. They are not supreme beings or saints. As a matter of fact, what does the fact that these two people made **you**, make **them**? Oh yeah. I know — 2 people who had sex.

Hmmm. Not so supreme. So now that *that* is revealed, I'd also like to point out that they really have no power to make your life miserable anymore – at least not without your permission. You need to remember that your parents' lame approach to raising you does not need to chase you and haunt you for your entire life. *That* can happen only if you let it.

So don't let it. Maybe they are just turds and no matter how smooth and shiny and great smelling you try to make them in your mind, they still are just turds. It's no big deal if they are. Lots of guys have turds for parents. You simply need to see them for what they are, so you can get over them and take your life back. *It's yours.* Not theirs.

Since you are an adult now, you need to sit back and consider the excess baggage that your parents may have sent out into the world with you. Is it good? If not, push it off the nearest cliff. Really. Just like My Mistakenly Unmarried Cousin (I mentioned him in Chapter 10), you should move away from the example that your parents set for you – if it's bad.

Do you want a real eye-opener when it comes to your parents? Then try looking at them this way: only *their* children – meaning you and your brothers and sisters – see your parents as powerful. Your parents can't control *anyone else* in the world, so why let them control you? You need to measure them realistically – as regular people. Consider what other adults think of your parents.

STOP GIVING POWER TO DEMANDING, CONTROLLING PARENTS. You can say **no** to them now. You're an adult. What are they going to do, spank you? Right. Guilt you? Only if you allow it. Cut you out of the will? Please! If they pull that one on you, tell them to go for it. Suggest they spend your inheritance on their much-needed therapy. If you keep on bowing down to lousy parents that don't deserve your respect just because you want their money when they're dead, then son, you are just a prostitute.

Be a man and tell your parents like it is, because here's a news flash. Parents *want* to know that their children have become functional, healthy adults. (Even the crappy, clueless parents want this, because they hope that you will take care of them when they're old.) They should have enough respect for you as an adult that they'll leave you alone to be happy – without their continual interference and/or constant 'neediness,' complaints and demands.

To fix old issues with your parents, all you need to do is stand up to them. They can't hurt you now, so don't live your life to please *them* anymore. Besides, standing up to them may actually cause them to suddenly respect you. It's true. Sooner or later, the tables will turn, and at some point, parents will even start to seek advice from their kids. So be a good grown-up and make your parents respect you. Don't worry about hurting their feelings. They will get over it. If they don't, then at least you are not at their mercy anymore.

Chances are, your parents will come around and you'll end up having a good relationship with them. You may even start to *like* them – on <u>your own terms</u>. Do or say anything you must to make them treat you with respect. Be nice, but strong. If they are still evil losers, then get away from them and stay away. *They aren't good for you.*

Ultimately, with regard to your future with bad parents, you have 3 choices:
1.	Stand up to them and possibly create a new, improved, and normal relationship with them – or discover that they are still idiots and then at least you'll know…
2.	Don't change anything, and keep suffering like you've suffered your entire life.
3.	Move to Panama and don't tell them.

PSYCHO DADS
Sorry if this sounds disrespectful, but not all dads deserve respect. Maybe when you were a kid, your dad always called you an "idiot" and/or other names. If so, then guess what… *your father was the IDIOT* – not you. Do not believe that the things that your verbally or physically abusive dad said to you or about you are true. They are not. He is the loser – not you.

> **What grown man with a functioning brain between his ears
> would want for his own son to feel stupid?** *Geez* people. **Everyone
> out of that gene pool, NOW.** We all know that when we see a
> ticked-off customer yelling at a counter clerk or cashier, it's not
> the clerk/cashier that is the loser. The loser is the one who is
> yelling — and looking out of control.

Perhaps your father was pissed at the world and he took it all out
on his family. This wasn't your fault. No matter what mistakes you may
have made to push his buttons, you didn't deserve to be treated brutally
by your dad (or your mom).

**A father who loses control and screams in the faces of his kids,
calls them names, and/or beats them, has a dent in his brain. You did
nothing to cause his explosions. You just happened to be there. Bummer
for you, but I'm here to tell ya, this was *NOT YOUR FAULT*.**

If you had a really rotten dad, and his issues are still hanging out in
your head, then call the head police, a *mind* sweep. If you feel that *you are
becoming your rotten dad*, carrying so much of his rottenness around inside
you that when you speak — *his* words come out of *your* mouth, you need
a counselor — so call one. He or she can help you, because do you really
want to be the dad to your kids (if or when you have them) that your dad
was to you? *I didn't think so.* So call the head cops and kick your dad's
clueless ghost out of your head now. Good riddance to that *Horse's Ass*!

MANIPULATIVE MOMMIES

Yikes. This is a bad deal if you have one. Oh, wait. She's manipulative,
and you're a guy, so you probably don't even know if you have one.

I'm not meaning to disrespect mothers either, but again, not all
moms deserve respect. (Remember that to everyone else, your mom is
just another female who had a baby.) I'm simply letting you know that
some moms have an absurd, twisted desire to keep their sons on a string
till one of them drops dead. *If your mom is one of these, then you have a real
problem, because usually that mother will 'innocently' or 'accidentally' cause
problems in your life and you won't even know it. She may create issues in your
love life, or it could be that your mom constantly needs your time. Whatever it
is, if it's making you unhappy or stressed, or causing headaches for you in any
way, then you need to have a sit-down with Ma.*

Tell her that you have your own life to live and that her constant butting in is a problem. If she won't get your *polite* message, then stop being polite. If it means hurting her feelings, oh well. Do whatever you must so that she'll leave you alone and stay off your back. She'll come around and accept who you are – and what *you* want – eventually. You are her *adult* son, after all. *She should love you and want for you to be happy.* If she doesn't, get away from her and adopt the mom of one of your buddies. If you're charming, the moms of your friends will probably fight over you anyway.

> You should be able to live your life without any interference from your mother. This means you cannot give her any power to cause problems for you. She cannot choose your mate for you and she shouldn't try to stick her nose into your relationships.

A good mom will be supportive and encouraging to her son. She also will let him live his life, learn from his mistakes and survive them on his own. Period.

We know there are many bad moms out there. Shame on them. But boys, *shame on you, too.* You have clearly helped create this monster by giving in to her and always doing *whatever* she wants. Don't make excuses for your pain-in-the-butt mom by saying, "But she's my *mom.*" So what? Don't forget that to the rest of us, she's a woman who had a baby, and that baby turned into you. Either way, she is crossing the line if she manipulates (or guilts) you into being her Beck and Call boy *forever.* That's right – *forever…* unless you stop it. Or she dies. And if you keep catering to her until she does drop, then she'll probably be sure you feel guilty about *that*, too.

Again, I'm simply suggesting that if you find yourself catering to your mother's wants and needs, without being happy about it, stop it. If her demands have taken a toll on your life and your own personal relationships, then you need to admit that maybe she is a problem. (Especially if you have 7 ex's that didn't really get along with your mother). And you need to fix it any way you can. Move to Tampa.

> By the way, don't subject your mate to your mom if your mom is a pain in the butt. Many mates would chose a red, oozy rash over an hour with your mother if she's pushy and obnoxious.

If you feel that you never get *or got* any attention from your mom — or dad — still follow the advice you just read. You will either gain respect, or you will know it's no longer worth it to try. <u>Move on</u>.

"Instant Asshole, Just Add *Alcohol*". (Sorry about that, but it's a bumpersticker.)

Your parents and alcohol... If one or both of your parents could be called an alcoholic, you probably had a pretty sketchy childhood. 'Happy Hour' in some houses clearly wasn't so happy. But if you are still struggling with negative old issues stemming from whatever nastiness may have resulted from your drunk mom and/or dad, get help. Many, many guys have lived through the nightmare of drunken parents, but it often requires outside help.

If your alcohol-related past still has a hold on you, you need to find a way to overcome it. Do you really wanna be miserable forever because you have bad memories of bad things that happened to you long ago? NO. Stop dwelling on — and suffering because of — that baggage. Change your focus from your **past** to your **future**. Stay away from the Whinery.

If you can't bring yourself to sit down and talk about your horrible childhood, then visit the bookstore and find your own personal reading section. You will find many books written by, for and because of kids of drunk parents. Start with one by Annie Lamott. She had a drunken, mean mom, but she still turned out great. Plus, her stories are all good, and they'll ultimately make you feel good. Our goal is to make you feel good – so that you can be charming. (If Annie's stuff isn't brutal enough for you to relate to, get any book by David Pelzer. Wow. And to think I complained because I had to be in bed by 9.)

HEY! If you have terrific parents, and/or in-laws... the easy-to-talk-to, always-there-for-you, listen-to-you, pat-you-on-the-back and we-encourage-you kind of folks, then I have instructions for you. Call or see them right NOW and say thank you, thank you, thank you! (Then figure out how to clone them, because there are millions of little kids out there this minute, suffering at the hands of clueless idiots that hooked up once, without a condom, and made a baby.) If you haven't been in touch with your parents on a regular basis, get into calling, e-mailing or writing them *once a month.* This will light up their world, and if they were good to you, they deserve that. If they weren't good to you - then maybe the shock of hearing from you will… Well. Nevermind. If they weren't good to you then be a good guy anyway and forgive them if you can. Just don't ever let them play with your head again. If they start the old games, get in the car and drive. Never look back.

Whether your parents were great or rotten, if you feel you now are emotionally healthy enough to help pave the way for a young guy who could use some guidance, think about becoming a Big Brother. Little guys these days have it rough. There aren't a lot of great role models out there for them, so if you feel you've got it in you to be a great Big Brother, do it. That would be *supreme* of you. And charming. Thanks.

Be Sure Your Life is a Victim-Free Zone. Just keep in mind that no matter what nastiness you have survived – YOU HAVE SURVIVED! No matter what you have done, or what's been done to you, you do not victimize - and you cannot be victimized. No victims allowed in your life. You can get over all of the garbage from your past by *deciding you want to get over it.* Take action to move from a yucked up past to an awesome future.

After the last 2 topics about your past - I'd like to remind you that YOU are in charge of your feelings — and your behavior… OK, again keep in mind that you can let go of — and get over — things once you decide to do it! Look, we can spend our lives focused on our past and all of the drama and bull that it may have involved. But today is the 1ˢᵗ day of the rest of your life. And unless you **get it** — I'll keep torturing you with statements like that one…

Why should your future suffer just because your past is an ass? Do you want to waste your future whining about your past? <u>NO</u>. Don't let your past own your future. Vow to stop sucking your thumb right now. This world is waiting for <u>you</u> to start having fun and liking your life, so toss the baggage off that cliff and watch it fly away.

Tips from Chapter 11: Getting Past Your Past

1• **Make every effort to get over a person from a past relationship.** That hang-up will keep you from being happy with someone else.

2• **Sex can cause Evil X's.** If there is an Evil X anywhere in your past... then avoid another one by giving yourself time to get to know the next person before sex, because once sex happens, the position of the relationship will change (from vertical to horizontal), and gets a whole new view. Maybe good, maybe not so good. Go slow.

3• **Don't let your past experiences keep you from moving ahead in a new relationship.** Simply learn from your past mistakes.

4• **Don't talk about how great or how bad old relationships were.** Be neutral and realistic if they come up with someone new.

5• **Be real about your bad parents.** If they weren't great, admit it to yourself. They're just 2 people who had sex, not saints *or dictators*.

6• **Forgive your parents if they were rotten to you, but don't continue to give them _any_ power over you.** You can say NO to them now. You're an adult, so take control of *your life*. Also DON'T believe that any bad thing they ever said about you is true.

7• **If you have rotten parents that you can't forgive, then cut ties with them and move on.** Counseling can help, you know.

8• **If your parents (one or both) were alcoholics, be careful not to follow their path into the bottle.** Get help if you know you should, so that you can have a great life without that bottled *monster*.

9• **If you have good, great or off-the-charts incredible parents, say "thanks!"** Right now. By e-mail, phone or face-to-face, get with them and say *"thank you."* Tell them how much you appreciate what great parents they are!

10• **Learn from your parents.** If they were great, copy them. Avoid mistakes they made with you, and if you are a parent, be a great dad to your kids. (Teach them good manners, too.)

11 • **Know that** *THIS IS YOUR LIFE.* No matter what baggage has been dumped on you by others, you can choose to carry it or not.

12 • **Consider being a Big Brother.** There are many kids out there who need you, and who could really learn from your experiences. Call Big Brothers and Big Sisters to see about signing up.

CHAPTER 12

The Great Date Guide

If you want to get a hot date, then you have to be one. This chapter will teach you how. Guys, these rules are set in stone, so do not think that you can skate on any of them. The happily ever after part of your life depends on your success while you are dating.

Let's refer back to the guy on the penny. He had a pretty sketchy (and humiliating) resume, but we still decided to elect him to be the 16th President of the United States, where he completely changed the world.

So what does this have to do with you? Well, it should tell you that other guys have risked rejection on a much larger scale than you ever will, so you should not be bummed that you haven't found the right partner – yet. (And that *IS* why you're dating – isn't it?)

YOUR QUEST FOR PERFECTION (Yes, this is repeated from Chapter 2)

Just out of curiosity, if you are in search of the "perfect" mate, what perfection will you be bringing to the table? Most guys have a long list of requirements when it comes to what they want in a mate. And that's OK as long as these guys have as much - or more - to offer a mate in return. But here's something my guy friend said once: *"I want someone who is slim and nice-looking, makes good money – without any debt. There shouldn't be any jealousy issues, and this person must like sex and want it whenever I do. My ideal partner needs to be independent and reasonably intelligent – preferably with a degree."*

Well, that's fair enough I guess – if this list of requirements came from the mouth of a male who met all of the requirements himself – but it did not. *He* did not. Bless his pompous little heart.

So let me suggest that as you pursue a partner, and create your "Ideal Mate Check List," you make sure that you have plenty to offer in return. Because if you are a mix of Airedale, Bull Dog, Lab and Cocker Spaniel, with bad breath, a bad habit of chasing cars or digging holes – and a gas problem, you really can't expect that a national champion, a winner of the Westminster Kennel Club dog show; a beautiful, sexy, smart Golden Retriever – would pick *you* to father *her* pups.

Remember this: **If you are fishing for <u>perfection</u>, try using something that at least resembles <u>perfection</u> as bait…** (OR: *Don't reach for the stars, unless you've put on your deodorant first.*)

THE BEST STRATEGY FOR FINDING A MATE

As I said before, don't be depressed over the fact that you haven't met your match… Here's an easy way for you to get one:
Stop looking for one. Seriously. As soon as you stop searching for a partner, *twelve* will show up at your door (– with a limo and tickets to box seats at the Super Bowl).

GET THEIR ATTENTION

How? By acting like you don't want their attention. Read on.

Following is the advice I gave to my friend, Pete, when he was going through a financial slump and bummed about being single. He followed the advice and suddenly he was in the center of a female feeding frenzy.

When you see someone that you would normally want to make a move on – or think about making a move on – DON'T do it. Fight the urge at all costs. When they think you are not interested, you will have the upper hand. Whether they want your attention or not, if they see that you are not into them, your interactions will have a completely different dynamic. (Most of us can tell when we are appealing to someone. So if our usual appeal doesn't work on you, we'll see that you're different and that will intrigue us.) Don't get me wrong, you shouldn't be too stand-offish, just politely *distracted*.

Try this. Be happy and friendly to *anyone* you interact with – without any strings attached. One way to do this – and the most effective – is by imagining that you have the greatest mate imaginable waiting for you at home. This is how you can come across as ultra appealing but not needy. That will show in your actions and then people will be interested in you. Try to present an attitude that says, "Wow, you are great and if I weren't already hooked up with perfection, we'd hop on a plane and go to Rio!"

Live your life for *30 DAYS* without any intent of *checking out* or meeting someone and see what happens. Keep thinking happy thoughts and coast along with no worries but to *brighten the day of everyone you pass.* Make that your only goal for 30 days. Every time you pass your reflection, stand tall, think back to a great, frisky & flirty memory and plant that comfy grin on your face. Keep the thought and the grin on. Start smiling at and saying HI to every female you see – short, tall, skinny, fat, all ages, all colors – every single female you encounter. (Say HI to the guys as practice, but really try to make a simple connection with the females as you say 'hello' to them.)

Remember: No checking out ANY girls – to ANY degree for 30 days...

SIDENOTE: If your attention causes someone to come on to you (invite you for coffee, ask for your email address) but you aren't as interested in her, welcome it anyway. Be her friend. If it won't physically hurt you, or cost you a million bucks, do it. You can talk and still only be 'flirty friendly' without leading her on. I recommend this for two reasons. One: because if you do not respond to her harmless little invite like this, it can hurt her feelings or make her lose face - especially if you turn her down in front of anyone. That will ultimately make you look bad to the women who see. Two: because it will teach you how to be friends with girls. This is very important. The more female friends you have, the more females will see you as a guy with 'something'. So play along – from a friendly, smiling distance - keeping her a little hopeful – but in a very gentlemanly way. (And start collecting female *friends*. You can gain untold fortunes by being on a friends-only basis with women.)

Here's the deal, you want for EVERY woman – the perfect ones and the not so perfect ones - to think you are a total sweetheart of a guy. Flirt with ALL women. It's flattering to them, and THAT will make YOU feel great, plus you will learn a lot about reading their feelings from seeing their responses. Do it in front of all your guy buddies, too. If they diss you for flirting with a non-hottie, diss them for being *shallow*. (You are just doing your homework... but remember that flirting should always be fun for the 2 people doing it. If it gets un-fun, it ain't flirtin'.)

As far as the *specific type* you are attracted to, keep in mind that you may be cutting your own throat by being so picky in your preferences anyway. Not that you are alone in this – or that it's a shallow trait to prefer a certain look or personality. But I know that it's very common for girls to become attracted to guys with whom they've previously had zero physical pull - until they got to know them a bit. This happens with you guys, too, so open your mind. Become friends and see what happens after you get beyond the 'she's not my type' thing.

If you're broke beyond belief, but still hoping to connect, here are a few suggestions that may help save some of your cash. Try making offers like, "Hey, I was planning to take a walk around downtown tonight. You wanna join me?" A night in a great city or town is perfect for window shopping, exploring, looking in people's windows (kidding), etc... and it's totally FREE. (Go explore your city and find the great walks, best time of the evening for sunsets, nicest places to catch a good view of the city lights, moon and stars, criminal activity. Whatever. Check it out before introducing/exposing a guest to it.)

Other cheap/free date options:
- ♥ A scenic drive, but with gas prices – I hope you have a Prius.
- ♥ Watching DVDs is pretty inexpensive if you go light on the food and wine or beer. (For healthier popcorn, avoid the microwaveable stuff. Get some Jiffy Pop, or a jar of popcorn and *an old fashioned AIR POPPER*.)
- ♥ Going for coffee won't break you.
- ♥ A stroll thru a city park is relaxing.
- ♥ A nice hotel lobby is a great place to sit and gab. Just don't be tempted by those elevators that are waiting to take you up to a *room*.
- ♥ A visit to Baskin Robbins won't break your bank (but may blow up your belly).
- ♥ Museums are usually free - or they will ask for a donation. To be safe, call ahead and ask if there is an entrance fee or what a typical and fair donation is. *Donating is like TIPPING – and your date is watching…
- ♥ Concerts in the park are free so watch for notices about upcoming music events.

FYI – always watch your local newspaper's Community Calendar and postings for local events. Keeps tabs on local bulletin boards where you can find quirky small scale events nearby. This way you will always have access to something inexpensive but entertaining to check out with a date. Community playhouses and small theaters often present shows that are fun and *cheap*.

Try asking women 'out' in a way that is completely *not asking them out*... and very non-committal. Let them know (enthusiastically) what you are planning to do later, and let them know that they could join you if they want. "Hey! I'm headed over to the Silverbow Cafe. At eight they're showing Casa Blanca (Reservior Dogs, Plan 9 From Outer Space) on the back wall. Would you like to join me?" If she declines, then smile and say, "No worries. Head over if you change your mind... I'll be there." She probably will - because you let her know that you are going there anyway - whether she goes or not - and your delivery actually implies that it doesn't matter to you if she shows up or not. People often like this 'no pressure' kind of approach.

Just be careful not to be too nonchalant. That can come across as arrogant or sore-loser-like... which is another reason your constant smile and friendliness is important. There is nothing worse than a transparent man with a bruised ego. If she says "NO", you don't ever want to say "FINE. I have people meeting me there anyway..." like you could care less. You should look like you care, but in a good way. You'd say, "OK... Well – have a great night! I'll tell you how it ends... ☺"

Like I said, Pete took this advice and it completely re-charged his batteries. You are more likely to attract someone if you are not trying to attract them.

a. Learn to FLIRT

Do you remember teasing the cute girl with the freckles and the long ponytail in 1st grade? Well, teasing *grew up to be* flirting.

Are you a flirt? Well – you need to be! Flirting is your key to appeal – which is the most important issue with regard to your *dating success*. Flirting is simply good natured teasing. It makes everyone feel good so you need to be doing it.

My neighbor, Vince, is a chronic flirt. No kidding - if it's sitting still – and he's awake – he is totally flirting with it; my dog, your grandmother, even the guy selling hot dogs on the corner. He doesn't flirt in a slimy way that's loaded with sexual innuendos. It's ONLY about making the person he's flirting with feel good. I call it *good natured teasing* and just to give you an idea of things he might say, here are some examples:

• To my dog as he pets her: "Hey Bailey! How's your love life? See any great looking legs that you'd like to settle down with today?" (OK – slight sexual innuendo there...)

• To your Grandmother: Hi Mrs. Thomas! You look *especially terrific* today... What's up? Do you have a boyfriend hidden around here someplace?"

• To the hot dog guy: Hey – it's the King of Great Hot Dogs - how's your day? Why don't you open a restaurant so that I can eat one of these amazing creations over candlelight with a date?"

Anyway, when Vince flirts with me, it prompts me to flirt back, so when we hang out, I shine and I know it. This is a great tool for me to tap into later. Whenever I need to put on some charm, I think of my last interaction with Vince to feel that flirty appeal again, and then I can pull rabbits out of hats.

So let me recommend that whenever you need to shine, you think of a moment when you know you were *totally ON*. And I DO NOT mean when you were feeling cocky or cool. I mean when you were feeling friendly and APPEALING. (Cocky and cool aren't bad things, but they can both be intimidating – or a total *turn-off* depending on the *over exaggeration level*). Friendly and appealing are welcoming and will pull people in to you. Any guy with a clearly friendly attitude is charming and *very attractive*.

There's a book called "Flirting 101". You should pick it up and learn that flirting can create *sex appeal*, but can also attract ANYONE. Not only does a flirty approach work in romantic pursuits, but it works in business, it works in family – especially with kids – *ref. Bill Cosby* – and in all of our interactions. Remember that flirting does not have to be sexual or romantic. (One of my best friends is a certified matchmaker and I can tell you that if she is not alone in a room, she is flirting. Everyone LOVES to be around her. She flirts with anyone from 3-year-olds to 90-year-olds and I can tell you that she always gets whatever she wants or needs from them!)

b. Just Ask
Wayne Gretzke said: "You will miss 100% of the shots you don't take." What does this mean to you? It means that if you don't ask, then the answer is always "NO."

There are around 6 billion people on this Earth. I'm pretty sure that 1 or 2 could be available and right for a relationship with you. But in order to meet the right person, you've got to put a smile on your face and get yourself out there. If you don't, the answer is <u>NO</u> for sure, and you get to be single for the rest of your life. Yippee.

If you've spotted someone you would like to meet and possibly ask out, don't waste days or weeks worrying about how to approach that person or what you should say. (Remember, people are naturally pretty aggressive these days, so I doubt you'll have to do all the work yourself.) Just prepare a quick, easy script in your head to open the conversation (more about that soon), then go up and say "Hi."

<u>Just do it</u>. Because if you continue to drool from afar, this person is sure to see that you are a drooler. Then we've entered into that stray-dog syndrome and you'll end up getting sympathy or pity and maybe a treat from your target and that's all. (Hey – this is a great opportunity for you to use your *testosterone*.) Go ahead and approach this person, because being watched too intently by an obvious chicken will creep most people out.

What's the worst thing that can happen? You'll get a "no." So what? *Can you say, <u>nnnnnext</u>?* Or maybe you'll get laughed at. *OHMYGOD!* Stop it! We talked about your self-confidence earlier. You know you can deal with getting laughed at – no problem, right? Good. Go up and start a conversation.

By walking over and talking to someone you'd like to meet, you probably will gain the respect of this person fast because you have proven that you possess the #1 requirement for charm: Self-confidence. If, when you approach someone, you are blown off right away, don't let it get to you. Keep smiling, be friendly and move on. It's *their* loss – not yours.

Of course, not everyone will respond to your attention with class. Some people are idiots, so if you happen to ask an idiot out, and they say "What? With *you*? Did you bump your head?"… then your response to them could be "You're right. *What ever* was I thinking?" They will look bad, not you. Most people will respond politely, even if they aren't interested in a date with you. Yet.

Either way, if you make a **good first impression,** then you have left the door open for them to come in later if they change their mind and decide to check you out a little closer. If I were you, I'd be really nice to everyone, considering the possibility of having a friendship with them. Contrary to popular *guy belief*, a friendship with someone you have the hots for is not a bad thing.

> "I'm comfortable being single. I may fall in love again — but for those who are listening to Bruce Willis — any relationship that isn't founded on friendship is just doomed."
> -Bruce Willis

(Many of the best — and hottest — relationships begin as *friendships*.)

When you go up to someone, be sure you are friendly and polite enough that they could imagine saying "Hi" and talking with you if they run into you again. Also, even if *that person* isn't into you, they may know of *someone else* who might be --- or they may decide they'd like to get to know you LATER. Make sure to mention your first name either at the start of your conversation or before you walk away.

> "Always remember that today's NO could be tomorrow's YES."
> -Marketing Guru, Steve Harrison

(Hey – it's *all* about sales…)

STARTING A CONVERSATION

If you have your eye on someone you would like to meet/date, don't start the introduction by handing over your business card. Meeting someone you may want a personal relationship with is not a business transaction, and even though you are basically trying to *make a sale*, your target shouldn't see it that way. If this person asks for your phone number, ask if your business card is OK. Of course it will be, but you don't want to come across as someone who throws his card out to everyone. Not in this instant anyway.

OK, here's an example of an embarrassingly *unsuccessful* two-way conversation – starring you. *You're at the gym. You see someone on the free weights. So you walk over and …*

You say: Hi. I'm Schmoo.

Response: I'm Kelly.

You say: Nice to meet you. Hey, I was wondering if you've tried the spin class?

Kelly: Yeah I have.

You say:	Really? How's the instructor?
Kelly:	Good.
You:	Right on. Guess I'll give it a try. Thanks for the input. (As you're walking away)
Kelly:	Yeah — no problem.
You :	Enjoy your workout, Kelly. (Said over your shoulder.)
Kelly:	You, too.

So this lifeless conversation didn't get anywhere did it? Well, that's what you think. In reality, you have just established yourself as a nice, self-confident and harmless guy to Kelly. So at the very least, the next time the two of you cross paths, you can say *in passing*, "Hey Kelly. How's it going?" Also, you ended the conversation first, so Kelly didn't need to worry about how to get away from you – if getting away from you was Kelly's goal, that is. This was very safe for Kelly and totally un-needy, un-drooly and un-desperate of you.

Also, you did not use Kelly's name until the conversation was over. That's because when you first meet people, using their name – more than once while you talk – can sound like you're trying to prove that you remembered it. Or you are wanting to get in there a little too close. Then there's a chance that you'll sound like that Used Car Guy in the plaid sportcoat. (Sorry Used Car Guys, but you know that *some of you come across as pushy beyond belief*.)

Whenever you would like to get someone's attention - in the grocery store or on the street – just look at them directly as you smile and say, "Hi, how are ya?" <u>as you walk by</u>. You've made polite contact and it could pay off later. Always keep walking unless that person *stops you*. In this scenario, you are basically making a *cold call*. Don't ever stop and corner someone or put anyone on the spot hoping that a relationship will begin right then and there. Just casually say "hello" and <u>keep walking</u>.

Perhaps the key to speaking to someone for the first time is realizing that you are not up in front of 400 people. You're simply speaking to another human being. Relax. Even if you're told to go jump in the lake, you can smile and say, "Sure thing – *I'll get right on it*." At least you tried.

If someone really dumps on you or puts you down, simply say, "Wow. Whatever." Never say anything like, "Oh yeah? Well F- you, too." Don't lower yourself to some bitchy, crappy level. Just think about how much you DON'T want to know that person. Think of it this way: getting spanked the first time you approach someone is actually <u>that person</u> doing <u>you</u> a favor. You want nothing to do with this person. And you would much rather see this "bitch" side of them in the first two minutes of your relationship than in the seventh week or eighth month, right?

And remember that if at first you don't succeed, (then sky-diving's probably not for you) go try again. Soon you'll meet your match.

c. Ace Your First Date With Someone New

A first date can be like a walk through the park or a tumble down a steep embankment. Decide which yours will be. Either way, wear comfy shoes.

DATING DEAL-BREAKERS! WARNING!

I'll get right to the point with the most important issues:

- **Your cell phone** – turn it off, don't put it on the table, don't check it periodically, don't even let your date know that you *have* one.
- **Bad personal hygiene** – too much cologne, body odor, dirty hands/fingernails, greasy skin or hair, dirty clothes. (Shower and clean up before any date. Brush your teeth, too.)
- **Bad table manners** – chewing with your mouth open or talking with your mouth full, sloppy eating habits (spilling or dripping as you eat), pigging out (have a snack before a date so that you're not starving), *holding your silverware like a little kid (see diagram on page 4).*
- **Bad conversation** – talking non-stop about yourself (how great you are, how many amazing things you've done, how much money you make), talking about your ex – good or bad talk.
- **Bad tipping** – leaving less than 15 or 20 percent.
- **Rudeness** – treating your server or anyone else rudely.
- **Flirting** – with anyone that is not your date.
- **Getting drunk** – there is no recovery from this.
- **A nasty vehicle** – with a dirty interior, dirty windows, etc.
- **Not opening doors for your date** – car doors, all doors.

Like I said, these are *deal-breakers*. These are the reason you won't get a second date, or anything else.

Now relax. Your first date with someone should be very casual. As a matter of fact, don't even call it a real date. I'm going to suggest that you simply plan to meet for coffee or snacks. Find a nice little spot, like the café or coffee shop in a bookstore such as Barnes & Noble, Books-A-Million or Borders, and offer to meet there. (Have a nearby backup location in mind, in case you arrive at the café to find that it is too crowded or closed.)

A Saturday mid-afternoon around 2 or 3, is typically good for a first meeting, because it can slide into dinner and even a whole evening together if you both seem to sense that things are going really well. But that will happen on a wait-and-see basis, so go slowly. Spend at least an hour talking and getting to know this person.

LOOKIN' LIKE A DATE MISTAKE? If things obviously head south after your first cup of coffee (order decaf if caffeine makes you edgy) still remember that the most important thing is that you relax and maintain your charm. Even if in the first 5 seconds you feel like you've bitten into an apple to discover half a worm inside, be an awesome guy anyway. Remember, you want the entire world to know you are a charming guy — and it will — especially if you can keep a smile on your face and a positive attitude **when you know there is half a worm in your mouth.**

Important: instead of feeling that the time you spend with a disappointing date is a waste, think of it as practice for future dates. Your image is a big deal, so you need to be sure that the reports about you that follow any date are great. That'll always happen if you are a nice guy – no matter how the meeting turns out.

If you immediately decide that this isn't going to happen, and you want to start inching toward the door now, <u>don't</u>. Be charming for the hour you have dedicated to this rendezvous – and chill. It will be over soon enough, and it won't hurt you to act charming – even if you feel the person is a total snore or worse. Practice asking questions - making conversation. Use the opportunity to become a <u>really great date guy</u>. You never know what may come of your hour with this person in the form of a terrific friendship or other good connections.

Honesty is great, and I highly recommend it. But don't drop the "Uh, you're just not my type" bomb. That could be painful news for the date, especially if the person really likes *you*. Be friendly, finish your coffee time and say it was nice seeing them. If you need a comfortable way to walk away, you could add that maybe you'll see them again sometime.

Here's a tip that you may choke on, but give it a try anyway: *Call your date the next day and say "thanks."* I know. If you don't want to go there again then you're probably thinking, "No way! Why would I do that?"

Here's why: Because even if you weren't impressed, you want to be a real charmer. So calling the next day will show true charm. Like 007 charm. (If when you call, you are asked about getting together again, just say that you probably shouldn't make any plans right now and that maybe you can talk later.) For sure, people will talk about what a great guy you are if you can get in the habit of doing things like this.

> SCUMBAG ALERT: One night I drove a young girl home from a restaurant. She was a stranger to me. She had a tiny baby with her, and she was overweight, but as my friends and I had our dinner, I witnessed her date abandon her there. When I offered her a ride, I discovered that it had been a blind date. Yeah, yeah. I know. She had a baby and she was overweight. Not the most appealing situation for many guys, but I defy you to prove that ANYONE deserves to be left alone like that. Get real. She cried all the way home. That guy who left her there is going to get his someday. **(I hope it makes the papers.)**

I suggested to her, that in the future, she avoid blind dates, and that on *any date*, she should hope for the best but plan for the worst. This will keep her from getting her hopes up and her feelings hurt.

Clue in to this, gentlemen. You have someone in your life that matters a lot to you, right? A mom, a sister, a best friend, a daughter, or *your Grandma.* Someone that you love and care a lot about? OK. You would never want to see this person hurt, right? So when you are with someone that doesn't appeal to you, just think of your own special person and be sure to treat the person you're with, the way that you would want for *your special person* to be treated. With respect and politeness. Not left alone and crying at a sushi bar. Good grief.

A BLIND DATE
*Remember this: If it's a **blind date**, always hope for the best but be prepared for the worst.* If the first sight of your blind date makes you wish you were blind, smile and be friendly and warm anyway. Do not ever treat someone badly because you aren't into the way they look. If you want to be charming, then you'll treat everyone you meet like you are <u>into</u> <u>everything</u> <u>about</u> <u>them</u>. Remember that a person's looks may tell you nothing about what's inside them.

Looks are a very small and superficial part of us. (If you can allow yourself to be attracted to someone because you really like who lives inside, without regard to their looks, then, Dude, step into the phone booth, and don't come out until there are two of you.)

> **"A wise man looks for what is within. The fool looks for what is outside."**   **-Yep. CONFUCIOUS said it.**

If you see someone you know while you are with an unattractive 'date' in public, hold your head up, smile, be positive and act like you are with the greatest person in the Western Hemisphere. Introduce the person, and if you can't remember the name of the person you've bumped into, present your date's name anyway. Just say "Hey! I'd like you to meet _____," (then your friend can relay his or her own name to your 'date'.)

Looking like you're happy about introducing this person, who may not be so hot to look at, will make you look like a really cool guy to both your date *and* to the person you've bumped into. If you act embarrassed, then you will show everyone that you are a jerk who judges people by their looks. And don't try to hide from, or act like you don't see the person who has spotted you. Very bad move. Obvious, too. This means you've been caught with someone you are embarrassed about being seen with and you'll never redeem yourself. Again, be enthusiastic in the introduction, no matter how you're really feeling, because if you aren't into your date, *nobody should know it.*

> Rent the movie "Shallow Hal" and get a clue from Hal. Be a charming gentleman no matter what. This will make you look great. (If you have a buddy like the Jason Alexander guy in that movie, you need to upgrade your buddies now. **I wanted to push him into traffic.**)

Again, regardless of whether things are looking good or looking bad at the start, always give your date the benefit of the doubt and try to stay for at least an hour. I'll repeat the caffeine thing – because you want to make a great impression, and if you get pumped or edgy on caffeine then you'll compete for *talk time* with your date. The first time you meet someone, you should hand over the microphone.

Just listen. Ask easy questions about your date (to keep them talking). That can help you figure out if the two of you are a possible match for a real date in the future. Try to show real interest in the person without coming across as *what's in this for me?*

WHERE TO TAKE A DATE

The *bistro* or the *bowling alley*? When you go on a *real date*, consider the atmosphere of the place you choose. Try to find a spot that's not too quiet, because a little noise and activity around you will be more relaxing for you both. Also remember that the foods you eat with your hands, such as burgers, sandwiches, ribs, chicken or pizza, can be messy and difficult for you to eat without looking like a toddler with Spaghettios. On one hand, that could be fun, but on the other hand, you may end up looking like a toddler with Spaghettios.

PICKING UP THE CHECK

Who's buying? Oh, I know. You are. As I mentioned in Chapter 1, if you ask someone out, *you are paying for everything*. It's the LAW. I know. It's not fair but it's the way things must be. Perhaps not every woman will admit this preference to you (plus there always exceptions), but plenty have admitted it to *each other* after your date. It is an *expected tradition*, stinky or not. So on the first few dates (3-5), unless you find yourself Powerslammed or in a Full Nelson, be sure YOU pick up the tab. If you decide that you do not want to impress your date, and on that date is NOT where you want to be, pay anyway. Consider it practice. Or feeding the Karma Bears.

As you are getting more comfortable with someone after 4 or 5 dates, you should start coming up with date ideas and things to do that don't cost a lot or are free. A drive through the country, a walk thru the park, a stroll around downtown, pizza and a DVD at your place (but don't expect sex just because your couch is handy. Follow your date's lead but feel free to say *'not yet'* if they get pushy about sex. If you are not ready to commit to that, then don't have sex.). Going for coffee is another option that is not likely to cost you a fortune. Even a visit to a bakery or a Baskin & Robbins can be a less expensive, fun option. (You'll get *fat* but you won't get *broke*.)

DO NOT 'GO DUTCH' OR 'SPLIT THE CHECK'

Yet. Hopefully, at some point the new person you are dating will say, "Let me buy this time". But when they do, *JUST SAY "NO"*. (Some girls will set this trap, so don't fall into it. They may offer to buy – but it may just mean that you are being tested. If you are strong and resist the urge to let them pay, you are *Batman*. If you gladly accept their offer to pay – then you are *The Joker*. Buh-bye.) The good news is that by buying, you are looking impressive. This is a hot topic among females. It's usually the first indicator of what can be expected in a new relationship and women like to talk about this buying/tipping thing all the time. Sorry if this is the first you've heard of it…

> My guy friend, Devon, came out with my girlfriends and me one night. It was his first time. He had never sat at a table full of females where he was not on a date or in a relationship with one. We spared him no embarrassment and talked about everything – all of our usual guy subjects – in front of him. He sat there the whole time, leaning in and wide-eyed just like a 1st grader learning to catch tadpoles. He even called us the next day to say **"thanks!"** (And **"wow…"**) If you ever have the opportunity to 'hang out' with some female friends, jump on it. **You'll learn more than you would in a semester at M.I.T.**

If your date insists on paying, say this: "No, I asked YOU out. If you would like to ask ME out sometime, go ahead, and I will let you buy THEN." If they try to get you to split the check, give the same response, but add, "If you want to treat or go Dutch next time, we can plan to do that. But I am paying for this one." Trust me here, guys. *Don't even allow them to leave the tip.* Don't allow your date to pay for <u>anything</u>. If you allow them to pay, then your date may guess you are a wimp, weasel or tight-wad in other aspects. I'm not saying that you have to pay for *everything*, all the time. Not EVEN. Just that you need to show your date that you are decisive and confident, and that you will not buckle on this issue. Sometimes it's really good to hear, "I insist". This would be one of those times.

TIPPING –

Size matters – *where tipping is concerned*. Again, we talked about this in Chapter 1: A HUGE factor as your date 'grades' you, comes in the form of the size tip you leave your server. (Don't groan as I point out that you are being *graded*. You know that you are *grading* your date, too. I'm just giving you some serious insider information here. Run with it or not.) Your date may have worked in the service industry at some point. And if you don't tip well, your date will inevitably think," *Yuck.* He's one of *those* guys…"

My friends and I watched a couple in a restaurant one night on what was obviously a *great first date*. They were totally into each other – really hitting it off as they laughed and talked for hours. But after the server came back with their tab, you could see her eyes zeroing in on the price of the dinner and she was CLEARLY turned off by the inadequate tip he left. The apparent chill that came from her frosted the whole place. We were pretty sure that *that* date ended early. I think the girl suddenly came down with the flu, remembered that she had to pick up her Aunt Lulu at the airport, or heard her mommy calling.

> I've seen women dig into their purses for cash to add to a guy's small tip. That is bad. If the service was great, leave 20%. If it was obviously rotten, leave less. But remember that anyone will be impressed when they see you leave a good tip even if the service **stunk** excessively. If your date asks why you would leave a good tip for such crappy service, just say, "Maybe it will encourage them to get better." (Then watch your date get all over you like... snakes on a plane.)

If you aren't sure about how much to leave, ask your date what they thought of the service and how much they think you should leave. I can tell you for sure that your date would rather have you ask them about it and prove that you are an open-minded, not-afraid-to-ask-for-someone-else's-opinion type of guy, than see you leave a crap tip. (There are credit card sized *tip calculation* cards that you can keep in your wallet. Order a few for you and your buddies from www.tipping.org.) Your tiny tips will tell a lot about you, and can make your date assume that there is no fun in a future with you because you won't part with your cash. So boys, unless the service completely sucked and you both know it, leave 15% to 20%. Otherwise, don't blame me when you don't get a 2nd date – or even the time of day - because bad tipping is usually a complete and total deal-breaker.

> FYI - If you are looking to SAVE money, leaving inadequate tips isn't the way to do it. I'm thinking that **dating** is probably not the best way to do it, either. Being alone is cheaper than not being alone – even you're Charles Schwab person will probably tell you that, regardless of tax issues. Dating and relationships definitely have fees attached, so consider your goals and decide whether <u>your</u> goal is to invest in your future love life and family (which <u>will</u> <u>happily</u> wrap it's arms around you everyday - **if you're a great husband and daddy)** or loading up your bank account (which <u>can't</u> wrap it's arms around you everyday - **but can pay for someone to do it...**).

(GOLDDIGGERS. *Beware of these alley cats.* There are plenty of people out there who are looking for a free ride. Not everyone is out to spend all of your money, but here's my advice if you aren't sure about someone's motives with your wallet: Give them a ride for as long as you want, then either end the ride or make them drive. If you have paid for 4 or more dates and they have made no effort to buy, or chip in, then start leaving your money at home (keep only enough for cab fare in your pocket) and find some activities that are free or very cheap. Hiking, biking, DVDs at home. If they aren't into you unless you are spending money on them, *why would you want them anyway?*)

> If you DO decide on the love and family thing, do your part to make sure yours is a **premium relationship**. Be sure you really DO invest in making it GREAT - because a **mediocre** r'ship can really suck especially when you are still paying for it... (then it's like making payments on a wrecked car.)
> Remember this word: **effort, effort, effort,** because everything good in life requires a lot of it from you.

If your date wants to have you over and prepare a meal for you...

When someone invites you over for dinner, offer to buy the groceries. Ask for the shopping list – a detailed shopping list complete with package/container size, lowfat or non-fat, with or without skin, wheat, white, kosher or not, organic, processed or still swimming. Remember that 'baked beans' to you may mean 'baked beans', but to your date it may mean Bush's Homestyle Baked Beans Seasoned With Bacon, Onion and Brown Sugar. Duh! You didn't know that?

Perhaps the two of you can go buy the groceries for dinner – together. If so, be sure you pay. Explain by saying, *"the least I can do, since you are making this fabulous home cooked meal for me, is buy the food"*. THIS WILL SCORE <u>MORE</u> MAJOR POINTS FOR YOU. In case the groceries have already been purchased, ask what type of dessert or wine you can pick up. Again, ask for details of their preferences. You wouldn't want to show up with the mighty *Silver Oak* if all your date is hoping for is a nice little *Turning Leaf*.

Wherever you end up, never complain about the service, the food, the atmosphere, high prices, or anything else while you're there. Save it. *Your date needs to see your positive side.* So let them see how well you deal with a crappy situation if you're stuck in one. Smile anyway. (But not with parsley in your teeth.)

> **Remember that most of us are great at smooth sailing.** The true test is how we deal with the rough waters. So when you aren't getting what you want or expect, stay calm and cool anyway. No temper tantrums starring **you** allowed. Especially on a first date.

You, acting like an ass/jerk/idiot because things don't go as planned or because your server has never had a job before this one, will only make you look like... uh, an ass/jerk/idiot. Be kind and understanding. Nobody's going to die over bad service.

Encourage your date to order anything they want. When the check arrives, place it directly in front of you until you're ready to pay (this tells your date and your server that YOU are paying). Also, after your meal, excuse yourself to the restroom to check your teeth for pepper, seeds or Spaghettios. **Lettuce pasted to a tooth when you talk will prevent your date *from hearing anything you say.***

If it becomes clear that your date is not into you, hold onto your charm anyway. Be polite and consider this as more practice. Keep the spotlight on your date, asking easy questions until the torture session is over. And don't let the fact that this person isn't interested in you mess with your self-confidence. If the person isn't into you, it's that person's loss. Soon you'll get with someone who is totally into you.

d. To Speak or Not to Speak (& the 6 Great Date Questions)

Here's something that people always say about charming guys: "Oh my God, he is so sweet and so interesting*!" How would they know he's interesting? He never got a word in edgewise... But you can see how he fooled them — simply by listening to them.*

The guy is 'charming' because he let the other person gab on and on and on about themselves. So I repeat, in your conversation with your date, keep the focus on that person. As you've read in earlier chapters, people LOVE to talk about themselves. If you show interest in hearing about them and NOT talking about yourself, you've already scored huge points. Ask them about the lightweight, fun stuff – like where they grew up, if they like to travel, where they've been, and where they'd like to go.

Here are a few key tips to a positive conversation:
- As you and your date talk, remember to ask questions about what's been said. This shows you are listening AND interested.
- Keep your eyes on your date. Don't let whatever is going on around the two of you take away your focus.
- As you are talking and getting to know each other, use your date's name periodically. (We all like to know that we are the center of your attention, and as you use our name while we talk, we'll know that we are.)

- You also can use the following positive comebacks:
  "You're right."
  "Great idea."
  "I agree."
  "Hmmm, I never thought of it that way."
  "That's interesting."
  "Good point."

These comments are encouraging, and they'll make your date feel like you understand their message while the two of you talk. (Of course there are many added benefits if you <u>do</u> understand their message — so <u>really</u> listen.)

- *Don't forget that you should never talk about a past relationship or partner.* **Whether it was a great experience or a nightmare on wheels. A date may be insecure enough at this point without having to be compared to that perfect (in your dreams) person from your past.**

- Keep up on what's going on in the world by regularly reading the paper or watching the news, so that you are awake at the wheel and knowledgeable in your conversations.

- Since you are basically *interviewing* your date, your date may be interviewing you, too. So be at your best.

- I've stated that you should focus on your date and try to keep the majority of the talk time on that person. But if you do find the spotlight is on you, and your date doesn't show that same respect, courtesy and interest in listening to you as you did, then maybe its curb time for them. You'll need to figure that one out as it unfolds.

- Asking about your date's first job is usually good to lighten the mood and help the conversation loosen up. And that can really help if the conversation starts to lag. That's partly because it will usually take someone longer to explain than current 'career' questions. Lots of other memories of the person's past will surface while recollecting that first job, and you'll probably learn a lot about the person. That means a lot more spotlight time for your date. Yay! And talking about first jobs can be relaxing and even humorous sometimes (unless the person is still at it), and it can take you both all the way back to high school or college. Or McDonald's. Wherever.

The 6 Great Date Questions

Here are a few questions that can really help you get to know your date and keep the talk interesting and fun:

1. Ask about the person's all-time favorite movie – music (CD or album) and book, too.
2. Ask who they would pick, if they could meet and spend a day with anyone *in history*, alive or dead, and why.
3. Ask what 3 things your date would do first with the money, if they suddenly received a million dollars.
4. Ask what your date would grab (other than a person or pet) if they woke up to discover that their house was on fire.
5. Ask what is their favorite animal in the world, and why.
6. Ask your date to describe their perfect Saturday morning.

Asking someone to explain a most embarrassing moment can loosen things up, too. Be sure you volunteer to share yours, as well. This type of open conversation can build trust and make two people feel like they've known each other a lot longer than an hour or a day.

e. A Summary of *1st Date* Guidelines

1. Use your date's name periodically as you talk.
2. Talk about foods, cooking and restaurants – they're easy subjects.
3. Don't talk too much about yourself. Spotlight your date.
4. Avoid controversial subjects like the death penalty or Roe vs. Wade.
5. If the date is an obvious mistake, treat your date like **royalty** anyway.
6. **Stay off your cell phone** – *turn it off*.
7. If *you have agreed* to a blind date, be ready for *ANYTHING*.
8. Be sure to introduce your date if you run into anyone you know.
9. Avoid caffeine if you must, to stay relaxed.

10. Smile, keep a positive attitude and make positive comments.
11. Be *nice* and diplomatic if you talk about past relationships.
12. Give compliments, but not too many.
13. Pay attention to topics that your date seems to like talking about, and stay close to them.
14. Always offer to order appetizers and dessert.
15. If you have a pet, mention it to your date *now* to avoid surprises later… just in case you're engaged to a hunter or an alergy sufferer by midnight.
16. Always grab the check with a smile. Be quick. *Don't split it.*
17. Leave a good tip. 15-20%.
18. Do not flirt with *anyone* other than your date.
19. If you go to a show or concert, offer to buy a souvenir for your date.
20. Never have sex on a first date. Sorry. (Never.) (Never.) (Never.)
21. Did I mention that you should never have sex on a first date?
22. No sex.

(**Guys be warned!** # 17 and 18 can be complete and total deal breakers.)

Here is a Top Ten *'Don't You Dare'* list - with regard to dating (this from AskMen.com):

DO NOT:
10. Use cheesy pick up lines. (Like: Who stole the stars and put them in your eyes?) *Gaaaaag.* Speaking of the Death Penalty…
9. Continually use profanity or bad language.
8. Make ANY noises with your body.
7. Talk on and on about yourself.
6. Constantly put a 'sexual' spin on any subject.
5. Get drunk.
4. Stare and drool over your date's body (or anyone else's).
3. Make fun of your date's friends or family. (Or anyone.)
2. Brag about whatever (or whoever) you've done.
1. Stare at or hit on someone else in front of your date.

Also, here are the 3 things you should *never* ask or say:

1. "What is that scar from?"
2. "I'll never get married (again)."
3. "Your friend is *hot.* "

(Thanks to my brilliant friend, Heidi, for those.)

This reminds me of my two hot friends, Laurie and Kristi. A guy had asked Laurie out to dinner (we'll refer to him as Clueless Guy #1), and wondered if she had a girlfriend that might be interested in a double-date with his buddy (now known as Clueless Guy #2). So Laurie called Kristi with the invitation and the four of them went out. Cool. Everyone was having fun until one of the girls got up to leave the table for a moment. At that time, her friend's date gave her what I'm sure he would refer to as 'just a friendly little pat on the butt'. Hmmm.

OK – first of all, on a first date, a guy should never assume that it's OK for him to touch his date's butt. Second, he should *really* never assume that it's OK for him to touch her friend's butt. No matter how many Grandes or bottles of Dom have been consumed, *do not smack anyone on the butt*.

"IF ONLY I'D MET YOU FIRST..."

Guys – I hate to be the bearer of bad news here (though I'm sure you're starting to get used to it), but I must point out the obvious and tell you that when you are in a new relationship, *you should not flirt with any of her friends*. This act is right above **bad tipping** on the loser list. You may be intrigued by (or totally ga-ga over) her friend or sister but do not trip on your tongue there. Stay focused on *your girl*. Many guys go through this "Uh, did I pick the wrong one?" flirtation phase, but press on. It's not unusual and you'll get over it.

In case you don't get over it and the intensity of your *hots* for the other girl is giving you a rash... then end the current relationship, wait a few weeks and go for the other one. Be prepared to die, but go for it if you must. Bottom line – girls have *other girl radar* and if you are into *any other female*, your girl will pick it up on her scope. Get over it and block it out forever or jump ship and hope the other girl will throw you a rope. Slim chance due to friendship loyalty, so don't say I didn't warn you if you find you've sunk to the bottom of Lake High and Dry.

If that hot friend happens to come on to you, just say NO. At the very least, just say NO – not yet. Then get out of the current relationship, and slowly get into the next (and hope you've made the right choice.)

f. A Message for Superman

Don't believe that you can change someone else's bad habits or change them into the person you want them to be. In other words, don't believe that you can cause a sexy new leopard to suddenly change its spots.

Although you and I know that you are special and amazing, this new leopard doesn't know that yet, so why would it change for you? Yet?

Guys (like girls – we're all guilty of this) notoriously believe that when they see a 'red flag' surface with a new partner in the early stages of the relationship, that *they* (guys) can fix the source of the red flag. A guy thinks he can change this person, and that whatever the unappealing issue may be that this new person has revealed, will miraculously go away now that this person has met *him*. Uh, where did this absurd idea come from? (Picture a spotted hippopotamus sprouting wings and a pink tutu and fluttering through the air, happily delivering chocolate-covered refund checks from the IRS to *everyone*. Because your ability to change someone who doesn't WANT to change, is about as likely as that.)

Believe me. I'm a female. I know about this. We've been trying and failing at changing YOU for centuries. *But you are open-minded now, aren't you?* So. If your new partner has an obvious flaw, like is a chronic flirt, is jealous or suspicious of everything you do, won't get off the cell phone, spends way too much of *your* money, tells lies or pees on the carpet, don't believe you can change or fix the defect.

There's a very slim chance that you are this person's first relationship, or the behavior in question simply developed overnight because the planets lined up. Or because this person decided to do it because they thought you might like it. Right. Whatever is occurring, they've likely done it before. This may just be their standard *M.O.* That warning also applies to a person's approach to sex with you.

If sex happens soon after you shake hands, don't believe that you, Master of the Universe, are the only guy who has charmed this person into the **whorizontal bone dance** so quickly. Not likely. This is probably the way they have done things before. (If afterward, you find you have the urge to question how many times this has occurred with other people – hoping you'll hear "never" – be sure to first ask yourself if you can handle, **and believe**, the answer.)

g. Ten Words About Online Dating

1*Tell* 2*the* 3*Truth* 4*About* 5*Yourself.* 6*Don't* 7*Believe* 8*Anything* 9*You* 10*Hear.*

Well, OK. I'll say a little more than that. I know a few couples that met online and now, 2 or 3 offspring later, they're still going strong. This is good. But there are about a billion horror stories about online dating, too.

Plain and simple: When it comes to online dating, I gotta tell ya… *it's a crapshoot.* (But when you think of it, what type of 'dating' *isn't*?)

> If you are shopping online for your true soul mate and/or the mother of your kids, be careful. People are notorious for lying online to paint better pictures of themselves, or simply to get into your wallet, your head – or your pants. The bad stuff gets left out, like the part about doing time for murder, the fact that they're still stalking their ex, or the part about how they owe $90,000 in credit card debt (due to a hot relationship with QVC.)

Granted, these issues all still can be present if you meet through a friend, or at the bakery, too, but communicating online doesn't give you the benefit of looking into someone's beady little eyes. It's much easier for someone to lie to you on a keyboard than it is from across the dinner table.

So be careful and go slow. Again, you could visit e-harmony.com. Let them do the screening for you. You still may end up being fooled, but at least you will be fooled by someone who has passed the '29 different dimensions of compatibility' test.

> **YOU ARE WHAT YOU EMAIL (Emails aren't protected.)** Don't send anything that you wouldn't want posted on the office (or world) bulletin board – where everyone, including your mom, might see it. Really. Your e-mails are running through public territory, and no matter how private you believe they are, they aren't. Beware that Geeks-R-Us can do anything - even catch you doing something wrong and then report it to your boss or your mate – who may be paying them. ALSO USE YOUR SPELL CHECK BEFORE YOU SEND ANY EMAIL !!!!!!!!!!!

h. Sex and the Single Guy

If you are dating just for the sex, then you AREN'T dating. You're trolling. And though your 'catch and release' methods are fun for you, your dates might not be so thrilled. (Rent MAID of HONOR and you'll get it.)

The next few paragraphs will give you a HUGE advantage if you find yourself back out in the Dating Zone.

THE FIRST KISS, AND SEX

My friend, Dan – in his thirties – was newly divorced and nervous about getting back out there, especially with the idea of being graded on kissing or sex with someone new. After all, he had been with only one person for at least a decade. So he signed up with a local matchmaker (FYI – finding a certified matchmaker is a great idea for you, too), and waited. As I said, he was nervous about his 1st date, so I made 3 strong suggestions for him.

1. I pointed out that if he's having a great time, he should say so. Then they'll both be more relaxed.
2. I suggested that if he knew that he liked her in their first hour together, he should find an opportunity to ask, "May I kiss you?" and get it over with. Then he should say, "Good. Now we don't have to be nervous about that anymore."
3. I told him NOT to have sex until they had shared several phone conversations and emails and had been on at least 4 dates.

He loved my first two ideas, but he was curious about why they should wait so long to have sex. I explained that as they got to know and like each other more, they would be more attracted to each other physically, especially if they kissed. I clued him in to the fact that sex is the ultimate thing they will ever do together so it should be the icing on the cake. (He confided that he was a little worried that his date might get pushy about the sex, but I pushed him not to buckle on that issue and to simply say he wanted to get to know each other better before going there.)

Soon he was set up for a date with an awesome girl. They hit it off right away as they had dinner and talked. He asked for the kiss as soon as he had the chance and conquered that unknown early, then they proceeded to have a blast. They had a lot in common and they loved the way they felt around each other. Over a period of days, they spent a lot of time talking, emailing and texting and became intensely attracted to each other.

Night after night, Dan would get home from his date and call or text me to gab or ask questions and whine about my NO SEX rule. Finally I told him to go for it. The next day I get an email telling me that they both were blown away to discover that it was the best sex either of them had ever experienced.

Ha! My point is that usually with regard to sex, the longer you wait to do it, the better it will be when you do. Getting to know everything else about each other before crossing that intimacy line just makes it loads more intense. (Sometimes it's simply better to wait for something, anticipating and fantasizing that it will be fabulous, rather than have it dumped unceremoniously on your lap. So guys, give this a try (and report back).

> "Don't have sex. It leads to kissing and soon you'll have to start talking to them."   -Steve Martin

SEX ISN'T ONLY ABOUT YOU

Well. Unless you're alone. Or paying for it (I don't recommend that either – perhaps reading this book can actually help you start saving some money.) You should make pleasing your partner a priority. Doing this will make it better for you, too.

What can I say about a charming guy under the sheets? Actually I'll say this: your charm is ultimately what got you under them, so with regard to the manners that you used in your quest to get there, use them once you've arrived, too.

Keep in mind that even though sex is obviously physical, to some people it's also emotional. So whether sex is a big emotional deal for you, it could be for your partner, so *charming you* should treat it like it is. Be nice and sweet. Or at least follow your partner's lead. (I guess if you get bit then you can bite. If handcuffs appear, that might mean you can disregard that emotional stuff I just mentioned.)

If you're unsure about what you should do to please your partner, just ask what they like. Then, if you can handle it, do it. Simple. If you're nervous about being good in bed and need some added confidence, go to the library or bookstore and find the SEX section. You'll probably find a few dozen shelves of books on sex. Seems to be a hot topic… (Try "Hot Sex" by Tracy Cox. *Hot book* — with detailed instructions.)

Use protection, too – unless you and your partner are into each other *only*. Or you're into the idea of 18 years of court ordered paycheck deductions. Or herpes. Or HIV. Shall I go on?

Be warned that latex has a shelf life. Condoms can get frightfully in-effective after a few dry months. So if yours have been sitting around for a while, don't trust them to effectively 'daddy-proof' you.

(**Here's a sexy secret:** Whether your goal with your partner is *all romance* or ALL HEAT, remember that a high level of eye contact during sex can make either approach an *intensely successful experience*.)

SIDENOTE: If you are invited into a bed, don't assume that it is an invite to sleep there all night. If you *are* begged to stay the night, you still need to remember that you may not necessarily want to be there when the sun comes up and shines its happy light on your morning face. Or *theirs*. (Especially if your invitation to that bed came via that 'Last–Call-and-Lights-On' thing. Don't forget that beauty is often in the eye of the beer-holder. You should also know that what looked and felt HOT at 2 a.m., might actually look and feel cold – like dead trout cold – at 9 a.m.)

I'm repeating the following two paragraphs from Chapter 10, *because it's very important that you get this,* and some guys benefit from being told more than once. Or 32 times.

You can avoid the relationship with the 'normal-turned-psycho' if you go slow. It's the only way for you to see what type of person you are getting involved with, before it's too late. Pay close attention to any little warning signs before you get in too deep because once you discover that a nightmare has moved in, and your place is suddenly decorated with silk flowers and Beanie Babies — it's too late.

Think twice before you have sex with someone if you know you don't want a relationship (or a baby) with this person. Otherwise, when you see their stuff moving into your place, you'll know it's because you let Junior in your pants get behind the wheel again. (Wow. Junior again...)

Don't forget that some people really do believe that once they have had sex with you, you are soul mates for life. Then the next thing you know, you're hearing an alien voice say to you from your kitchen, "Did you pay the rent and take out the trash yet, Sweetie Baby Pookie Cheeks?"

TIP: You've heard that employers should "Be slow to hire, quick to fire"? Well, in the case of *first sex*, if you are certain you don't want a relationship with this person then, "be quick to dump, slow to jump". You should be certain that you really want to go there before you *go there*. If you see any red flags, run away. Those red flags can get waaaay *redder* once you've had sex with that person. And don't jump and dump. That is so cliché.

PORN
Be careful here. Porn can be addictive, and if you've been into it for a while, by yourself, then the reality of *actual* – not *virtual* – sex between

you, and a less digital... less inflatable, *less looks like your hand* partner, could be disappointing for both of you. Wean yourself of pornography. Return from your Fantasyland and focus on the 3-dimensional things that live and breath - and walk on two legs – like you.

However, if you find a mate who is into the same things as you are, such as porn, S & M, Kinky Boots, well then ... you'd better cuff that one to the bedpost. (But remember that if you choose to record your most intimate moments on film, they could end up posted on the Internet. Just ask Tommy Lee. Of course if *your* recording features *you* with Pamela A., well then, *you go boy...*)

BABY, BUG AND BULLET-PROOF YOURSELF

What I'm going to say now is reeeeeeeally important so listen up. Like everything else in the book – it's for your own good. **Do not let the** *heat of the moment* **make you an instant daddy. Remember that you make up 50% of a baby.** And if a girl *sucks* you into sex, (pun intended) *pregnancy can happen.* So now imagine yourself in the worst relationship on Earth, with someone who's dark presence actually sucks the air out of a room. If you get *her* pregnant, then you won't be sharing the next 18 years, and custody of your little kid, with Snow White. You'll be sharing it all with *Cruella DeVille.* Yikes.

Put it this way: EVERY form of birth control has failed. So be sure you understand that she *can* get pregnant, and if she does you are tied to her for *18 years.* (It's true. They can prove the dad is you.) This means that if you don't want to marry her or live with her, and *she* is a clueless or rotten mom to your kid, then you simply get to stand by and watch a psycho raise your child. The child you get to see on Wednesdays and every other weekend. And remember that the psycho may want to make your life miserable every chance she gets. Then gee, what could she use to do such a thing? Oh yes, your kid.

Another thing: females **do not** get pregnant "by accident." EVER. Have you ever seen a girl slip and fall on a loaded penis?

Me either. So always be sure that if you do not want to be a daddy in 9 months, you take proper precautions. Don't trust that she has handled the birth control (or the disease control). Let me rephrase that. Don't trust anyone else to pack your parachute, OK? Your life depends on this. There's nothing like those two little words, "I'm pregnant," to slam you into the "GROW UP NOW" or the "LIFE AS YOU KNOW IT HAS JUST ENDED FOREVER" lane.

Either of those signs *suck* if you aren't ready. (But there are two other spooky little words that can make an unplanned pregnancy seem like a winning lottery ticket. They would be "I'm positive." So suit up, Studly.)

Speaking of 'suck,' here's a terrifying little bedtime story for you: Once upon a time, in a neighborhood like yours, a guy and a girl were fooling around. For some reason, this guy decided that he did not want to have intercourse with this girl, but decided that he would take her up on her offer of oral sex. (Imagine that.) Then 10 months later, this very sneaky girl showed up with a baby and said that it was *his*.

Wait! No deposit was made at that bank! How could this be? Well, a blood test proved it was true (see, I told you…), and then a judge slapped the gavel, declaring that this guy would be financially responsible for this child for the next 18 years. Now that's just not right. That sneaky semen thief admitted that she had impregnated herself with what this guy had left behind. Does *that* not <u>totally</u> suck or what? My buddy asked, "what kind of skanky viper would do that?" Uh, that would be the skanky viper that your kid could end up calling "Mommy".

The moral to that particular story is that if you leak at all – no matter where – beware. A handy little turkey baster can do much more than baste turkeys. So be choosy when picking the person you will share your DNA with, and where you decide to leave it. (Don't forget about that blue dress/Oval Office thing.)

WATCH WHAT YOU SAY AFTER SEX!
Here's a little advice for you in case of an "emergency after sex meltdown". Typically guys experience a loss of logic immediately after sex. So with this in mind, do not be tempted to propose marriage immediately after *disengaging*. Your brain is still in a funky state (temporary loss of blood flow…) and just because the extraordinarily hot (at the moment anyhow) person beside you made your back arch for a second does not mean you actually want to spend the rest of your life with them. Besides, if after the next 10 times you have sex with them, you are still thinking that this person is perfect for you — then you'll need to plan a perfect proposal for them anyway. Not in bed. One that she can be proud to talk about with her mom and the minister, pastor, clergyman, or ship captain who performs the wedding. Discover 12 reasons — other than amazing (or not) sex — to marry her. Then propose.

If after sex you find that the heat of the moment has created an urgent need for you to say something profound to mark the occasion, instead of saying, "Let's get married", say "I love you". Obviously you think you do, so it's not a lie. But once the blood returns to your big head, if you feel differently, then those words are waaaaay easier for you to 'retract' than a proposal will be. (Good luck with that.) It won't be an easy task either, but compared to a proposal (which I'd love to see you get out of without a scar) it's my only recommendation.

Note to Divorced Guys: I want to warn you that getting back out there after you've been in a long-term r'ship can be tricky. For one thing, unlike your earlier years in dating, not everyone in your age range is single. (Or *skinny*.) And going into a bar to meet someone at your age will not get the same results for you now as when you were in your twenties. (Have you tried this? How's that workin' for ya?)

So let me suggest that before you set your sites on meeting someone great, you make sure you ARE something great. Join a gym or start exercising. This will make you feel terrific physically AND emotionally. And losing your extra flab and building back your self-confidence will make you *very attractive*.

Next, find a *certified matchmaker* in your area. They are in most major cities and they can save you a heck of a lot of frustration, wasted time, money and *heart hassles*. Consider your track record so far. If you have awesome dates anytime you want one, then you're set. Drop this book. But if your methods aren't exactly getting you what you want, then talk to a matchmaker. Once again boys, I'm telling you about a *trained professional*. Don't be afraid, a matchmaker will do the screening for you and you'll end up with fewer bad date choices/crazy people in your life. All it takes is money, and you and I both know you can afford it if you want to. So go for it.

(Visit www.matchmakinginstitute.com. Your next relationship lives there. You'll have to give them your first name and email address, but considering that you are shopping for your most important purchase ever, grin and bear it. These guys can give you great mate choices and you won't even have to step foot in a bar.)

Tips from Chapter 12: Dating

1• **If you are looking for something great, you need to BE something great.** Try to present yourself as whatever you are attracted to. Be your own bait.

2• **Flirting can get you a lot of positive attention.** It makes the people you flirt with feel great about you, too.

3• **Stop worrying about hearing "*no*" when you want to ask someone out.** You stand just as great a chance of getting a "*yes*." Letting your fear of "*no*" stop you from asking will guarantee nothing but "*no*'s. So ASK. Like our buddy Doug says: Don't *ask*... Don't get."

4• **Don't wait for weeks and weeks to approach someone.** You must do it *before* that person notices that you are totally into them. *You've got self-confidence*. Use it. Besides, the worst that can happen is a NO, and you know that getting one of these is not going to stop your clock.

5• **Don't rule out becoming friends with someone if you'd like to be more than friends.** You may disagree (most guys do), but a friendship with a hottie isn't deadly – and actually it's the way that many intimate relationships will begin. Just ask Bruce Willis.

6• **Be friendly and easy-going when you first talk with anyone you are interested in a possible r'ship with.** Even if the person isn't interested at that moment, they may change their mind later.

7• **On a *first date*, go for coffee and focus on your date.** Treat it like a casual chat, getting *that person* to talk more about them than *you* talking about *you*. Be understanding and friendly – not a know-it-all.

8• **After your first time out for coffee with someone, call and say "thanks."** No matter how you feel about that person, calling the next day to thank them for the chance to get together, will show that you are a truly amazing guy. (If you really don't want to talk to the person, plan your call to their home or work when you know they won't be there. Just leave a voicemail. Painless. Easy. Do it. But plan a quick conversation in case they answer the phone – or use caller block – # 6 7 – so they won't know it was you who hung up when they answered.)

9 • **If a blind date looks disappointing, be nice and charming to this person anyway.** You never know what lies in store for you through your connection to that person. Remember your reputation. (And let's also consider the importance of KARMA, so do the right thing, be a nice guy, and hopefully, it will come back to you.)

10 • **If you run into anyone you know while on a date, introduce the two in a positive and friendly way.** If you aren't proud of the way your date looks, act like you are anyway. That is *charm*.

11 • **Always pick up the check on a date.** Be sure you leave a good tip. You are being graded on your generosity or lack of it.

12 • **Learn and use "The 6 Great Date Questions" in this chapter.** Keep up on current news and what's going on around the world, too, so that you can talk knowledgeably about different topics. **Boring guys rarely get second dates (or sex).** Beef up your personality so that you are fun and entertaining. Or at least not excruciatingly difficult to spend five minutes with.

13 • **No drooling over your new girlfriend's hot friends.** If you've already picked the blonde, then you can't have the brunette. (Unless they are extremely open-minded.) Flirting with, or otherwise pursuing the friends, sisters or mommies of your new relationship is grounds for *something really bad*.

14 • **You cannot change a human if they don't want to change.** After you've had a few great dates with a seemingly perfect partner, and you discover a few spooky or bothersome traits you had not seen before, don't think that you can change them. Accept the flaws or run away.

15 • **If you date online, be prepared for anything.** Just like the original blind date, 'hope for the best, but plan for the worst'. And <u>be careful</u>. Remember that online, 'criminally insane' can look just like a beer and a bag of chips. Also, no marriage proposals online. (Or after great sex.)

16 • **No sex, ever, on the first date.** No sex on the first date. No sex.
(But be sure to have a condom handy anyway.)

17• **Kick your addiction to porn.** Trade it in for ant farming.

18• **Protect yourself from everything that you do not want.** Babies, STDs, angry lovers with guns. Use protection and good judgement. Don't go there if you don't want to *live* there. (Just in case.)

19• **Be careful with what you say after sex.** Those three little words can cement a deal that you may not be certain yet that you want to be cemented to.

Visit www.greatdateconsulting.com for more about being a *great date.*

CHAPTER 13

Attention Teens and Young Guys…

"Youth is wasted on the young." Clearly that statement was made by a jealous, old person. *But listen to those old guys. They have knowledge and experience. YOU, on the other hand, have the huge advantage over them of being able to actually remember what they tell you.*

It's true. You will stand a greater chance of success at the prom or at the casino if you can absorb the wisdom the old guys are always trying to force on you. So be sure to <u>listen and learn</u> from them while they still have a pulse.

> **If you lay down with dogs then you'll get up with fleas.** I know. Goofy saying. But the things that you allow into your life will mold you into a person that fits with those things. Ya wanna be a great snowboarder? Then hang on the slopes with someone who is better on a snowboard than you are. If you want a strong, hard body, hang with someone at the gym that can lift more than you can. **Surround yourself with talented people who will push your limits to match their own.**

Look to the older guys. They usually are less pre-occupied with their own images than you guys are, and they probably won't mind having you around. (But if you want to be a total loser, just hang with a gang of losers. It'll take no work, and you'll be exactly like 'em in no time.)

While you are still in school. What's your goal? To be cool? To be smart? Whatever you want to be, you *can* be, if you focus on YOU — in that way or image. Really. VISUALIZE yourself in the place you want to be. But don't sacrifice yourself to any one segment of your teen society if you don't really wanna act like they act, dress like they dress, listen to the music they listen to — and be smart enough to know whatever else they may want from you — then *give it.*

Your best chance at total and complete success is to learn to be comfy in your own skin. Build yourself into a guy that you want to be. Forget the other kids and what they have or do. The most appealing *you* — is the one who is happy with who he is. **Read "Life Strategies for Teens" by Jay McGraw and "The 7 Habits of Highly Effective Teens" by Sean Covey.** Both of these guys have big name dads, but don't hold that against them. These are not their daddy's books. Their books are good and they are each talking to you with the voice of a young guy, so don't worry... you'll get it.

"If you can't tell the difference between a spoon and a ladel – you're fat." -Demitri Martin

There is no such thing as FLABULOUS. If you are overweight, then it's because you are livin' LAZY and feeding on <u>crap</u>. So get your pudgy self up off the couch or **away from the computer** and do some sit-ups, push-ups and wake up to the fact that <u>you</u> <u>are</u> <u>in</u> <u>total</u> <u>control</u> of what you weigh and how your body looks and feels. **(Tell your mom to stop buying chips and ice cream.)** Take over, Dude! <u>It's</u> <u>all</u> <u>you.</u> So control what <u>you</u> eat. No one else can. (Rent the movie "Sixteen Candles".) Yep, it's another old movie but you need to watch Anthony Michael Hall's character in it anyway. Then watch an episode of "Dead Zone" starring him now. You'll see that how you look now has no bearing on how you can look in your physically fit and totally *hot* future. Only you are in control of your body and how it looks.

IF YOU ARE A GREAT STUDENT: Go to your teachers and offer to tutor the kids that could use some help – even if it means you may miss out on some fun stuff once in a while. This is ultra-charming, and it will no doubt pay off for you now or later *or both.*

When you have the answer that the person you are helping needs, then **you** **are** **the** **total** **expert**. And what guy doesn't want to hear, "Oh my God! You are so good at that!" or "Wow. You make this look so easy!" or "I never could have done this. I'm so glad you helped me..." Hmmm?????? If you've read anything else in this book – other than the sections on sex – then you know by now that the best way for you to feel great about yourself is to help other people. Think about it. They'll <u>worship</u> you. (How would you like to be <u>worshipped</u>?)

Remember these two things:
1. *You can have anything you want in life if you'll just help others get what they want first.*
2. *What goes around comes around.* (a.k.a.: Karma, Earl.)

While you're in school, be cool to the teachers and faculty there, but more importantly, be cool to everyone else, including the kids you don't know. Say 'Hi" to everyone and be open to making friends *with everyone.* Don't be afraid to get to know the people that are clearly different from you – because of their looks or otherwise.

As you attempt to meet people, don't worry that anyone is gonna blow you off. Sure some will, but who cares? You know what you are made of (amazing stuff) and if someone is too self-absorbed and judgmental to want to find out who you are... *their loss*. They will become adult idiots and life will never satisfy them. How could it? *Nothing could possibly be as great as (they think) they are.*

Give everyone a chance by never judging the way they look. Find out what's inside them. If your buddies are snobs or egomaniacs, ignore them if they try to talk you out of being a nice guy. You know what's right, so do it. *Always do the right thing.*

If you are failing or struggling at school, find a way to get into a Sylvan Learning Center (1-888-EDUCATE / www.sylvanlearningcenter.com). The people there are miracle workers. I knew a kid from the country who moved into the city for the first time when he was 14. He had lived in a mountain cabin his whole life – without running water or electricity. His city dad finally convinced his woodsy ex-wife that it was time to introduce their son to toilets, TVs and telephones – which were all mysteries to this kid.

Needless to say, the poor guy was clueless in school. He was used to home school and no other kids. After several really tough weeks, Dad enrolled him in Sylvan. Within a few weeks in Sylvan, he was a totally new kid. Not only could you see him becoming a star student, but he also was becoming a star athlete. It's like his confidence was suddenly on steroids. This proved to me that Sylvan *rocks*. Find a way to help your family afford it – and go.

Shake your family tree until a teen who isn't broke falls out. This is what most teens know about personal finances: "My pocket has money in it." OR "My pocket is empty."

If this is you, start doing something to improve your pocket situation. Go to the bookstore or Amazon.com and get *Personal Finance for Dummies*. If you can learn the secret of keeping your pocket "un-empty" now, then holy smokes, Chuck! You'll have a jumpstart on your financial future and a much easier time of keeping it *full* later. Please don't get me wrong. Money can't buy happiness, but full pockets just seem to make unhappiness *suck less*...

> "Academic qualifications are important and so is financial education. They're both important and schools are forgetting one of them."   -Robert Kiyosaki

IF YOU ARE A THIEF:

Understand that there is no way you will become a ka-billionaire by stealing car stereos. Or the cars that go with them. And although I'm not saying that you need to get a college degree to become a huge success, you <u>do</u> <u>need</u> to get a clue about where the illegal crap will actually get you. That would be jail - or worse. Seriously. To succeed as a career criminal, not only do you have to be reeeeally good at it, but you must surround yourself with other people who are equally reeeeally good at it. Then you'll need to be sure that they aren't so jealous or power-hungry that THEY will set you up for a bust. (Watch Law & Order. You'll see that there is nothing new, it's all been done, and after running and hiding and looking over their shoulders, everyone gets caught. Eventually. Or they'll remain paranoid and sentenced to a life of always looking over their shoulder.)

> "A man who has never gone to school may steal from a freight car: but if he has a higher education, he may steal the whole railroad."   -Theodore Roosevelt

Chris Rock says: "you can get *some money* and buy knew wheels for your car. Or you can get *a lot of money* and buy the company that makes the wheels." (And you won't get *a lot* of money by stealing crap from other people.)

Here's a better, more 'proven to work' suggestion for becoming King of the Hill: Have lunch with a millionaire. Find an adult who clearly has no worries about money. You may know him or her by the clothes he or she wears, by their car, by their house, business, or by the fact that they always wear a smile. (If a person has all of the "things" I just listed, then that person probably has money, but they may only have lots of debt. If he or she always wears a smile, then maybe they have money and maybe they have NO money, but they obviously have **no worries about money** – they're **smiling** - and THAT is your goal. Either way, again, money can't buy happiness, so learn how to NOT worry about money.) Ask this person to lunch to talk about his or her philosophies on money. THEN LISTEN CLOSELY TO EVERY WORD THEY SAY. (And start a savings account today. Go do that now.)

Are you disgusted with all rich people (Nathan)? Why? Not all of them own Veyrons and Vacherons. Bernard Kouchner founded Doctors Without Borders in 1971. Gardiner Hubbard founded Nat Geo in 1888. And even though Bill Gates may have the ultimate CRIB – he sure isn't hoarding his cash. He's given about 30 billion to charity (behind every great man there's a great woman – saying "write the check". You go, Melinda!). You can do whatever you want with your millions, too, so get rich, then save the planet.

OK, if you have a job... or if you plan to have a job *someday...*

Think about this: These days, the work force under the age of 20 can be pretty sketchy, so many employers firmly believe that the majority of young people are LAZY and unmotivated. And if that's true, then all you need to do to put yourself at the top of the food chain is *work harder than your co-workers*. Learn your job and do it very well. You won't even need to step on anyone's toes to get ahead. Just DO YOUR JOB. Do it very well.

When at work, leave your phone and your music in your car or in your locker. Don't think that your personal calls, texts or playlists are acceptable at work unless your boss says they are.

No matter what your job is – or who you work for – be a self-starter. Figure out what needs to be done and do it before somebody has to ask you to do it. Really. Kick ass at any job you ever have, and one day you can dominate Corporate America, MTV, Capitol Hill. Whatever.

One problem with being under 20 years of age is that you think *you know* what's best for you. I know that. And maybe you do know what's best for you at the moment. But you aren't looking at the big picture. You're looking at *this hour, this day,* maybe *this week* or even *this summer.* And that's about as far as eyes under 20 can usually see – or plan. No problem. Have fun while you can. Leave the thinking and the planning for the adults who keep telling you what to do.

Before reading the next several paragraphs, please note that I am completely neutral on the subject of the U.S. military (just so you know that I'm not a *recruiter*). But I am for sure against young people without any hope for a successful or happy future - wasting their lives doing stuff that will get them <u>nowhere</u> or worse. *You are a great guy, so why not get out into the world and let the rest of us know it?*

> **If you are out of high school without the option of college,** and have no idea of where you're going, call your local Job Corps, the Peace Corps or consider joining a branch of the military. Extreme? Maybe for some. None of these options are parties. Sorry. But they can sky-rocket you into a great place. And if you are struggling with your focus and are wasting time or getting into trouble, then these options can save your ass and your soul.

Seriously. In just a couple of years, the military can teach you a new way of life *and* a new skill that can pay off for you when you get out. Not to mention give you great *and* countless life experiences. If you've gotten into trouble and you have an arrest record, call a recruiting office anyway. Tell the recruitment folks about your offense and ask if you still can get in.

It's rare that a young guy with no real direction or focus joins the service and regrets it. Some get in and stay in, building a 20-plus-year career there. That can actually be a pretty cool option, giving you a guaranteed paycheck, health insurance benefits – medical, vision and dental coverage – *and retirement checks.* (By the way, health care in the military is top notch these days. Nothing like what your dad or grandfather experienced. Uncle Sam has obviously given his doctors a raise.)

So as you're just coasting, consider this: If you're scattered now, you could come out of the service as a sharp, focused, healthy, buff, capable and confident guy, ready for a life with more opportunities than you could even dream of now.

But be sure that you make a **good impression** in the recruiter's office. Otherwise he may tell you to get lost. Tell him that <u>you are the man</u>. Then live up to that statement. You'll see that you can do it, and soon you'll have a clear shot at ruling the world.

If you are already in or headed for college, hear this: Don't blow it. Everything you do right now is dictating your future. So pay attention and stay focused. Don't party each semester away. If you are in with the party crowd, set goals and limits for yourself. More on this coming up.

If you're feeling resentful about being at college, or if you've got a chip on your shoulder for any reason, *get over it!* Deal with it. Sort it out and get over it. Talk to a counselor or your parent or any person you trust to give you confidence in yourself and in what you are doing. Someone who knows you can convince you that what you are doing is right. You are where you need to be and you will realize this later.

Think of it this way. Listen to the 'voices of authority' that you may be sick of hearing right now. I know you think it all *blows*, but your bad attitude will go away, and I can guarantee that you are not wasting your time at school. Finish, because whatever else you feel you could be doing – instead of college – will still be available once you're *degree'd up*. Have fun, but focus on getting good grades and getting your education over with. If you are struggling with *anything* at school, talk to a school counselor. That's why they're there.

To make this weird and stressful time a little more relaxed for yourself, check out the following books as you are coasting to (or through) college: **"It's OK If You're Clueless: And 23 More Tips for the College Bound"** by Terry McMillan, **"A Student's Survival Guide: Everything You Need to Know Before College"** by Matthew Turner, and last (but probably most entertaining): **"The CollegeHumor Guide to College: Selling Kidneys for Beer Money, Sleeping With Your Professors, Majoring in Communications, and Other Really Good Ideas"** by The Writers of CollegeHumor.com. There are many great jokes, and many great ideas in that last one. Good luck with figuring out which is which.☺

SET GOALS

You can totally kick butt and accomplish anything you want by doing one thing. *Set goals and write them down.* (Most millionaires will tell you they do this.) Get a dry erase board and place it in a visible spot. Then list your goals and slash through them as you complete them – even list getting your laundry done on Sunday night. The visibility factor is the key here. Your goals will see when you're screwing off and they'll give you crap for it.
("Hey. You didn't do me yet."
"He didn't do me yet, either."
"Loser.")
Allow yourself some party time only after you've completed a goal. You'll be more fun and feel more like partying after you've slashed through a few of your goals, anyway.

YOUR PARENTS

If your parents are nagging you about your grades and your achievements at college, just remember that they do this because for some reason, that's what they are programmed to do. Which is really bizarre because they won't gain anything from your degree. This is why I think they must really just be *programmed* to do it. It is in their blood because take it from me — there is a hell of a lot more in your college degree for <u>you</u>, than there is for <u>them</u>. They must be nuts.

Regardless, forgive your parents their delusions, bite the bullet and snag your degree. Then watch as doors start flying open for you and opportunities start grabbing your arm and jerking you in. (And you can retire at the tender age of 30, while your parents, for some reason, are jumping up and down and cheering on the sidelines...)

At college, remember that you should be learning **how to use your mind** - but NOT **what you should think** (or **how** you should think). <u>You are not there to be programmed.</u> The key to your success after college is to be able to process any info you receive and formulate your own opinions about it. Yes, 2 + 2 will always equal 4, but when considering whether there should be a Republican or a Democrat in the White House, the answer should require some heavy duty debate in your head.

Read Chapter 11 – "A few words about sex."
(Rrrright – as if you haven't already.) If you are foolishly going to have sex, then be sure that your big head does the thinking and planning to protect you, capisce? (Because that little head of yours couldn't care less about your overall wellbeing, your other body parts, or your future – and on occasion will actually try to get you killed. The ultimate purpose of your penis is to deliver fertilizer. And that is what will cause child support to fall out of your pocket at an unbelievably high rate of speed. Tattoo a flying dollar sign on yours to remind you.)

FYI – since I'm not a teen, in order to provide the info here, I consulted several teens, with a wide range of IQs and life experiences, and one total smart-ass in Kansas. So this isn't my generation talking. It's yours.

IF U R A HORN-DOG
As you spend the next few years of your life focused completely on finding any opportunity for sex, you need to learn now how to deal with sex like a good guy. You should be <u>safe</u>, polite, knowledgeable, charming and appealing. So do your homework on this topic. Not with porn, but with books that can actually teach you how to be the best at whatever it is that you want to be the best at.

For some bizarre reason, group sex is trendy right now, but don't *EVEN* go there. That is so *not* charming. Why would you want to reveal to *everyone*, what you are like sexually? You are opening the door to be judged on <u>so</u> <u>many</u> levels. Geez — save that action for behind closed doors, where a little mystery is a really great thing.

An air of mystery about what you do or don't do is much more intriguing than a signboard strapped across your chest, providing a glaring insight into your sexuality. Keep your mouth shut instead of bragging to your friends if you score. Don't have casual sex with someone you care nothing about. Connect with your partner if you are going to commit the most intimate act that two humans can commit. You hear what kids say about other kids, and you see how rumors get started, so avoid that - or the rumors will be about you and your really odd Johnson or your one funky testicle.

Who cares if your friends or other kids are doggin' ya about group sex (or other avenues to your own private Hell)? You may not even know them next year. Why would you sacrifice yourself to the God of Stupidity on behalf of some pushy jerks or idiots that you will probably never see after high school anyway?

Be smart about the choices you make – you know right from wrong. Remember to do the right thing, even if it means that you must stand up to the peer pressure (or the beer pressure).

WHAT ARE YOU TALKING ABOUT?

Get comfortable at making conversation. If you are nervous about talking to others because you are worried you'll say something stupid, then learn to ask questions that will encourage people to talk about themselves. Refer to the "6 Great Date Questions" in Chapter 11. They're the types of questions that will allow the person answering to gab on for 5 days. Then listen closely to the answers because they will give you a whole new herd of questions to ask them. This will keep them talking about themselves – and keep you out of the spotlight… if that's what you want.

WHAT'S YOUR FAVORITE LETTER, *U* OR *I*?

If you prefer talking about yourself to listening to someone else talk about themselves — or other *non-YOU* topics — then you need to sit down and shut up. Keep your mouth shut and start listening. **You are not the**

center of the Universe. But if you can be a great listener, then everyone will soon think you ARE the center of the Universe. Start listening and stop yakking. We may all decide that you really are as great as you want us to think you are, and then we'll all want to hear *everything* you have to say. But you need to hear what others want to say first.

YOUR LIFE PLAN

This idea may help you with your overall success: statistics over the past few decades have suggested that the majority of guys who are happy, successful and financially secure throughout their lives have followed the same simple scheme. Here it is:

- **First, they finish high school/go to college and/or get a job.**
- **Second, they get married or settle into a permanent relationship.**
- **Third, they have kids. LAST. They have kids last. (CONDOMS!)**

I know. It sounds so Ozzie and Harriet. Oops – you don't know who they are. Sorry. OK, it sounds really old fashioned – maybe like your grandparents or great-grandparents. But it works. It's proven to work. In that order. Because as you follow these steps, you will learn about, *and learn to get good at* <u>commitment</u>. Starting with the easiest commitment first.

The first: Your job or career. You'll gladly commit to this one because it will cause green to appear in your wallet... And in your new Scottrade account. (Remember that when it comes to your job or career, typically the more education you have, the more you'll get paid. *So study!*)

The second: Your relationship. Which will happen to be best after you've discovered that there is green in your wallet. Earning money will put you in a good mood, then you are more likely to score a great relationship with a great person, which will keep you in a good mood. Then you'll want to start <u>practicing</u> for the *third*.

The third: Kids. Well, what can I say? They're kids. And after you've had them, you'll learn the REAL meaning of committed. (You'll stand at the admission counter in the psych ward and say, "I want to be *committed*.") Not really. Well, hopefully, not really.

> **Kids will change everything about your life.** Having them when you aren't sweating the cash each week will mean they're a good change. Ask any dad who has the cash, the savings account and the steady job to buy Pampers and trips to Disneyland, and he and Mom will tell you that kids **rock.** The unemployed guy who lives in the efficiency apartment with his unemployed girlfriend and her kids or his kids or their kids at the end of **Life Sucks Boulevard,** will no doubt tell you something else.

If you don't want kids – no problem. Kids are a lot of work anyway, and they definitely won't make you any money. No financial advisor will tell you that kids are a great investment. (They're a labor of *love* – so be sure you have a lot of love to give before you take part in a DNA mix.) If kids are in your future, have them *after* you've made a few bucks – and you know how to make more.

Be sure you've found the love of your life and you've committed to *that* **before becoming a dad,** because with a great partner, life is much better and easier on YOU. The two of you will treat your kids like good parents treat their kids, and your kids will grow up to know that their daddy was *the best*. (Do yourself another favor and make a pact with the guy in the mirror to not have kids until you are over 25. Trust me on this — you will be a better, more successful, and popular daddy and husband. Take a cold shower.)

Back to that "Life Sucks Boulevard" thing... even if you are on welfare or state aid, you can be a great husband and dad. Just remember that all it takes for you to succeed at anything is your EFFORT. You can do <u>anything</u> in your life is your effort.

(Keep in mind that if you are single, you are much, much, much more marketable without kids — and if you happen to get a girl pregnant, there's no guarantee that YOU won't end up with complete custody of your baby, soon to be toddler, soon to be asking you for 20 bucks and the car keys, etc, etc, etc.)

If you are a teen guy and you already have become a daddy, without the possibility of a good job and enough money to pay *ALL OF THE BILLS* each month without relying on FOOD STAMPS, join the military. I know. There it is again. But you'll have a guaranteed paycheck, a house or apartment to live in, schooling (basic and advanced) and FREE medical coverage for you, your wife (marry her) and baby (ies). Not to mention self-respect *and a future*. By the way, DO NOT have another baby until your financial picture improves. HUGELY improves. I repeat: take a cold shower — or call in the Trojans.

OFFER YOUR TIME TO AN ELDERLY PERSON (don't call them old)
Old people can be a total crack up. (I mean elderly, don't call them old.) Think about it. They have no need to try to impress anyone – they are so over

that. Especially the ones in retirement homes or nursing homes. They really don't care anymore about what you think of them, so the things that often come out of their mouths can leave you rolling on the floor. (The things that come out of the other end can actually leave you passed out *on the floor.)*

If you have grandparents or other older relatives who live near you, go and visit them regularly. Daily, weekly, or monthly – depending on how near or far they are. As nature would have it, these people will keel over soon, so now is your chance to get to know them. Plus, your visits will give them something to really look forward to. Keep your word if you say that you're going to go visit them. (Otherwise, the Karma Bears will shred you someday.) Think about what you already know about them and from there, ask more questions. Learn more about their lives. Remember that they were your age once, and to them *that* time of their life probably seems like 'yesterday'. (They'll probably tell you that a lot.)

The older people have seen so much in their lifetime, and no matter what you read about in history class, you will learn loads more about any event if you can actually learn from someone who was there.

Imagine what you could hear from your grandmother who was at Woodstock. Well... depending on whether or not there were mind-altering drugs involved. In which case she may not remember squat. (But that's a common risk with old elderly people anyway, isn't it?) So ask and see what you'll hear.

If you don't have any older relatives, then adopt one. Call a local nursing home or retirement home and ask the staff there if you can volunteer with some social interaction. You could read to someone, or play checkers, or maybe you could help Sam, the little 97-year-old retired sailor snag a date with Gertrude, the 95-year-old retired shrimp boat Captain.

There may be nothing about being around old elderly people that sounds good to you. Fair enough. They smell funny and they make odd noises, plus, sometimes they talk to the door knob. But think of it this way: imagine how you would feel if you were old. And all alone. Go to a nursing home and take a look at what the future may hold for you or your mom and dad. *That view may motivate you to get off your butt — and be a success.* Regardless of how you connect with an older person, you could be giving a great gift (your time) to an older person who may have *no one*

— in the whole world. Imagine having no family or relatives. Or friends.

Here are a few things that you need to be aware of or do, in order to make the rest of us believe that YOU are charming.

1. Keep clean, from your hair and scalp, to inside your mouth, to inside your nostrils and inside your ears to your fingernails, toenails, your belly button and your butt.
2. Don't be discouraged if your face, back, and/or chest is broken out. Get to a dermatologist for a prescription to zap your zits now. Industrial strength acne medications exist, you know.
3. Bad breath and grungy teeth are a huge turn-off, so be sure to keep your mouth healthy and clean. Tooth decay and gum disease can affect anyone and new studies show that they are *contagious* and *transferable*, so go to the dentist twice a year for cleanings and check ups. More often when you're over 25.
4. Careful with the cologne or body spray. Use two squirts – MAX. Too much will make you smell like the 8-year-old who discovered his dad's old 'Polo' under the bathroom sink.
5. No matter what you like to wear, make sure your clothes are *clean*. Unwrinkled would be good, too, though that's probably asking too much. (Learn to iron.)
6. **Wear clean socks and underwear everyday.** *No exceptions.* **Watch your boxers or shorts for brown stripes. If you have them, fix your problem. Refer to page 145-146.**
7. Always wear socks with your boots and closed shoes to absorb sweat and avoid stink.
8. **If your feet stink**, soak them in Listerine. Then get new shoes.
9. If you have chronic stinky foot syndrome, buy some sandals. Doc Martens, Birks, Tevas. Open shoes can prevent sweaty/stinky feet.
10. If you aren't sure what you should wear in a certain situation, then wear something nice. You would rather be over-dressed than show up lookin' even a little bit sloppy.
11. Keep physically fit. If you are overweight, start working out. Run or something. No matter what your age - *fat* is out.
12. Have good posture. Stand and sit up straight. You'll be *taller*.
13. Keep a smile on your face. Get comfy with this - it's important.
14. **Be a nice guy. This is huge when it comes to appealing to other people. Nice guys are accessible and that's what you want to be, even to your best friends little brother.** *Be nice.*
15. Speak clearly and look at the eyes of anyone you talk to.

16. Buy Webster's New World Pocket Desk Set to improve your vocabulary. Visit www.wikipedia.com, too.
17. When you want to impress a date, or someone you want to date, ask questions about *THEM*. Think of how un-nervous you'll be as you sit and listen to them talk and talk and talk about *themselves*.
18. Think before you speak, and think about what response your words may bring on.
19. If you need help in your conversations, go to Borders, Barnes & Noble or any bookstore and look in the self-help section. Find a book that addresses how to give good *conversation*.
20. If you tell someone you will do something, do it. Always keep your word. You said you'd call? Then ya better call.
21. **Work hard for your boss. Impress them by bustin' your butt anytime you're on the clock. Make everyone else look lazy.**
22. Casual sex is not going to do anything good to build your self-esteem or your image as a great guy. Save your DNA for someone who means something to you.
23. If you have an old elderly relative in a nursing home or a retirement home, find a way to go and visit them on a regular basis. If they are too far away to visit, then write them nice letters and send them photos of you often.

BAG THE ANGST

If you are constantly preparing for *departure*, stop it. I can guarantee that whatever is happening to you now has happened to someone else before. There is a fix for you – remember that wherever you are right now is temporary. Everything is.

If you've gotten a girl pregnant, that sucks, but it's not the end. If you're into booze or meth or anything else, that's a total bummer – but not insurmountable. If you've come to the realization that you're gay, I'm sure this may be spooky to you also, but not life-threatening. Here's some contact info for you:

In case of a pregnancy, call 800-448-3000 (Boystown.org)
Meth Helpline: 866-535-7922 – www.methhelpline.com
Gay Youth Talkline: 800-246-7743

Your parents will survive any of this news, too, and you can all still live happily ever after. (But if your parents become more balistic than cooperative after hearing your news, then go to your boss, your best friend's parents, a school counselor or call a crisis hotline. There are plenty of people out here that want to help you.

Tips from Chapter 13:
Attention: Teens And Young Guys

1• **Determine who you want to be,** then choose your friends based on that goal. Hang out with the people who are going to where you want to go. College? Jail? Hollywood?

2• **Lay off the groceries and the computer if you are fat.** Get your *ass* in shape! You can be flabby and unhealthy when you are 75.

3• **If you are still in high school,** do the absolute best you can. You've got the rest of your life to party and have fun, but what you do now will dictate how much partying you can do later.

4• **You create your own weather.** When you are energetic and happy, that's what you attract. If you are feeling down and out, that's what's gonna knock on your door. So control your bait.

5• **Be a great guy to everyone.** Learn to be a guy that YOU will like. You can make a huge difference in the lives around you by giving your positive attention to other kids.

6• **If you're really struggling with your grades,** then try talking to a counselor and/or find a way into a Sylvan Learning Center. STOP partying, obsessing over sex or doing whatever you are doing that is taking your head away from the books.

7• **Only a really good thief can make a living at it.** So unless you are a rock star at breaking the law – don't quit your day job.

8• **Stop judging rich people.** If you become one, you can do great things with your money. (Just because someone is filthy rich doesn't mean they're filthy.)

9• **If you are out of high school and have no chance for college, get a job.** Find 3 job options and pick the best of those. Then stick with it until something better comes along. **Volunteer.** (If your resume says "Volunteered" anywhere on it, we'll all want to hire you. While volunteering, you can make great connections with other volunteers and Program Directors, too. Don't forget that it's not only what you know — but WHO you know that will put you on top.)

10• **Consider the military, if your life seems like it's at a dead-end already.** Dude! Get the hell out of there. The military will guarantee you a paycheck, a place to live, 3 meals a day, health benefits, gyms for workouts, travel and friends. Talk to a recruiter from each branch – Air Force, Navy, Army, Marines, Coast Guard and the National Guard. Then locate and talk to a regular guy from each of those branches to see which sounds best to you.

11• **Call your local Job Corps (or Google them) and/or your local Peace Corps office.** Your future can go from dark and depressing to bright and totally right on.

12• **Set goals for yourself.** Write them down on a dry erase board and make it the focus of your space. (Also create a *dream board* so that you can visualize what you want and focus on it each day.)

13• **Regarding your parents:** if you want to continue to battle with your parents – knock yourself out. But keep in mind that as long as they're paying for *your life*, they get to call the shots. If you wanna run your show, then move out. Take your tent.

14• **If you are having sex, use protection so that you don't become a daddy soon, or get a disease that will make your penis fall off.** Trust me when I tell you that fatherhood is a lot more pleasant when you are older, wiser and there's cash in the bank. But no matter how much cash you have, STDs still blow. Be smart and safe with sex. Consider the consequences of a stupid move, and don't let anyone talk you into anything you know will cost you. Think with the head on your shoulders — not the one that's always trying to get you killed.

15• **Girls lie and condoms leak.** Well. Not all girls lie and not all condoms leak. But hear this (and read it to *The Sperminator* behind your zipper), to avoid babies – believe they all lie and leak.

16• **If you have already become a daddy, make it work out well for you, your wife and your baby (ies).** Be *committed* to your new life and family. DO YOUR BEST. If your financial picture is looking grim, think about joining the military. (Or you can get on welfare. I'm sure you've been dreaming your whole life of the day you could get your 1st food stamps. ---- *Loser Central! Avoid it.*)

17• **Pay attention to the elderly people in your life.** If you have none, go and borrow a few. Do something good for them once in a while and the Karma Bears will push you closer to winning the lottery.

18• **Stop eyeing the exhaust pipe.** Your 'bummed' state will pass so ride it out and watch your future get better. You can make the change you need.

> "...the real role models to teens shouldn't necessarily be the athletes or entertainers. They should be people in their own community, the people that they can talk to when they have a problem. People that they can see on a daily basis and watch how they carry themselves. Because if they look up to entertainers or athletes, all they're seeing is their successes."   -Nelly

Jay McGraw says in his book, "Life Strategies for Teens", that the people that have your attention in life are typically trying to create a perfect image for you to see. (So no matter how Ferrari-like someone seems to be on the outside, keep in mind that on the inside they are probably just average... like an innocent little *Neon*.)

CHAPTER 14

More *Sex*, Anyone?

Would you like to have more sex? Then read every word in this tiny little chapter, as well as every word of this book.

I know. This chapter title was a ploy. But the chance of more sexual activity for you will improve dramatically if you read it and understand it.

The foreplay begins the moment you lay eyes on a potential partner. (Even if you are already married to them.) That the old saying "Sex begins far from the bedroom" is absolutely true. Because even though the thought of sex may be all it takes for you to rise to the occasion, for some people – namely females – a little convincing that you are the *greatest* (or some serious unconvincing that you are the *grossest*) might be required. Everything you do or say is being assessed and could ultimately decide your sexual future.

Look at it this way: You do or say something. And your target thinks either YUM or YUCK. You do or say something else. And they think either YUM or YUCK. You do or say another thing. Again, inevitably they think YUM or YUCK.

Your words and actions cause a reaction. Where as you may not be affected by all of *their* words or actions, YOUR words and actions have an "OOOh". That turns me *on*, or an "OOOh", that turns me *off* – effect.

So it's important for you to remember that even though sex is on the minds of most people – to some degree, quite often – the thoughts about sex with *a specific person* are more involved than you may have thought. For instance, many women will look at a potential partner and think (or say) "Oh my God – can you imagine sex with *that*?" This may be a good *that* or a bad *that*. Meaning she thinks he's a hot "that" or she thinks he's a troll "that". Appealing or *appalling*. Often to her, there's is no 'in between'.

Guys will typically not acknowledge the possibility of sex with the *troll*. That idea does not even develop in his brain. So if someone doesn't turn a guy on, then he is simply not turned on. But if someone doesn't turn a female on, there is a very strong chance that she will not only not be turned on by that person, but she could actually be turned off by them. Do you see this dangerous difference? *You* aren't interested in someone and that's all. But when some females are *uninterested*, it can be as if she's *ALLERGIC*. In other words, when you are not into her, you don't care. But when she is not into you, she may be thinking, "HA! When *Hell* freezes over."

So you need to keep these thoughts in mind as you cruise through each day. And it does not matter if we are talking about your interactions with your wife, your neighbor, the hottie behind the counter at Starbucks, or your next date. **As simplistic as this may sound, it's all about sex. So be sure that as you exist, you are aware that everything you do and say will affect your chances of success in that area.**

> One day a grown son asked his mother how he could find 'the right woman'. She told him to concentrate on becoming 'the right man' and the right woman would find him. <u>Great</u> <u>point</u>.

OK GENTLEMEN – start your engines...

You've completed (and survived) Charm School. You've actually made the effort to make some improvements in yourself by reading this book – and chances are you have succeeded. Well done you! Not only have you put your hands on hundreds of valuable tips, but you have laughed off a hell of a lot of sarcasm here, too. *That* in itself is a major accomplishment *for any guy*.

The information that you've discovered in this book will not only help you improve what you see in the mirror, but it also will help you in your job/career and in every relationship you build in this journey called *your life*. You can be anyone you want to be and do anything you want to do. Don't forget that you are in charge. Stay focused on the positive things that you want to see in your future. **Keep your eyes on the prize and that prize will be yours.**

At night, before bed, grab this book and go over the points you feel will make the biggest difference in your life. Fold the corners down on the important pages. Highlight or circle the points that you want or need to connect with. Study them and *focus on them*. Refer back to those points as often as you want. Remember: **Practicing a new behavior for only 21 days will turn it into habit.**

Look at your image in the mirror, too. Follow a checklist each morning as you prepare for the day. You have the tools to be charming and appealing to *everyone* you meet. Don't be lazy on this one. Take your vitamins. THE WORD OF THE DAY – EVERY DAY – IS *EFFORT*.

At the end of the day, think about the conversations that you participated in throughout your day. Are you OK with what you said? Grade yourself.

Use what you've read here and watch your life improve. Each day, do your best to be this charming new guy. It won't take long for it to come naturally and soon, that charming guy will simply be YOU.

With those words in mind, don't believe that you'll do something good for yourself or start making changes in yourself – tomorrow.

"The poor, the unsuccessful, the unhappy, the unhealthy are the ones who use the word 'tomorrow' the most."
-Robert Kiyosaki

DON'T WAIT. **Get out there right now and be the best, biggest and most influential person in your life.** *And pay attention to the road you are on at this moment, because you are living your "future past" right now. Next week, this moment will be part of your past so fill it with great experiences, memories and accomplishments.* Be happy, and try to remember this quote:

"Life is what happens to you while you're busy making grand plans for it."   -John Lennon

Congratulations.
Good luck, spread your charm and keep me posted.

Hey Charming Guy!

Don't set this book down to gather dust. Keep it for reference. Pass out the order forms in the back, too. Order one for your most un-charming buddy and sit on his chest until he agrees to read it. Spread the charm and help save our planet.

(And remember that even birds must fluff up and do a dance to get what they want. So now you can, too.)

Final Side Note: I'm sure as you've read through this book, you've had the same thoughts as many of my guy buddies. "*Girls* aren't perfect." "I know women who do *that*." "How come she's picking on *us*? Women do rude things, *too*."
I get the message, so Charm School for Girls is next... and it's totally *loaded*.

YOUR READING LIST. Here is a list of books you may find useful:

- **Painless Grammar** by Rebecca Elliott
- **Webster's New World Pocket Desk Set (3 in 1)**

- **From Clueless to Class Act** by Jodi R.R. Smith
- **Essential Manners for Men** by Peter Post

- **Feel the Fear and Do It Anyway** by Susan Jeffers

- **The Leader in You** by Dale Carnegie

- **:60 Second Anger Management: Quick Tips to Handle Explosive Feelings** by Michael Hershorn
- **Beyond Anger: A Guide for Men: How to Free Yourself From the Grip of Anger and Get More Out of Life** by Thomas J. Harbin

- **How to Win at College: Surprising Secrets for Success from the Country's Top Students** by Cal Newport
- **It's OK If You're Clueless: And 23 More Tips For The College Bound** by Terry McMillan
- **A Student's Survival Guide: Everything You Need to Know Before College** by Matthew Turner
- **The CollegeHumor Guide to College: Selling Kidneys for Beer Money, Sleeping With Your Professors, Majoring in Communications, and Other Really Good Ideas** by the Writers of CollegeHumor .com.

- **The Doctor's Book of Home Remedies** by "Men's Health" Books

- **Massage For Dummies** by Steve Capellini and Michael Van Welden

- **Hot Sex** by Tracy Cox

- **His Needs, Her Needs** by W.F. Harley

♣ **Relationship Rescue** by Dr. Phil McGraw

♣ **Men Are From Mars and Women Are From Venus** by John Gray

♣ **Booby Trapped: Men Beware!** by June Marshall

♣ **The Caveman's Pregnancy Companion: A Survival Guide for Expectant Fathers** by Port and Ralston

♣ **Tales From the Delivery Room: "I'll Never Have Sex With You Again!"** by Bleidner and Zutell

♣ **How to Raise Kids You Want to Keep** by Jerry Day

♣ **500 Great Things About being a Dad** by Steve Pelsohn

♣ **So You're Going to be a Dad...** by Peter Downey

♣ **A Child Called "IT"** by Dave Pelzer and **My Story** by Dave Pelzer

VISIT

WWW.BN.COM

WWW.BORDERSSTORES.COM

WWW.AMAZON.COM

FOR MORE DETAILS OF THESE BOOKS — AND TO ORDER.

For your great (or really bad) breath visit www.oxyfresh.com

Check out www.charmschoolforguys.com to continue your education in charm.

Charm School FOR GUYS!

✎ QUICK ORDER FORM

Order Online: **www.charmschoolforguys.com**
E-mail Orders: **orders@charmschoolforguys.com**

Have your credit card ready. (Amex, Disc, MC, VISA)

Please mail _____ copies @ $19.95 each, plus $4.95 S&H to:
(include $3.00 S&H per additional address)

Name:_____

Address:_____

Apt. #:_____ City: _____

State: _____ Zip Code: _____

Phone #s: _____ / _____

Email: _____

SEND AS A GIFT TO:

Name:_____

Address:_____

Apt. #:_____ City: _____

State: _____ Zip Code: _____

PAYMENT TYPE:

CREDIT CARD: ❏ Am. Express   ❏ Discover
             ❏ MasterCard   ❏ Visa

Card #: _____ Exp.:_____

Name as on card: _____

TOTAL AMOUNT PAID: _____

Charm School **FOR GUYS!**

✍ QUICK ORDER FORM

Order Online: **www.charmschoolforguys.com**
E-mail Orders: **orders@charmschoolforguys.com**

Have your credit card ready. (Amex, Disc, MC, VISA)

Please mail _____ copies @ $19.95 each, plus $4.95 S&H to:
(include $3.00 S&H per additional address)

Name:_____

Address:_____

Apt. #:_____ City: _____

State: _____ Zip Code: _____

Phone #s: _____ / _____

Email: _____

SEND AS A GIFT TO:

Name:_____

Address:_____

Apt. #:_____ City: _____

State: _____ Zip Code: _____

PAYMENT TYPE:

CREDIT CARD: ❑ Am. Express ❑ Discover
❑ MasterCard ❑ Visa

Card #: _____ Exp.:_____

Name as on card: _____

TOTAL AMOUNT PAID: _____

Charm School **FOR GUYS!**

✎ QUICK ORDER FORM

Order Online: **www.charmschoolforguys.com**
E-mail Orders: **orders@charmschoolforguys.com**

Have your credit card ready. (Amex, Disc, MC, VISA)

Please mail _____ copies @ $19.95 each, plus $4.95 S&H to:
(include $3.00 S&H per additional address)

Name:_____

Address:_____

Apt. #:_____ City: _____

State: _____ Zip Code: _____

Phone #s: _____ / _____

Email: _____

SEND AS A GIFT TO:

Name:_____

Address:_____

Apt. #:_____ City: _____

State: _____ Zip Code: _____

PAYMENT TYPE:

CREDIT CARD: ❏ Am. Express ❏ Discover
❏ MasterCard ❏ Visa

Card #: _____ Exp.:_____

Name as on card: _____

TOTAL AMOUNT PAID: _____

ABOUT THE AUTHOR:

"The odds are good, but the goods are odd."
This common euphemism in Alaska, regarding the
historically unbalanced ratio of men to women there,
was the principal inspiration for "Charm School for Guys!
How to Lose the Fugly and Get Some *Snugly*".

The saying about single men in The Last Frontier put our
author on a path of research and development of sorts.
With her marketing background and an investigative
zeal, she embarked on a mission to document the various
aspects of 'guy behavior' and the complaints that the
behavior often triggers. This book is the result of her
study and a veritable *Encyclopedia For Guys*.

M. Marshall is a successful Dating Consultant. She works
closely with Certified Matchmakers in assisting men and
women create their own brand of stand-out charm and
appeal. Founder and CEO of *Great Date Consulting* and
Get Off the Couch Books, she currently lives in Anchorage
with her partner, Jon, and their Alaskan Malamute, Bailey,
'The Mighty Fat Dog'.

FOR GUYS!

FOR GUYS!

FOR GUYS!

FOR GUYS!

FOR GUYS!

Sex causes babies
and other funky occurrences...

USE CONDOMS.